The Americanization

of God

COME OUT OF HER MY PEOPLE

How America Has Changed God Into Its' Own Image
And Got Everybody Off Track

Ronald Barksdale

ISBN: 0997893206
ISBN 13: 9780997893205
Library of Congress Control Number: 2016917150
TKOH, California, CL

"The world will not be destroyed by those who do evil, but by those who watch them without doing anything" - Albert Einstein

"Bear ye one another's burdens, and so fulfill the law of Christ."
- Galatians 6:2.

Table of Contents

Acknowledgments

GRACE BE WITH YOU, mercy, and peace from God the Father, and from the Lord Savior Christ, the Son of the Father in truth and love.

I acknowledge my dad Alvin and mother Ruth for laying down a foundation of spirituality and faith in the most High Father and His Son Immanuel.

Also, "Mother" Smalls, a grand 92-year-old Hebrew, who taught me the truth back in the late 50's.

My brother Harold with whom I've had so many theological, philosophical and political debates.

My precious wife Shiloah who has supported this journey through thick and thicker.

My children Ryan and Catrina, who've given me much food for analysis. Pastor Abel Tamez, who gave me some of the most critical feedback to shape the outcome of this work.

Which led me to Malak Yisrael, who helped complete the journey, thus far.

To all friends, family and acquaintances, I am grateful.

Blessings

He Who Has The Most Toys Wins

THERE IS AN AMERICAN SAYING, "He who has the most toys when he dies wins". This speaks to the intense rat race to accumulate the biggest, best and most expensive items which includes but is not limited to all the houses, cars, jewelry, clothing and money one can accumulate.

The problem is that once we die, we can't take any of these "toys" with us. Ironically, the American Christian church supports pretty much what society promotes which is the idea that if we're not keeping up with the Joneses materially, we are "suffering".

This is the very same idea the commercials try to sell us. The church teaches that if a person is well-to-do, it is likely that because he's well-to-do he has had tremendous faith in God. Conversely, God's criteria is way different, He states the measure of our blessings is determined by how much we give away, to help the poor.

Our fear of not keeping up with the Jones supports the supposition that we are experiencing horrible trials and persecution. To resolve this problem, we are covetously taught to give to the church, so that we might receive the prosperity on earth that we deserve, which is a distraction from the "real" goal, which should be that we are to build prosperity in heaven.

Indeed, our mantra should read, 'He who has the most toys stacked in heaven wins', for it is in heaven that we'll enjoy our treasures for eternity.

Our Savior says, "Lay not up for yourselves treasures upon earth...but lay up for yourselves treasures in heaven...for where your treasure is there will your heart be also."

So where are our hearts? What do our hearts really value the most? Our hearts should value heaven. In the "pursuit of happiness" we tend to seek wealth in this life today. But if we see what God says to pursue, happiness is to pursue wisdom and understanding.

"Happy is the man that findeth wisdom, and the man that getteth understanding. For the merchandise of it is better than merchandise of silver and the gain thereof than fine gold. She is more precious than rubies: and all the things thou canst desire are not to be compared unto her. Length of days is in her right hand; and in her left-hand riches and honour and happy is everyone that retaineth her." Proverbs 3:13-22.

"The fear of the Lord is to hate evil: pride, and arrogance, the evil way, and the froward-mouth do I hate." (Which is the opposite of the way society has groomed us.) Prov. 8:13.

"Riches and honour are with me; yea, durable riches and righteousness. My fruit is better than gold, yea than fine gold; and my revenue than choice silver!" Prov. 8:18,19. "Receive my instruction, and not silver; and knowledge rather than choice gold, for wisdom is better than rubies; and all the things that may be desired are not to be compared to it."v.10

What are the durable riches and righteousness? What fruit is better than gold and choice silver? Life is. Not this physio-chemical existence we live today but real Life.

Who gave us the impression that this air dependent existence we experience today is Life? This existence which requires food to live isn't Life.

The second that Adam chose to eat of the wrong tree he died, and man has been dead ever since. What is better than gold, silver, rubies and all things desired is Life.

The very fact that we can die means we are dead already. Any organism with the capacity to die is not alive.

Material gold, silver, rubies, cars, houses, large bank accounts have value to us because we are dead. If we were alive, these things would not have the same meaning.

'Things' are not comparable to Life. Being subject to things proves we are not alive. We admit we are mortal, thus we admit we are dead. Thus, the words, mortician, mortuary, mortal.

We should be teaching people how to prepare for their eternal existence. Churches need to prepare folks not for escape from the burdens of life on earth but prepare folks for Life in the Kingdom of Heaven.

How do we even demonstrate we value the Kingdom of Heaven? Well for the most part that means a denial of the attention, time and energy to the things of this earth.

Many reading this book are heavily involved in Church activity. We serve as an usher, deacon, we sit on the church board, we teach Sunday classes, count the offering, lead praise and worship, hold bible studies, cast out demons, anoint with oil, are Bible or Faith based or spirit-filled and we're on fire for the Holy Ghost. Our church has a great choir and the preaching is so God inspired it's off the charts. Perhaps our church is pulling in new souls by the droves, baptisms occur almost weekly, and our youth program is "rockin"!

Our church may have all night sit-ins, prayer services, no one smokes, drinks or fornicates, but everyone is living right. Our church fasts, as a group and as individuals, and pleads the blood of Jesus over our lives. We also have a powerful women's ministry and we hold a revival not once but twice a year. We keep the Sabbath day perfectly; no one works on the day of worship. We keep the commandments perfectly. There is a retreat every so often in which the members dedicate their time to seeking God. Most our members attend an annual church convention. The pastor is a wonderful man, and everyone loves his wife. At every worship service, people are "delivered", and our church does discipleship, whereas sinners are brought to Christ. Our church keeps all God's ordinances, we dot the i's and cross the t's.

But when God asks, that amid doing all of our church work, behold in the day of our fast, we find pleasure, and exact all our labors, what does He mean? What might He be saying?

All the spirit inspired praise and worship services, all the shouting, loud rejoicing, great music and all the wonderful people in fellowship, may still be exacting our own pleasure, because in this we fulfill our own ideas of how to please God, but do not make the effort to please Him in the way He asks us to.

In God's eyes our hands are still rendered bloody and we are what is considered defiled even though we fasted to have our voices heard on high. Our hearts are still wrong if we are not doing the job God is really concerned about, which is "to loose the bands of wickedness", or in other words where there is injustice to fight for justice.

Why is it our hands are rendered bloody? Well if little girls and boys continue to die of starvation in near and far away places, if their parents are slaughtered with machetes and the pop, pop, pop of semi-automatic weapons, if they are mistakenly or deliberately targeted and exploded by bomb and missile fire and their limbs and flesh are splattered to pieces everywhere and their bodies crushed in the rubble, that blood is on our hands if we're not doing all we can to stop such atrocities.

Bands of wickedness? Despite the political leanings of most Christian churches, there is a stark fact about the American governmental system. It was not inspired by God, but is a government created by men. The American government is not a Theocracy (a government from God down), it is a democracy (a government from the bottom up), the government founded by people, for the people, not by God, for God. Thus, the government or form of government is by no means biblical, Christian or sanctified by the Holy Ghost. Consequently, the American governmental system and this country itself, is not a designated sovereign state on earth of the Kingdom of Heaven.

The United States of America is not by pedigree, heredity or by unction right, just because we live here and claim to be "one nation under God indivisible with liberty and justice for all."

The American church aligns itself with a government that despite its' high moral statements can be and is often corrupted due to the ulterior motives of the human beings that operate it.

It does not make us a better born again Christian because we espouse "God and country", nor is that idea somehow biblical. The beliefs and policies of the United States government are not biblical. It promotes a separation between Church and State. We uphold that separation dearly, and dearly it should be upheld because the State is as secular or opposed to sacred as possible. Yet it would be better if we promoted a theocratic government run by God almighty.

Nor could it possibly make us a better Christian just because we claim to be a neo or ultra-conservative or a moderate or bleeding-heart liberal. None of these opinions is located in God's sovereign world which judges the heart of man; something no man can do. Yet because the American Christian church has attached itself to this secular or Godless government, it often adapts what the government wants it to think.

Maybe because the church takes the quote from Romans 13 too far and applies it to every heinous philosophy the rulers may endorse due to their own self-interest the church's role as moral compass and fighter for justice is compromised and reduced to scraps.

Where the ideology of a political party conflicts with the ideology of God in heaven, then a fight against the oppression of poor people, and fatherless, strangers (immigrants), the homeless, and those incarcerated must begin. Instead, the church invents, as does the military, an attractive concept of loyalty to man and man's government. Basically Romans 13 is saying we are to pay tribute or pay taxes to the powers that be and in this way, you are showing support to those who are placed in office to protect us.

Paul writes, "render therefore to all their dues: owe no man anything, but to love one another." In short don't short the IRS. Just as Our Savior said render unto Caesar the things which are Caesar's, Matt. 22:21.

However, if people are being exploited and oppressed due to government policies, philosophies, or positions in this country and in the world, it is the church's job not to stand by the government and support the abuse but rather to speak truth to power. The church must realize that the friends of the American government, the wealthy, and the corporate oligarchs are exploiting marginal peoples.

Poor people are getting poorer while the rich get richer by deliberate design. The healthcare system is going further and further out of whack and is unobtainable by the poor masses, by deliberate design. Court systems give the advantage to those who have the most money and thus does not function equally on behalf of poor persons, by deliberate design. Prisons are sinfully over-crowded and yet there is an unreasonable "need" for too many more prisons, by deliberate design (Micah 7:1-6).

At the same time, the justice system is compromised and overwhelmed due to financial self-interest, therefore many who are innocent, are incarcerated. An innocent man or woman incarcerated is a crime against humanity. (Habakkuk 1:3-4).

Meanwhile pedophilia and child sexual abuse is increasing by deliberate design. Beside uncles, cousins, dads and granddads, corporate and religious officials are often involved.

We have same sex partners adopting and raising children in unmarried and married unions. Sex outside of marriage appears to be the norm and thus the abortion debate rages on. Legal and illegal drug use is on the rise, and there is government sponsored and sanctioned "illegal" drug sales going on for the purpose of raising revenue for governmental and personal activities.

There are prisoners being held for political reasons rather than criminal activities and there is immoral gambling pervading our society in the form of the lottery and the Indian Casinos. Even in this, funds that should be earmarked for the public good are being diverted unscrupulously by "upstanding", public thieves.

Wars; or the killing of innocent peoples for financial profit, is being propagated and condoned, justified and ignored, by people who claim to have the love of God in their hearts. Such people either support these kinds of activities with blind loyalty; do little to no research; or ignore one specific tenant; you cannot hate your brother who you can see, and love God whom you cannot see.

Because The Prophet's Wickedness Fills The Land

Or
When the Prophets, Profit

BUT THE CHURCH WANTS TO BLAME THE DEVIL, and the sinners for the condition in this nation, when it is the church which has abdicated its' role and is responsible for things going down the drain the way it has. "Because the prophets, wickedness fills the land". Jeremiah 23:14.

The church justifies away its' own shortcomings, as a part of being "human", instead of grabbing itself, shaking itself up, humbling itself and praying for its' own condition (2 Chronicles 7:14).

"Amos 6:1-7, Those are looked upon as doing well for themselves, who do well for their bodies; but we are here told what their ease is, and what their woe is. Here is a description of the pride, security, and sensuality, for which God would reckon. Careless sinners are everywhere in danger; but those at ease in Zion, who are stupid, vainly confident, and abusing their privileges, are in the greatest danger. Yet many fancy themselves the people of God, who are living in sin, and in conformity to the world. But the examples of others' ruin forbid us to be secure. Those who are set upon their pleasures are commonly careless of the troubles of others, but this is great offence to God. Those who placed their happiness in the pleasures of sense, and set their hearts upon them, shall be deprived of those pleasures.

Those who try to put the evil day far from them, find it nearest to them." (Matthew Henry Concise Commentary on the Whole Bible).

In this country, we suffer from a condition which sympathizes with an atmosphere of greed, of I'll get mine, and you get yours. We say, "pull yourself up by your own bootstraps". We celebrate the Buffalo Bill pioneer who destroyed millions of Buffalo in order to destroy the Indian nation.

We extol the pioneers who scalped Indians for money, while the Washington government displayed the scalps on the walls of the White House.

This evidences that the ways the American church believes, acts and models is just not Christ, but is flesh or carnal. There is the absence of the father protector in the home censoring dress styles, teaching morality, controlling dating practices, and teaching adulthood responsibilities.

The results of the flaws and errors which much of the time we accept as "oh well its' just a part of life" have causes which begin with how we think, and how we believe, thus how we conduct our lives. Many of these wrong thoughts can result in:

1) Anxiety
2) Depression
3) Despondency
4) Bipolar
5) AHDH
6) Stress
7) Cuttings
8) Body Augmentation
9) Tics Tourette's Syndrome
10) Mental Illness

When the father is absent though present, and the woman becomes the head of the house, and the dad lives a self-absorbed spoiled lifestyle, though he may have a job, he abdicates the real leadership role of the family to the wife. If there are boys who grow up under this condition, the boys having a natural proclivity for being leaders then begin to imitate the feminine leader model they see acting out on the stage of life that is their home, and thus are subject to what we call effeminate ways of acting.

The same thing is true of the girls who grow up under such a dysfunctional arrangement when the man has abandoned his position as high priest of the home. The girl can take on a dominatrix or father deprived role, which can confuse her as to her sexual orientation also. She may for a lack of a father's attention and leadership take on masculine roles in her career in order to prove something to herself and to her father, sometimes sabotaging long-term attachment with a male partner.

Such distorted lifestyles to what God ordained can often lead to weirdness in the children. To add to that psychosis, the church will go on appeasing the women in the congregation and empowering them in their dysfunction while further alienating the man, and further reinforcing perverted roles in the home, instead of plainly telling the people of their sins. "[The priest] commit adultery (having intercourse with both good and evil), and they love dishonesty. They encourage those who are doing evil instead of turning them away from their sins. These prophets are as wicked as the people of Sodom and Gomorrah once were." Jeremiah 23:14 God blames the ministry, but are the people exempt from blame? "For these are rebellious people, deceitful children, children unwilling to listen to the Lord's instruction...which say to the seers, See not; and to the prophets, Prophesy not unto us right things, speak unto us smooth things, prophesy deceits" (Isaiah 3: 9-10). God's people want to hear lies. We don't want to deal with upsetting truthful things. We want "smooth" things, stuff that's easy on the mind. We don't want to hear truth in regard to our own destruction.

When pastors become men pleasers instead of God pleasers it causes distortions and perversions in our society, and as a result we witness broken and distorted lives all around us.

When we'll go spend time seeing that extra movie or participating in that extra shopping spree, but won't spend that same time raising funds to feed a hungry child or write a letter to our government officials regarding a negative social issue, there is something wrong with the picture.

What happens is that we Christians won't keep up a constant fight to censor the violent or sexually explicit shows and commercials that appear in the media; instead we spend gobs of time engrossed in these same shows.

Fornication Has Consumed the Land

When fornication or premarital sex is the norm, and virginity until marriage is the exception to the norm, then the fornication has consumed the land. Premarital sex as the rule of the culture is wanton. And again, the church does not raise its voice as a trumpet and shout against it. Too many toes might get stepped on. Even when the church does boldly tell the people of their sins in this area, the people shun the message as archaic and not doable. When we are proud and exalt the fornicators, but turn around and debase and shame the virgin, we are thoroughly corrupt.

I Cor. 6:9, states a criterion for receiving or not receiving eternal life. If eternal life is the goal of our Christianity and the criteria for receiving it is plainly stated, then go no further, just look at it and obey. "Know ye not that the unrighteous shall not inherit the kingdom of God? Be not deceived: neither fornicators, nor idolaters, nor adulterers, nor effeminate, nor abusers of themselves with mankind…". Verse 13. "Now the body is not for fornication, but for the Lord; and the Lord for the body." v. 18, Flee fornication. Every sin that a man doeth is without the body; but he that committeth fornication sinneth against his own body. v. 19, What? Know ye not that the body is the temple of the Holy Ghost…?"

The corruption of the church expresses itself in the form of fornication and adultery. When a church is fat, self-satisfied, comfortable, about creature comforts, about self-pleasures, about greed, about status, about consumption, about sense, about money, about medicating, about wealth accumulation, about the pride of life, the church is committing fornication. This is because it is operating in the lust of the flesh. In that it states that Christ is its Savior, it commits the equivalent of adultery (I John 2:16).

When we take pride in this world's highlights we neglect to take pride in this world's lowlights, which entails sacrificing for the needs of others. The numbers of parents put away in nursing and convalescent facilities is a testament to that (I John 3:16-17).

The level of activity of physical sexual fornication that is tolerated by its members is often a mirror of the religious fornication of its purpose.

The fornication in the land is also a reflection of a church that is fornicating with the idols to which it is attracted, the created things such as watches, fine jewelry, big stock holdings and the like. Such wealth orientation is akin to enjoying a sexual relationship with a whore. What about the movies we watch, the entertainment that dominates our time, the music we fill our heads with and the television shows that consume the few productive moments we have in our day?

Our intimate interaction with the Godless, hedonistic secular culture makes us, if we proclaim Christ as our Saviour, adulterers. We thus live spiritually, in sin. We have intercourse with a life of sin instead of suffering the reproach of the world, for the cause of the Kingdom of God (Hebrews 11:26) "Ye 'adulterous' people don't you know that friendship with the world means enmity (makes us an enemy) against God? (James 4:4) The issue in our land is not mainly abortion because abortion for the most part is the by-product of the deadly practice of fornication. Fornicators will receive eternal destruction (I Corinthians 6:9). Why eternal destruction? Fornication dilutes the marriage union. It pollutes the specialness or sacredness of the union of marriage. It is no wonder the divorce rate in America is so very high. We have no idea how strongly God loves the marriage union. He hates divorce. Once married always married in His eyes. Earthly marriage typifies the coming spiritual marriage of His Son the bridegroom, with the
church. God wants to insure there will not be another divorce!

The father as head of the house under our Savior and God the Father, has to be the hands-on leader of his wife and children. When he abdicates that position, the family crumbles under the pressure of the weight of the sins the world places upon them. But something very vile has occurred in the Christian church in general. The pastors have taken up the position as leaders of the families due to the submission to them by the wives and mothers of the families.

To trust the pastor over the husband as spiritual leader of the family disrupts the flow of the Holy Spirit and perverts the leadership in the home. The father is no longer the final authority under The Messiah and the preacher becomes trusted as the intercessor for God, this too is adultery. God needs no intercessor, the father must stand-up in his role as spiritual leader in the home and be a direct channel from Christ to the wife, cleansing her and washing her regularly with the word, Ephesians 5:26-27. This is why women must keep silence in the church (I Corinthians 14:34; I Timothy 2:12).

The Sexual Problem

The raw truth is that the attitude of 'empirical selfishness' to the degree that we abuse the weak for self-gratification and advantage, is a greater danger to our society than is fornication. A culture that devalues a young girl and encourages, even expects her to sully herself with a young man or men prior to marriage, an act which corrupts the marriage institution itself, and ignores the divorce and unhappiness rate that results, that culture is profane. Fornication is the sullying and disdaining of a virgin for premarital self-gratification. It is the destruction of purity and holiness in the family bloodline. It is the abuse of the weak and unprotected virgin girl or boy and corrupts their sanctity with God.

The hardness of a mindset that blames the poor for being poor, or blames the weak, for being weak or blames the less blessed, for being less blessed is the same one that regard children as objects to be abused. The excuse is that we want to give them things we've never had, which is why we are willing to sacrifice relationship.

There is a cultural mindset that appears hypocritically loving in public but is hateful at home. Hatefulness is thought of as normal. This attitude of greed and lack of generosity, of me first, and thinking God understands is the primary source of the production of the perverted lifestyles we see today. No wonder God gives us deaf, blind, physically and mentally challenged peoples, because if He didn't, we humans would race off the cliff into oblivion faster than we're already going. And yet we as a society put pressure on the challenged to be "normal!" As a whole we lack compassion, we do not support them, we don't care. We care solely about self. We often give lip service but do very little hip service.

A culture that as a norm puts away its parents and old people into a nursing home because it is inconvenient to personally care for them, is empirically selfish and evil.

We also have a culture of saying so we got to have "law and order" or there'll be anarchy in the streets. We preach the law was nailed to the cross, but we espouse on the "flesh level", a militant "law and order" over a humility and sensitivity culture. We create the atmosphere of violence and then solve it with violence.

We promote a prideful arrogant, self-righteous, me first, and "God is in my pocket" culture that is intolerant, which has made us neither thankful; but [we] became vain in [our] imaginations, and [our] foolish heart darkened. Professing [ourselves] to be wise, [we] became fools, Romans 1: 21-24.

Look at Romans 1:25 and see what Paul says to Christian believers about why God has given some of us over to a perverted and reprobate mind. Verse.25, "Who changed the truth of God into a lie and worshiped and served [created things] more than the Creator, who is blessed forever. For this cause, God gave them up unto vile affections: for even their women did change the natural use into that which is against nature: And likewise also the men, leaving the natural use of the woman, burned in their lust one toward another'...", thus the production of the gay culture.

We don't acknowledge that Sodom and Gomorrah were destroyed as much for their indifference to the poor and needy as for their perverted sexual lifestyle. To be insensitive to the needs of the weak is perversion, Ezekiel 16:49-50.

God says "Behold this was the iniquity of thy sister Sodom, pride, fulness of bread, and abundance of idleness was in her" …which describes perfectly America today. "Sin City" Las Vegas, has spilled over into the mainstream… "they were haughty, and committed abomination before me; but thou has multiplied thine abominations more than they… And has justified thy sisters in all thine abominations which thou has done…*THOU (The United States of America) HAST MULTIPLIED THINE ABOMINATIONS MORE THAN THEY, THEY (Sodom and Gomorrah) ARE MORE RIGHTEOUS THAN THOU (United States of America).*"

What goes on in this Christian nation is what Christians have talked themselves into tolerating. When we are not about what's on God's heart, all the religious verbiage and genuflecting is done in vain. When we are perverted toward the poor, the homeless, the immigrant, the weak, the challenged, the children, the elderly, we cultivate a people that begin to manifest perversions in the flesh in egregious, promiscuous, aggressive and lewd ways.

The arrogant attitude of such a culture produces a number of adults who take on such a selfish and calloused worldview, that they are willing to destroy powerless, weak and helpless little children for their own perverted pleasure. As a result, a good number of these victimized children become predators themselves, and a portion even become gay.

Many theorize that many gay persons are born gay, but the Bible states that the gay person is produced by a people with an attitude of heart that is stubborn, arrogant, filled with hate against the poor and weak of our society. When a church is out of line with the attitude of God's heart, then that can result in a society that produces variant lifestyles that negatively affect the community. The question is who is to blame, the fruit of the tree or the tree that produced that fruit?

If we then factor in the "boneheaded" perversions that the Catholic or Universal Church have covered up that take place in their "hallowed" halls in regard to those in authority who persist in the molestation of the weak, the vulnerable, the children, even little boys, it is a wonder that there isn't a larger gay and homosexual community in the larger society than we already have. But less well known yet hidden in plain sight is the fact that the evangelicals are not far behind, and some say even exceed the Catholic church in the molestation of vulnerable children and so I would be remiss if I didn't include the evangelicals who are giving the Catholic priests stiff competition in this category. Yet again an even deeper mystery is the indulgence of pedophilia in the practice of those who claim the Talmudic faith.

The disgusting irony is that many of our religious organizations have propagated some of the major ills we suffer in our society today and then turn around and in a pompous, "hard-ass" self-righteousness manner, preach 'fire and brimstone' against the very sins we've created in order to cover up our own despicable darkness.

Where are the so-called Christian churches that God says are to resist and fight against injustices, why aren't we standing up and staging a war against these bands of depravity that cultivate such a degrading culture as this?

The Drug Problem

We Christians are thus anesthetized, caught-up in concerns of everyday living, work, family, friends, bills, health and problems, and so there is no real intention, no real overt effort being made. There is no sacrifice (except for church activities) no loss of life, pleasure or comforts. We practice a form of godliness, hearing, reading, teaching even studying the Word but doing no real work, bearing no real fruit (John 15:8). The resultant problem is we otherwise fail to forward the Kingdom on this earth (James 2:14-15).

It is probably because we're not teaching people to do His commandments. We're not teaching people what those commandments are. We're not teaching people the importance of doing the commandments (John 14:21). We're not teaching them how to accomplish really doing the commandments. We talk about Him, about calling on His name, about the fact He is the way the truth and the light that no one can come to the Father except through Him, about how He died for us, His grace and His mercy, about how good He is, that "this is our season for blessings" and the like, but we fail to talk about the "part" we are expected to play. We're not thoroughly teaching the people the "cross" that we must bear. (Matthew 16:24). We're not explaining how that must be manifested in order to receive eternal life. That to "take up our cross" is to forsake the comforts of this world. It is to take up a burden for Our Redeemer.

The "cross" are the sacrifices we're making to implement the Kingdom by implementing Isaiah 61:1, into this world. The cross alters our priorities away from self and toward the benefit of others who are most "less blessed". It is what we must pick up and carry each day. It is to shun the 'flashiness' 'glitter' and 'glamour' of this world, to shun the "things" of this world, to shun the "pride of life".

To bear the cross means to lose self and find others (and not the other way around) Luke 9:23. The cross is death to self, to sacrifice our self, our time, our attention, our energy to lay down our convenience, and let others have the priority over us. It is "carrying [our] own execution". It's the "willingness to take up the cross and to crucify upon it [our] own interests". Not to be like, but to be unlike everybody else, it is to be despised due to our humility on behalf of others. The cross is the burden upon us of the poor, the sick, the helpless, the least of the people. The cross is to neglect creature comforts, it is to serve the needy and not the greedy. It is to take on the burdens of those who are in despair. It is to give up what we'd prefer to do at our own expense.

When we fail to pick up our cross each day we tend to drift into hideous lifestyle choices to appease our selfish desires which may include, misusing another human being's body for our own pleasure, without being legally married to that body. Going from body to body can tend to lend itself to the need to medicate the void in the soul it creates. The need to medicate the void calls for overeating, alcoholism, smoking, and or drugs legal and illegal. All the things that are wrong to do even if they appear to be the norm exacts a price that must be paid. That price is especially steep for those who claim to be the "called out ones". Abuses are occurring that create pain and that need a cure.

The United States of America leads the world in legal and illegal substance use and abuse. Could it also be leading the world in the abuse it does to others?

We as the church know that since drugs are in the streets, that the authorities know their location and where they are being dealt. We know that since the authorities know this, then the drug trade should be stopped. But we also know that key folks in authority are "on-the-take" and they profit from the drug trade. We know the trade can continue only with their permission. We know that this corruption is the only way the drugs can get into this country and be successfully distributed. We know that these authorities need to be removed or the drug trade will simply continue to increase. We the church know that we have not confronted this issue in earnest and forced the illegal drug trade to stop poisoning our society.

We know that the Vietnamese war was essentially fought to control the "Golden Triangle" which comprised the three-principal drug producing countries of that day: Vietnam, Thailand and Cambodia. The Vietnamese war was a drug war. The war in Afghanistan is essentially a continuation on the same theme. Wherever that much money is being produced (uncountable trillions) in the growing and export of opium there is no chance we're going to pull out of that market until another country becomes the apex of opium production. Just as the Sandinistas, Columbia and Panama were being exploited to create revenue for the United States corporation, the war in Afghanistan is also being fought to increase this country's Gross National Product (GNP) under the guise of American self-interest.

Thus, the war on drugs goes on and on, it's a war that Nixon and Reagan declared long ago, however the war is for control of the drug market and not for its' destruction. And where are most of those drugs being sold and used? Right here in the good ol' U.S. of A. Why is it that the church hides from these facts? Why is the church not concerned with the forked tongue double dealing of this dear heartthrob of a country they love so dearly? Why are we still singing her songs, singing her praises and pledging our allegiance to our hi-jacked nation? Why isn't the church fighting a bitter battle to stop her moral decay? The USA and the UK are essentially the largest drug cartels on the planet. Our troops are over there protecting the poppy fields. Lives, young and old, American lives are being maimed and killed to protect a business enterprise that is further destroying and killing lives on our very shore. There is horror story after horror story of addiction and the destruction this debauchery brings to people's lives, families and children.

And the church ignores this?! The church would rather look the other way and look at the bright side of things? There is no bright side of things with this thing going on. If this horrible atrocity is allowed to occur and we do nothing, we are accomplices in this crime. And the church looks away? The church sings praises on Sunday or Saturday, but does not actively stand up against this illegal, immoral and decrepit enterprise? The church is so in love with the American government that it looks away? Whose church is this anyway? It must not be God's true church.

Do we feel that because we're sitting in a "good" church, a church that represents God and the beliefs of our family that because we're a part of that church we're sitting in the "honeypot"? Do we believe we'll obtain salvation by association?

"Remember that there will be difficult times in the last days. People will be selfish, greedy, boastful, and conceited; they will be insulting, disobedient to their parents, ungrateful, and irreligious; they will be unkind, merciless, slanderers, violent, and fierce; they will hate good; they will be treacherous, reckless, and swollen with pride; they will love pleasure rather than God; they will hold to the outward form of our religion, but reject its real power" (2 Timothy 3:1-5 GNB). Churches are preaching "Jesus", that He is our risen Lord and Saviour and how we must give our hearts to Him. But the people in the congregation are manifesting these very dysfunctional traits, why? The people are not even trying to keep God's commandments. We're not being taught we need to keep the commandments.

We're an immobile Christian if we make no real effort to help anyone or do anything more than would the average person in our society. We are commanded to love God and love our neighbor.

Nothing Is as It Appears

God says to the churches, temples, synagogues, mosques the good ones, "(You) seek me daily, and delight to know my ways, as a nation that did righteousness, and forsook not the ordinance of their God: (you) ask of me the ordinances of justice; (you) take delight in approaching to God. Wherefore have we fasted, say (you) and thou seest not? Wherefore we afflicted our soul, and thou takest no knowledge? The Lord answers, "Behold, in the day of your fast ye find pleasure, and exact all your labors.

Behold, ye fast for strife and debate, and to smite with the fist of wickedness: you, shall not fast as ye do this day, to make your voice to be heard on high."

Conversely:

God says the fast He (God) Has Chosen, is to "loose the bands of wickedness, to undo the heavy burdens, and to let the oppressed go free, and that (we) break every yoke.

To deal our food to the hungry and to bring the outcasts to our house. When we see the naked to clothe them that we do not hide ourselves from our own flesh" (our own infirmed parents) (Isaiah 58:2-7).

We can be as righteous in religious practices as we want, sitting in the "honeypot", but if we neglect what is the "heart of God" if we neglect the "Kingdom of God and his righteousness", if we perform miracles and move mountains and give our bodies to be burnt and have not this "charity" if we give hundreds of cattle, sheep and rivers of oil, millions of dollars to the church but if we don't have this "charity", [mercy, judgment, faith] it amounts to nothing. We are a culture of desperately taking care of our own needs and hiding our face from the needs of others.

We are a culture of neglecting by omission the needs of the poor, weak and less blessed peoples, which spawns an atmosphere of despondency and pain that is perpetrated throughout the land. Thus, there is as a result a perceived need for a police gang, or a sworn vigilante group within law enforcement to put down with military force the threat of revolt created by the neglect and deceitful repression taken against the lower class, the weak, the vulnerable, to put down the 'slow-riot' set in motion.

Going out to preach the gospel to the world and "save souls" or proselyte is no substitute for doing what God requires. Neither does God allow the excuse that we have to make a living to feed our families. God says, that He that clothes the lilies of the field will also much more so clothe us; we are to worry not nor be anxious but seek first the Kingdom and His righteousness. Whose righteousness? God's righteousness.

And when we do what he asks, "Then shall your light break forth as the morning, and your health shall spring forth speedily: and your righteousness shall go before thee: the glory of the Lord shall be thy rereward. Then shalt you call, and the LORD shall answer." If we fulfill God's requests of us, He will show up on our behalf for all our requests, Isaiah 58:8-9.

So, what is a real believer? What does a real believer believe? When we know that, then we should not forsake assembling ourselves with them.

So much of what the American church is doing is pseudo Christianity, or everything but the REAL thing.

What kind of heart does God require, except a contrite heart? (Psalms 51:17). God wants us to be like little children, simple, Matthew 18:3.

"Whoever receives one little child like this in my name receives me; Whoever CAUSES one of these little ones who believe in me to sin, it would be better for him if a millstone were hung around his neck, and he were drowned in the depth of the sea" Matthew 18:5,6.

Are churches causing little ones to stumble and then blaming them for walking away from the church? Many youths once they get to college go buck wild. Some we never regain.

Our culture today is creating a Brand Name Christianity that is commercially attractive, but off track. As scripture says, such a church might be keeping all the ordinances, it's people are even giving as never before, it is afflicting the flesh to have its requests heard on high, but it fails to do what really counts to its creator.

The evidence of this corruption can be found in how the church views money. Through the lens of its attitude toward money and how the church corrupts what God teaches regarding finances and the adoption of the philosophy of capitalism as a tenant of American Christianity the church has taken us off course in our quest for God's will.

"And through [getting people to covet] shall they [the ministry] with feigned words make merchandise (money) of you". Getting the congregation to pay money to receive their "piece of the pie", their earthly rewards is bad business. "While they promise them (the new believers) liberty, they themselves (the ministry) are the servants of corruption (which is covetousness): for whom a man is overcome, of the same is he brought in bondage..." again:"for of whom a man is overcome, of the same is he brought in bondage..."

"For if after they (the new believer) have escaped the pollutions of the world through the knowledge of the Lord and Saviour Jesus Christ, they are again entangled therein, and overcome, the latter end is worse with them than the beginning" (2 Peter 2:3, 18-20).

Instead of preaching abundance on earth we should be willing to give up things we covet such as houses, lands, material things and adverse familial relationships for the Kingdom's sake; instead we are told by these leaders that we are entitled to all these things, and the Lord would see us prosper and not lack, thus it is the thrust of our conversion to receive these things in this life, which fulfills the lust (desires) of the flesh and the vanity of the mind (what seems right) 2 Peter 2:1. We are teaching riches are evidence that we are being blessed because we're paying great amounts of tithes and offerings to the church rather than that giving away our money to the poor is a sign of being blessed. We need to be told that when we lose according to God's will, we win.

Self Wins Every time

If there is one area in which the church today has been consistent it is in the area of financial corruption. YET FROM THE DAYS OF YOUR FATHER, YOU HAVE GONE AWAY FROM MY ORDINANCES AND HAVE NOT KEPT THEM, Malachi 3:6-7. The result of such a corruption though we've grown to accept it and abide in it, is devastating to the point of putting us in line for very severe correction.

For example, a new church doctrine is spreading throughout the Christian community that tithing is a Bible command, demand, badge of Christianity, proof of righteousness, means of reciprocal economic enrichment or a biblically sanctioned means to fund the work of the church and to position self for a windfall of prosperity.

I was introduced to the concept of tithing when my mother became a member of the 'Radio Church of God' which became the 'Worldwide Church of God' (WWCG) back in January 1963. I learned through their teaching that we were to observe the Old Testament/Jewish laws and statutes while at the same time acknowledge that we have a risen Savior who was crucified for our sins. In short, we believed that salvation could be earned or loss by our works even though The Messiah had died for our sins.

The principle of tithing was also taught and practiced as found in the Old Testament. The church financially flourished and became what we call today a 'mega-church', one of the first of its' kind in that day. While the church hierarchy became prosperous, I also noted that its' rank and file did not. However, prosperity was promised to the people if they remained faithful.

I noted that tithing works for church growth, but it does not work for the people. Every church has its' "rich" person. That guy tends to dazzle our vision, and we simply "keep hope alive", that we will be blessed like that, one day too.

What we fail to realize is that some people are born with the ability to find gold in a mountain of horse manure, and the rest of us aren't. That's just the way it is! It has nothing to do with tithing.

When the church growth began to occur at WWCG, many other church leaders began to inquire as to the secret of this corporate church's success. WWCG literally had churches all over the country and around the world including Europe, Asia, Africa, Australia, South and North America.

It had "three", not one, but "three" college campuses, "three", not one but "three", radio and television studios and it broadcast worldwide. It had a magazine circulation in the tens of millions, successive private jets including the 'Learjet', access to countless world leaders and generated hundreds of millions of dollars in income annually.

What many discovered was that the tithing practice had contributed greatly to the church's meteoric ascendancy. Upon observing what made WWCG such a mega successful organization, many church observers proceeded to incorporate the principle of tithing into their church doctrine as well.

Having tithed unfailingly for years, I decided to research the subject more thoroughly. I particularly enjoy research and was surprised at what I found when researching the subject of the 'tithe'. I literally found that though to tithe is a command in the Old Testament, a fabrication or spin-off had been added to the command by the Old Testament priests which got embraced by the Worldwide Church of God (WWCG) but does not line up with what the scripture is saying. I am happy to say; the WWCG no longer practices false tithing methods today. But tensofthousands of other churches have not yet come to their senses.

In our astute society, people take great pride in investigating what percentage of the charitable money they contribute gets to the actual problem instead of to "administration" costs. People are miffed when they find out that 90% of the funds don't even reach the target, and don't let someone misappropriate the charitable funds altogether, this invariably causes that charity to go under.

However, when it comes to churches, the church people take little to no stock on investigating what percentage of the money goes where, to whom and to what. Is the use of the money in line with God's instructions? Is the money being properly appropriated or is there an air of embezzlement taking place? WHAT PERCENTAGE OF THIS MONEY IS GOING TO CHARITY?

Think for a minute, should your money go to a church organization or to a love organization? If apparently as humans in authority are prone to do, the priest assumed the position of collectors of the tithe, and it didn't get distributed to whom God intended, should we continue to give it to them? (Malachi 3:5, 8-9). What happened was the priests who felt underpaid and deserved a bit more of the 'pie' than the Lord had designated them, fabricated a year to year tithe which failed to get to the widow, fatherless and foreigners. On top of that they collected tithes from wage earners! A definite no, no!

It is very interesting that in today's world the two 'Bible' commanded tithes have been eliminated from the equation, and the fabricated man-made tithe remains in place. Apparently if the tithe were taught the way the Bible teaches, it is to be paid every third year, in the year of tithing.

It is the fabricated man-made year to year tithe to the 'priests' that we investigate here and demonstrate is a robbery of God and his people. That's the point, we and God are being robbed.

Financial Corruption, Corrupts Absolutely

If there is corruption in our church's use of the money, there is corruption in our Christian walk with God. God says He is Love and thus loving in terms of money according to Him is giving to the needs of the needy. Lusting in terms of money is trying to hold a portion of our money back for self; a position which is the antithesis of love or God. There are numerous churches that preach awesome "word" and do awesome "works". The false teaching as regards to tithing however places a question of plausibility in our inner core. We want to know, what is the REAL purpose or motivation of the churches' operation. The suspicions thus make many of us who are savvier, doubters. As many members that such churches gain, many more members are lost because they feel an intuitive lack of plausibility. Lies always come back to bite us, and the lack of transparency regarding the money will be no exception.

That church operates in the fulfilling of lust or in short, the incestuous program of promoting itself through the preaching of The Messiah Christ. Such a church is a business. It thus demonstrates little to no power. It is not interested in The Savior, but the promotion of itself and its' own ideas, by using the teachings of The Messiah Christ.

That church builds a monument around a preacher personality that attests to God's specialness in that preacher's life. Thousands then follow in the wake of the glory that God has cast upon that preacher.

Such an operation of lust is incestuous in that it loves itself, its own flesh, but has little time to love others, others who have needs that are way past what has been provided for in the church's vision for itself. Churches who have not written into their vision plan, sacrificial love, but focuses on self-sustenance, have failed to understand that sacrifice leads to Godly sustenance. That church does not understand that it is inferior to sustain itself. God promises more if we trust him to be our sustainer and go about doing what He asks us to do.

Thus, we see an extension of this same inward spirit portrayed in the society to whom the church is meant to be a light. We see the ramifications of the perversions acted out in the church, acted out in society that demonstrate a church that can hardly be said to be set apart from the society if distinguishable at all.

It is the leadership of the church who is responsible for teaching God's people true 'Kingdom' economics, which is that none should have too much, and none should have too little (Exodus 16:18; Acts 4:32-35).

The Kingdom economics model pertains to the forgiveness of sin which is the forgiveness of offenses, which is the forgiveness of debts, and is interested in the redistribution of wealth, also called 'Sabbath' economics. In the Bible, in the Sabbath or seventh year, all debts were to be forgiven, slaves set free, and wealth redistributed so that none had too much, and none had too little.

For this to work successfully our economic hearts must be fully about the 'treasures in heaven' and not the treasures on earth.

The false teaching in regard to tithing is an example of one of many selfish positions many churches have taken, that ultimately steers us away from the true teaching in regard to what is really important to the Lord.

The false teaching as regards to money is a gauge as to the church's heart, and what in truth is its' REAL motivation.

Our true condition should be to act justly, to love mercy, and to walk humbly with our God. Our true position should be to give up our own works and pursue the Kingdom works of God, and our true mission should be to heal the sick, feed the hungry, fight for the oppressed and make disciples of all men.

Tithe$, Are We Crazy?!!!

CONSIDERING WHAT WE'VE JUST SAID, why is a discussion about the church's false doctrine regarding tithing important? The false doctrine of tithing is a symptom of how the truth can get twisted in God's name and how easily, deceit and the shadow of lies can take everyone into the pits of hell.

Is tithing in the Bible? Yes, it is! But not the way we're doing it; the way most of us do it, we're doing it in vain. Having our sights on the money transforms us out of the unlimited Kingdom world into the limited material world.

Let's get this money thing straight! In Matt. 23:23, Christ confirms that we should continue to tithe, and Malachi 3:8 states that God had been robbed of tithes and offerings. Upon repenting as a nation, Israel brought again, their tithes to God (Neh.10:38).

You can see that in the Bible, God clearly lays out the pattern by which we should live financially, whether in offerings, land Sabbaths, conditions of the jubilee, supporting the poor, lending, usury, slavery, but what about the so-called 'priestly' or 'Levitical' tithe, which some call the "first" tithe.

The "first"? If there is a first, then there could be a second? Wait a minute, what's going on? It is widely assumed based upon the historical accounts of Josephus, the Mishnah and other sources that the Jews tithed properly according to scripture and that they paid a yearly first tithe to the Levites, in addition to a second called the festival tithe, and even a third called the "poor" tithe! Whoa, how did things get this crazy? Well, when it comes to money and people, things can easily get "crazy"!

If we look further into the Bible we find that a directive to pay a "year to year" tithe to the priests or in today's vernacular, pay 10% out of every paycheck to the "church" is missing. What do you mean, "Missing?!" Yes, 'was never there'! 'Un-there!' Hocus Pocus! A-void! And there is no reasonable way we can imagine that on top of paying offerings, then paying a first tithe, we're to turn-around and pay a second, and then every third-year, a possible third tithe!!!

Say after taxes, you have five hundred dollars left of your paycheck, you would then have to pay $150 of it in tithes not counting offerings. That leaves you $350 to work with.

Whoa!

What's the problem here? Is God broke? Does he need our money that badly?

No, but the preachers do!

Once you are off the floor, let's 'disgust', I mean discuss, this thing, civilly.

God's Financial Blueprint

Does God give us any instruction as to how He intended for us to manage our finances in relationship to Him? Of course He does.

First, look at the financial commands in Deuteronomy 26:1-16 (NKJV). It is here that God gives instructions as to how He wants for His people to pay offerings and then the tithes.

God gives the scenario and depicts the nature of how He intended the offerings and tithes to be paid.

First the offering, v. 1-11, God wants the people to bring the first of all the produce of the land and offer it at a festival time to the priest. He also wants the people to be thankful for the fact that He has delivered them from bondage and unto a land flowing with milk and honey, the promised land.

Secondly, God requires a tithe every third year. Regarding the tithe v. 12-16, God states that the third-year, is "the year of tithing", and that the tithe that year, is "the holy tithe".

God assures us that we can be certain that in this third-year we can say we have removed the "holy tithe" from our house and have given it to the Levite, the stranger, the fatherless and the widow according to all the commandments the Lord has given us. We can also be assured that at the end of this third-year we can say we have not transgressed God's commandment, and "we have done all that the Lord has commanded us." Notice that God states this clearly and directly to us, and carefully encourages us in this.

So, we know for sure, we are required to pay offerings annually, and a tithe every third year. These instructions are clear and concise.

The iGNORED tithe

Okay, so why has the church not passed on to us these simple instructions? I think we are not given these instructions in the church today because the ministers want us to pay a tithe to them every year and that tithe is not shared with the widow, fatherless and foreigner. If we would pay the ministers that tithe year to year, and then they ask us to pay them an additional tithe every third-year, it would sound like they are asking for way too much.

So, should the preacher not ask for the tithe every third-year which takes care of the widow, fatherless and foreigner so as not to jeopardize receiving his tithe year to year? We say No! So we ask, if the preacher were to leave one tithe out, which one should be left out? We say certainly not the one that God clearly and specifically commands, which is the third-year tithe.

So let's review, if the preacher is receiving offerings, and a tithe, year to year and also a portion of the third-year tithe, wouldn't that be too much money going to the preacher? We say a resounding yes!

The every-third-year tithe is traditionally coined the "poor-tithe". However, this is a misnomer when you understand it's purpose. Notice that in the biblical rendition, the recipients of the 3rd year tithe are not all the "poor" of the land. You can read about how the poor are to be cared for in Deuteronomy 15:7-11; 24:19-22 and Lev.25:35-38.

This tithe is deemed "holy" because it goes to those closest to God's heart. It is the tithe ignored.

Ironically this is not the tithe being preached in the churches today. The Bible says that this tithe is to be paid every third-year and is to be paid to the widow, the fatherless, the alien and the Levite. What happened to this tithe?

Could it be that the church doesn't preach this tithe so that it can push for the other tithe which they claim we must pay out of every paycheck year to year?

Realize that it is not the peculiar burden of the 3rd year tithe to be the total care for the poor. In this light, the 3rd year tithe might be considered a supplemental support to a designated class of people whom are identified as the Levite, the stranger, the fatherless and the widow, all who have no inheritance (Deut. 26:13; Jas.1:27).

God addresses this tithe four (4) times specifically by name (Deut. 14:28-29, Deut.26:12-16, Amos 4:4 and Malachi 3:5). It is the third-year tithe that determines whether we've kept God's commandments, because it cares for what is most important to Him, the Levite (priest), the stranger, fatherless and the widow. The Levite, stranger, fatherless and the widow combination in fact identify the tithe that God is speaking of in Malachi 3:5-12.

Because the Levite, stranger, fatherless and widow are mentioned in the "tithe every three years" in the previous three references, then that mention of them in Malachi 3 identifies the tithe being spoken of here of which God is being robbed. It would be this tithe, the tithe of blessing that include the same four elements, the Levite, stranger, fatherless and widow. This is no random coincidence that the Levite, stranger, fatherless and widow are mentioned in regard to the third-year tithe, the holy tithe, the tithe that signifies we've kept all His commandments by which we will be blessed in "all" the works of our hands. It is very significant that the four participants are mentioned here in Malachi 3:5, in regard to the priest having robbed God and even the whole nation.

Because of this robbery, the whole nation who had paid the tithe to the Levite which should've been distributed or divvied up between the stranger, fatherless and widow had been robbed. The importance of the tithe going to the stranger, fatherless and widow cannot be over emphasized. It is downplayed by the clergy today who insist on receiving a year to year tithe, but God insists this tithe be placed in the storehouse so all who He's named can have access to the produce they will need to sustain them. These folks the stranger, fatherless and widow are special to God. Unless we are walking in their shoes we don't understand their level of distress nor their challenges. It's not the majority that God is most concerned about, it's the minority to whom He gives priority. God has the greatest heart for those on life's fringes. And so must we.

Whereas God gives the greater emphasis, man gives the least emphasis to the 3rd year tithe. And since by this tithe He considers we have kept His commandments and deserve "blessings", of what other tithe would He feel robbed if not this 3rd year tithe? (Mal.3:8)

After all, which tithe is consistent with the statement, "Bring ye all the tithes into the storehouse, that there may be meat in mine house, and prove me now herewith, saith the Lord of hosts, if I will not open you the windows of heaven and pour out a blessing, that there shall not be room enough to receive it"? "All nations shall call you blessed", Mal.3:8-12.

The New International Version states specifically, "At the end of every three years, bring all the tithes of that year's produce and 'store' it in your towns." The KJV says, "lay it up!" Malachi 3:10 says bring the whole (all of it) tithe into the 'storehouse', that there may be food in my house." (NIV). The Malachi tithe includes the same four factors, Levite, stranger, widow and fatherless, and it is to be "stored".

The Malachi tithe is obviously referring to the third-year tithe which our fathers had gotten away from since the beginning. The priests ignored this tithe hundreds of years prior to this writing and have ignored it thousands of years hence. The preachers are ignoring this very same tithe today!!! This is the 'storehouse' tithe to be laid up so that the individuals to whom this tithe is so designated could have access to it throughout the year.

Think about Malachi 3 very carefully. If failure to pay tithes was how the priests were robbing God, to whom were they to pay tithes? To ask the question another way, since the priests were the receivers of the tithe, how could they have robbed God by failing to pay the tithe? Since priests had no tithes to pay then how are they then guilty of robbing God? The primary income of the priests was the offerings. These offerings were extended to them three times a year from the produce of the people. They managed to mess up the offering to the Lord on the sacrificial altar by offering Him the sick and inferior stock. So back to the question, who were the priests supposed to tithe to, when we know that they were the receivers of the tithe? How if they were receivers of the tithe and had no one whom to pay, were they robbing God?

The context of Malachi 3 tells us that the priests had gotten instruction to divvy up or make the tithe available to the widow, stranger and fatherless by placing it in the storehouse, so they all could have access to it. It is clear the priests did not distribute the tithe to those closest to God's own heart, His greatest concern, and so by this they were robbing God Himself.

The subject matter speaks also of the "storehouse". The storehouse was setup so that the widow, fatherless and foreigner could have produce available to them for their sustenance. This produce was to be laid up within the gates, Deuteronomy 14:28-29, for easy access. Again, what tithe were the priest required to pay and to whom would they pay it? They had no produce, no inheritance, no permanent means of sustenance. Their dependency was upon the offerings the people gave them. The tithe was to be a supplementary bonus to the offerings they had received. However apparently, the priests got selfish and greedy and instead of sharing it with the three other folks, they kept it all to themselves.

Therefore, God felt robbed and called it robbery. So, because they misconstrued the proper use of the tithe they robbed God and even or 'also' the whole nation. They were stealing from the nation because they were supposed to share it with those appointed to receive it. This inaction on their part amounted to fraud. This fraud deprived the nation of the blessings God promised them because now the widow, orphan and foreigner weren't receiving the tithe to which they were entitled. So yes, the nation was also being robbed, robbed, robbed of their blessings. This very type of disobedience led that nation into captivity. One form of disobedience leads to another until we slide into complete destruction.

If you ask the ministry today, they will obviously downplay this discussion as an unimportant and useless debate to get our minds off of the centrality of the gospel which is Christ and Him crucified. However, the Lord of the old testament is the same Lord of the new. He claims He was being robbed, and the nation was being robbed, even as this robbery goes on today. I say that if these folks, the widow, the fatherless and stranger are neglected by the church even today, not just of tithes but of care, attention and financial support, even by the churches that don't preach tithing, there will be a reckoning. These people's situations are the centrality of the gospel of The Savior because they are at the heart of His concern, and I don't see why we would think it has changed today. Can we claim that because He came and died for our sins and saved us that a special support for the fatherless, widow and foreigner is no longer at the utmost heart of our Father God's concerns today? No! Might we not be crucifying Christ afresh every time we neglect those closest to His heart? Yes!

Read again Deut.14:28-29, "the Levite, and the stranger, and the fatherless, and the widow which are within thy gates, shall come and shall eat and be satisfied; that the Lord thy God may bless thee." The tithe of the third-year is the only one with a promise of "blessings" (Deut.14:29; 26:13-15; Mal.3:10).

The Holy Tithe

The third-year tithe is not just the "poor" tithe, as it is traditionally coined, but it is the "holy tithe", "poor" being in God's sight the "richest" folks of them all (Deuteronomy 26:13), "holy" being the highest order of all. Why are the churches not requiring us to pay the "holy" or "hallowed" tithe? Is not our God holy? Aren't we required to be holy? Are we not called "saints of the most High God"? If we're saints we're required to be holy, and if we are holy we must pay the "holy tithe".

So why do we not pay the holy tithe? Why do we not pay it in "the year of tithing"? Why do we neglect "The" year of the tithe? The year of the tithe is clearly the year that we should pay the tithe, so why don't we know about this year of the tithe? Why isn't this "holy tithe", the most divine or Godly-tithe, preached at church? Why isn't the year of the holy tithe preached? Why is it that when this tithe is paid, then (and only then) we can say we've "kept all God has commanded us"? Conversely if we don't pay this tithe in the year of tithing we have failed to keep all God has commanded us? Why, why?

Why is this very same tithe called the "sacred" tithe? Why are we not taught to pay this sacred tithe every three years? Why are we not taught that the third-year is the "year of the tithe"? That if we're not paying the "sacred tithe" in the third "year of tithing" do we fail to do all that God has commanded us? Yes! If we fail to distribute it to the Levite, widow, fatherless and stranger, can we say we've done all the Lord has commanded us? No! If we fail to pay this God-ordained, hallowed, sacred, divine tithe, are we subject to God's wrath? Yes! So why have the preachers let us down, placed us in jeopardy with our God and not taught us to pay this, the sacred "holy tithe"?

It might destroy the tithe system we are taught today, because we are taught to pay a tenth of our income to the church every week. It would question the notion that it is alright to apply the tithe to help maintain the church operations, lights, bills, rents, salaries and so on.

Deuteronomy 14:29 states that when paying this "holy" "third-year" tithe the Lord will bless us in "all" the work of our hands. Well if He's going to bless "all" the work of our hands with the payment of this holy third-year tithe, then why pay a year to year tithe exclusively to the church?

And since this tithe 'fulfills' the tithe command requirement, why pay a year to year tithe exclusively to the church? According to the scripture, upon paying the 1) yearly offering and the 2) tithe every third-year we'll have done "all" that we're required to do.

So why are we taught to do something else, while neglecting these directives from our God?

Why are we being misled? Abraham paid a tenth to Melchizedek and the law of Moses instructs us as to how we're to pay our tenth. Moses instructs that we pay to the Levite, widow, fatherless and stranger, every third-year, a "holy", "sacred" tithe. And that because it goes to the Levite, the widow, fatherless and foreigner it is considered a payment as unto the Lord.

I believe we're being misinformed. We love the people who teach us the Word and of course we're going to love them, but are they telling us the truth, the whole truth and nothing but the truth? In fact, they may not know that they've been deceived. When that happens, the responsibility is on us to stand up and make a difference in their lives, and we must not back down. So, when they reply, 'so you don't believe in tithing?', you say, 'Yes I do believe in the biblical tithe. The tithe is holy. The biblical instruction says we are to tithe the holy tithe every three years and it is to be stored up for four categories, the Levite, widow, fatherless and the foreigner.'

Confusing Tithes with Offerings

In the Biblical record, are the offerings and tithes somewhat confused and convoluted, without distinction?

In truth, the offerings and the tithes are not confused biblically or symbolically. Also, as is sometimes suggested, the tithe is not a way of regulating the offering. The two serve entirely different purposes.

The convolution of the two gives weight to the argument that a "priestly Levitical" tithe is to be paid year to year, because the offering is regulated by the year to year harvest season around which the feasts take place.

Confusing the offering and the tithe as indistinct, veils the fact that there is no direct command stipulating that there is a supposed "priestly" tithe to be paid year to year to the church.

What is being ignored is that the offerings always mentioned first are the primary sustenance for the Levites, the priests or ministers, since they have no inheritance (Lev.7:28-34; Deut.18: 1-8).

The offerings came in the 3 prominent harvest seasons (Ex.34:23, 24; Deut.16:16, 17). They are the great and dynamic support of the priesthood (Deut.18: 1-8).

The offering is the most important feature in the biblical record beginning with the incident of Abel and Cain and the significant trial of Abraham offering Isaac.

It points to Christ The Lamb, our Savior, "THE OFFERING" and His great sacrifice of death on the cross for us. It is also the Church giving of herself unto Christ, her husband, who gave Himself for her salvation.

The offering is the first giving of ourselves. It is the only giving out of our "own money" because the tithe already "belongs to God". The offering is not based upon income percentage, but upon the substance we have gathered according to how God has blessed us (Deut.16:17) and how much of it we voluntarily give back to Him.

The offerings can also remind us of how insignificant we are and how great God is, and that we are to give of ourselves to Him, humbly. The offering further shows God how grateful we are for all our riches and that it is He who has blessed us and not we ourselves. Offerings come from the heart; the proportion we give is voluntary, so it is a true measure of our heartfelt appreciation for how He has blessed us.

Offerings embody the total worship of the Eternal. God assures the Levite priests they would be sustained by the offerings, it is their due, God's portion of their inheritance, "a covenant of salt", Num.18:19-20.

Whereas the tithe plays a comparatively supplemental role, the offerings are the key support to their livelihood (Lev.7:28-34; Deut.18:1-8).

Did Abraham Set the Priestly Tithe Precedent?

Tenth and Ten Commandments. Unless the tenth given every third year is kept, all the commandments are not satisfied. The tenth is the first-fruits we are to give, and the ten commandments are the premier Laws to be observed in our life. Abraham set the 'priestly' tithe precedent, the exclusive 'priestly' tithe. One tenth shall go under the rod. The tenth is Holy as is the ten commandments. (Lev.27:32)

Abraham's grandson Jacob did promise to give a tenth unto the Lord upon being blessed by God, because there was an apparent law of animal sacrifice for sins, prior to Moses' law of animal sacrifice for sins. (Gen.28:22)

The breakdown of how to tithe as explained in the book of the Law of Moses was that the tithe is to be split between 1) the priest, 2) the immigrant, 3) the fatherless and 4) the widow.

Abraham tithed. He demonstrates that due to the fact he was wildly blessed when his life was in jeopardy He tithed a tenth of the spoil to Melchizedek, the priest in the land. This priest may have performed animal sacrifices for sins.

The tithe command that is reiterated in the Book of the Law is stated twice (when you look at the common denominator that it should go to the fatherless, widow, stranger and Levite).

If the priest were to receive an entire portion of the tithe exclusively, then he'd be receiving two tithes for himself. This would amount to extortion. Thus, when we acknowledge the third-year tithe commandment that God gave in the old covenant then we realize there is no exclusive year to year, every year tithe to the priest. The tithe command given to Moses supported the work of the Levitical priests who sacrificed the animals for our trespass of the covenant. This tithe is holy and pre-belongs to the Lord but is supplementary. The Ten Commandments already belong to the Lord, but is supplementary also, for it hands on the two main commandments, love God with all our heart mind and soul and Love our neighbor as our self.

It is in ignoring the third-year tithe that the priest have suckered the people into believing in a tithe that goes exclusively to the church year to year. It is only the tri-annual tithe that determines whether we've kept God's commandments, because it cares for what is closest to God's heart (Jas.1:27), the Levite, the stranger, the fatherless and the widow.

As regard to Abraham and his tithe to the High Priest Melchizedek the apostle Paul states; "For there is verily a disannulling of the commandment going before for the weakness and unprofitableness there-of" (Hebrews 7:18). In short, the tithing command which was covered under the law was eliminated, along with the Levitical priesthood which was rendered ineffective. That is why despite all the ordinances, laws, regulations and traditions established in the old covenant, The Lamb of God our Lord and Savior The Christ had to come and give His life for us. "If therefore perfection were by the Levitical priesthood, what further need was there that another priest should rise...?"

Paul states, "For it is evident that our Lord sprang out of Judah; of which tribe Moses spake nothing concerning priesthood. And it is yet far more evident: for that after the similitude of Melchizedek there ariseth another priest. Who is made not after the law, of a carnal (fleshly commandment) but after the power of an endless life." Conclusion: There is no record that Paul, Peter, James, John, or any of the apostles asked the church to tithe. After the death, burial and resurrection of The Lamb, the law of sacrifice for our sins was fulfilled once and for all.

That is to say, there being no more need for the law of animal sacrifices on our behalf, there was no need to support the Levites with our tithes. Christ came to fulfill the need for the law of sacrifice once and for all.

Thereby the function of shedding the blood of animals for our sins which was handled by the Levites, was removed. Thus, the need to tithe to them as compensation for that work performed on our behalf was eliminated. Their function being now thus eradicated, the only other participants of the tithe are the widow, fatherless and stranger. Ex. 22:21-22; Zech.7:10; Mal.3:5. The widow, fatherless and stranger are now the standalone concerns of the Almighty. It suggests that these three which include the poor and hireling are still sensitive in God's heart.

Thereby, those with plenty are to share their all, with those who do not have enough as occurred in Acts 4:31-37 and sold their lands and their houses and laid them down at the Apostle's feet. And distribution was made unto every man according as he had need. v. 36...[Barnabas] a Levite, and of the country of Cyprus, Having land, sold it, and brought the money, and laid it at the Apostle's feet."

The properties were turned into money. The money laid at the Apostle's feet was distributed to the brethren. But then of course the Apostles maintain the theme of caring for the fatherless and widow, (James 1:27), even in the New Testament.

In summation, it is no longer about giving our tithe to the priest for if we do, that which is part and parcel of the sacrifice of animals we deny faith in the Messiah and the sacrifice He gave of Himself for us. The tithe He demands of us today is to sacrifice our whole life for each other, as living sacrifices, by which we prove we accept the sacrifice He made for us, and we are thereby forgiven of our transgressions. Thus, they sold houses and lands, turned it into money and distributed it to the people.

Before Our Redeemer died for our sins, tithing was still in effect even while He walked the earth for 33 1/2 years. When He stated, we should emphasize "judgment (righteousness), mercy and faith" and not leave the other (tithing) undone, the Law of sacrifices were still in effect. (Matt.23:23).

He came to fulfill the Law of animal sacrifices by making Himself subject to an unjust death. He did this because the old covenant Law of animal sacrifices, was insufficient to cover our sins, Heb.9:1-28; 10:1-10

Our Redeemer came to give His body so that upon our violation of the old covenant Laws our sins could be forgiven, and we would live. This is how the death of Christ marked the fulfillment of the old covenant Law requirement of sacrifices, Matt.5:17.

Israel was a sacrifice honed society. Their entire salvation was dependent on the animal sacrifices because there was a covenant between them and the most High. If the covenant was broken, it could mean death to them. A covenant or vow is to the death. So you don't break it, because you've vowed that you would die before ever breaking the covenant. So the Law of animal sacrifices was added to the covenant Laws as the way to obtain forgiveness for transgressing the covenant Laws. To believe

Christ, the Lamb of God came to replace the sacrificial Laws was hard for them. Faith that His sacrifice replaced the animal sacrifices had to be encouraged. Ultimately the sacrificial Laws could not save us from the breaking of the covenant Laws. But when Our Redeemer Christ sacrificed His life for us He fulfilled the Law of sacrifices for the breaking of the covenant Laws, so that upon calling upon Him we might be saved.

Therefore, now it is no longer the Law of sacrifices that must be offered to save us, but it is the sacrifice of Christ that saves us from the fleshly man within us, the heart of stone that transgresses the covenant Laws of God. Now it's Christ's sacrifice in whom we have faith, and not the Law of animal sacrifices. When we accept Him as our sacrificial Savior, we get forgiveness if inadvertently we trespass the covenant Laws. This is why the scripture says, it is by faith (in Christ's sacrifice) we are saved and not by works (the works of animal sacrifices).

He removed the death sentence the breaking of the covenant Laws placed upon us, thus redeeming us from the trespass of the covenant Law into the life of the spirit. When we accept His sacrifice, we walk in the spirit and not in the works of the Law. The spirit cleanses us from all unrighteousness. The Law exposes how far we fall short and the spirit absolves our shortcoming. By this we keep the Law perfectly in spirit and in truth.

In our flesh, we come up short of keeping the Laws, but because of the Holy Spirit released to us through Christ, Our Savior, we are cleansed from all unrighteousness.

Is the Law evil, bad or good? It is good, but it is our flesh which wars against the Law in our mind that causes us trouble. It is by the acceptance of The Lamb as our sacrifice that we are saved from the curse that our flesh imposes upon us in light of the Law. In acceptance of Christ The Lamb we no longer walk in the flesh but after the spirit of everlasting life. (Romans 7:12-25)

If we think that in keeping these commandments we do them perfectly, we are of all men lost. We cannot and will not keep them perfectly. If we trespass any of them in one point, we break them all. So, it is necessary to have a blood sacrifice to atone for our sins in coming up short of perfectly keeping the Law, especially in our hearts. There were never enough animals that could be sacrificed to make up for our shortcomings, even though we were going through the motions of Law keeping. In Christ Our Redeemer, our Law keeping is perfected because His perfect life redeemed us from our shortcoming in keeping the Law which was negated by our flesh man and its enmity against God.

So now by His spirit Christ overcame the enemy of the flesh man in us which caused us, to come up short of keeping the Law perfectly and by His perfect sacrifice has absolved us of all unrighteousness.

Can the Law save us? No! It is Christ who saves us. Is the Law thereby eliminated? No! The Law is rather intensified, the Law meaning the ten commandments.

We now keep it in the spirit with our whole heart, selling all we have and giving it to the poor, visiting the sick, fighting for righteousness for the fatherless, oppressed, aliens, enemies, clothing the naked, all as a way of life, religiously, and teaching men to do so.

To teach the commandments are done away once we accept Christ in our hearts as our personal Saviour, is not honest. To think by keeping the commandments we ignore what Christ did for us because he is the fulfillment of the commandments, is not honest. To think that by keeping the Law we are now a debtor to do the whole Law, is not honest. It is the sacrificial Law that we must not keep, so we do not negate what Christ did for us, and so that we are not a debtor to the whole Law. The rest of the Law, other than the sacrificial portion of the Law, the commandment portion of the Law, we are to keep, Romans 13:8-9. What we have been deceived into believing is that it's either one thing or the other. It's either Law or faith. However, it is evident it is about the Law and faith, Revelation 14:12, "Here is the patience of the saints: here are they that keep the commandments of God, -And- the faith of Jesus." This "And" implies we must do one in addition to the other. We are to keep the commandments and -Additionally- have faith that His blood sacrifice forgives our sins.

As Paul said, if we keep part of the Law we must keep them all. However it is apparent that since the Law exposes our inability to keep them perfectly, because in our hearts as was shown by the rich ruler the Law doesn't solve our need to love the poor and needy, to sell all we have and give the proceeds to the poor, or as in the case of the good Samaritan to bend down and help lift up our neighbor in need or as in the case of the tax collector to give half of all we've earned to the poor or in the case of Cornelius the Centurion to give alms to the poor and needy, even though we keep the commandments

42

perfectly from our youth as did Saul who proceeded to murder the Christian Jews who were also keeping the commandments or in the case of those who failed to visit the sick, imprisoned, feed the hungry and give drink to the thirsty, if we keep the commandments perfectly and don't have the love of God, it profiteth usnothing.

So, it is not in the keeping of the commandments that our salvation is assured, but it is in extending the love to our brother which is the blood sacrifice that God now requires of us to atone for the shortcomings in our attempt to keep the law perfectly. Our "sacrifice" of our time, money, energy, our lives for each other good and evil alike, lives the love Christ requires of us, just as He lived and died for us. As He laid down His life for us, He commands us to lay down or give away our lives for the needs of each other.

When we keep the law, we are guilty of breaking the whole law if we transgress in one point, James 2:10. However, we are forgiven of breaking the whole law in one point when we perform the deeds of charity toward a hungry brother.

Verse 13. "For he shall have judgment without mercy, that hath showed no mercy", in other words we will pay for our sins if we don't show mercy, "(However) mercy rejoiceth against judgment." In other words, "mercy" defeats or rejoiceth against any shortcoming we may have in keeping the commandments. And how do we obtain the mercy that forgives our sins? We obtain this mercy through faith. And how is this faith demonstrated? This faith is demonstrated when a brother is naked or hungry, we must clothe and feed him. It is by these works a man's sins are forgiven. It is not faith alone, James 2:24. Faith in Christ alone is not what justifies us, but it's the works of faith in Christ alone, which forgives us of having broken the Law.

It is self-evident that we can save others more effectively by the sacrifices they see us do for one another, than all the preaching in the world, (I Peter 2:12). Then on top of that Peter makes the cornerstone statement of his entire book, "And above all things have fervent (intense) charity among yourselves: for charity shall cover a multitude of sins", I Peter 4:8. Charity (love) is sacrifice for one another. Sacrifice will cause us to suffer for the needs of the brethren, even as Christ our Messiah also suffered for us.

"Greater love hath no man than this, that a man lay down his life for his friends," John 15:13. The rich man kept the physical law perfectly his whole life but could not keep the spirit of the law which was to lay down his life for his brother. The "sacrifice" is the fulfillment of the law! "This is my commandment, that ye love one another, as I have loved you", John 15:12. "Hereby perceive we the love of God, because he laid down his life for us: and we ought to lay down our lives for the brethren," I John 3:16. How is life 'laying down' demonstrated? I John 3:17, says, "But whoso hath this world's goods, and seeth his brother have need", ..that's how 'laying down' of life is demonstrated which atones for our shortcoming when we fail to keep the commandments perfectly. Even as the sacrifice of Jesus Christ laying down His life for us atones for our shortcomings. However, His sacrifice cannot and will not atone for our shortcoming in keeping the law if we fail to accept His sacrifice as our payment for the penalty of keeping the law imperfectly. And we fail to accept His sacrifice of payment for the curse of the law if we fail to do what? Love, "in deed and in truth", v. 18. "Do whatsoever I command you..." John 15:14.

In mimicking the sacrifice of His life for us by sacrificing our life for our neighbor, we accept the blood sacrifice of Our Savior for our sins of imperfectly keeping His laws and we are thusly saved unto eternal life.

Law keeping only distinguishes us as His called out chosen ones. Suffering through the laying down of our lives distinguishes us as inheritors of His Eternal Kingdom. "For all the law is fulfilled in one word, even in this: Thou shalt love thy neighbor as thyself." Galatians 5:14.

The laying down of our lives for our brother fulfills the "spirit" of the law in which we are to walk. When Our Savior said, I came not to destroy but to fulfill, the fulfilling of the law was the blood sacrifice of Himself. It is that He laid down His life for us. The laying down our life to save the life of our brother is the highest love. There is nothing that tops that, John 15:13. Especially when we lay down our lives for our enemy. When we do it to save sinners, the unholy and the unrighteous, this is its ultimate fulfillment, Romans 5:8-10. Charity for our brothers is the fulfillment of the law.

We're to walk in the spirit and not the flesh. So, of all the physical sacrifices that the law required of us, if we cannot lay down our lives for our brethren, we won't be forgiven of our sins because we've proven we have not accepted the sacrifice of The Lamb and are thus doomed to eternal destruction,

Matthew 25:41-46. We live in a suffer-avoidance society. Our Messiah came to suffer, I Peter 2:19, 21. If He came to suffer we must also suffer, especially for the right thing. "This is my commandment that ye love one another", John 15:12. This is my commandment that ye 'suffer for one another'. This is where men shall see our good works and glorify our Father in heaven.

Our sacrifice for our brethren ultimately makes up for our lack of keeping His commandments with our whole heart, mind and soul, for in that area we would always come up short.

This is the way in which we must have "faith" in Christ and the sacrifice He made for us.

Many say we live by grace only. However, where there is no law, there is no need for grace. If there is no law saying that we should not exceed the speed limit, then when we exceed the speed limit, we do not need grace.

It is when we kill someone that we need grace. If there is no law against killing someone we would not need that grace.

Only when there is a law do we need grace. So, grace is the proof that there are commandments required for us to obey. Then if we break those commandments we require the grace that's been made available to us through the blood of Christ, Romans 6:2. In Matthew 5:17, The Savior said, "Think not that I am come to destroy the law, or the prophets: I am not come to destroy but fulfill". He fulfilled the law by becoming The Sacrifice.

Galatians 5:26, "But if ye be led of the Spirit, ye are not under the law." The key point is that we must not walk in the letter but in the Spirit of the law, (Matthew 5:27, 28). The Spirit of the law more than covers the letter of the law, and thereby proves that we're not under the penalty of the letter which is death. What is the spirit of the law? The spirit by which we must be led is the spirit contained in the sacrifice of our own lives for our neighbor. "For all the law is fulfilled in one word, even in this; Thou shalt love thy neighbor as thyself", Galatians 5:14. So when we are led by the "spirit of sacrifice" as was Christ, we "fulfill the law". We are then no longer under the curse of death when we un-intentionally break the law. So, the spirit of the law is to lay down our lives for our neighbor. What does that really mean? "...he that hath two coats, let him impart to him that hath none; and he that hath meat, let him do likewise", Luke 3:11. I was sick and ye visited me: I was in prison, and ye came unto me," Matthew 25:36.

Removal from Idolatry

When we get away from idolatrous worship we move toward the laws of God. Our lives are empty without His natural laws. We fill our lives with Easter, Christmas, and Sunday worship or absent of that we fill it with Unleavened bread, Pentecost and Shabbat observance. The removal of the idols and covetousness backs us into God's holydays and laws, but these days and laws are not an end to themselves, but merely a marker for the salvation works we are to perform in laying down our lives for our brothers, even our friends, as Christ did for us.

The key is we cannot be a believer and be immobile. We must act as a friend of The Word, an adopted son of the most High. It is the "sacrifice" which is the "spirit" of the law. It is all about the "sacrifice" of self. The ten commandments have two parts, the sacrifice of self for our brothers, and to abstain from idols, fornication and lewdness. We are in fact to be a "living" sacrifice, Romans 12:1. We must be dying daily for our brothers. No "sacrifice", no "spirit", no forgiveness, utter damnation.

If we fail to do good on the sabbath day we have done evil. The reason for that is because unless we do good on the sabbath day we have rested in it only in the flesh but have failed to rest from the works of the flesh by exercising the works of the spirit in sacrificing ourselves for the needy, helpless, oppressed and sinners, Luke 14:1-6; Matthew 12:9-13.

Sacrificial offerings of meat and drink were presented by the priest of old every sabbath day (Numbers 28:9) and so in the same way we should offer ourselves as a living sacrifice for our brothers every sabbath day. Is it not lawful to do well on the sabbath day (Matthew 12:12)? Christ made the point that if according to old covenant law it is pro-law to rescue a sheep, goat, ox or other animal that might be in distress or stuck in a pit or ditch of some sort, then how much more pro-law would it be for us to work to rescue a needy brother who is in some type of distress, especially when it's on the sabbath day?

The work of sacrificing is still a demand and even a command today! It is the labor of the heart we must accomplish to enter that "Rest" today! Jesus went out of His way and away from self to seek out the sick and broken, the maimed and the laime, on the seventh day. He could have relaxed and rested at home, He could've healed them on another day, but worked so hard on the sabbath day until He had become famished, and illegally fed on the grain and corn in the field.

The seventh day was made for man says Mark 2:27; made for the support and healing of men in need. We are to walk in the spirit, to do spiritual works on that day, which is done by inconveniencing the self to serve others. It is also as Paul called it, "dying daily", (I Cor.15:31). It is also called "labor to enter into His rest". It is the labor that produces the fruit Our Savior demands we produce, John 15:2,8. It is the labor that enters us into His rest, spiritual rest. It is the labor that must cost us something. v. 8. "Herein is my Father glorified, that ye bear much fruit; so shall ye be my disciples."

It is in this labor in which we walk in the spirit of Romans 8:1. We stay away from drunkenness and revellings or partying and uncleanness and we live in the fruits of the spirit as stated in Galatians 5:22...love, joy, peace, patience, kindness, goodness, faithfulness, gentleness, self-control; against such things there is no law. "And those who belong to Christ Jesus have crucified the flesh with its passions and desires."

How We Walk In The Spirit

When a person dies we say His spirit has gone back up to the Lord, or "to be absent from the body is to be present with the Lord." When a life dies, it releases its' "spirit" from that body. A thing must die for the spirit to be released. When we "sacrifice" our self, our "spirit" is being released", and so we are thus walking in the "spirit".

It is why when we die to self, we walk in the spirit, John 12:24.

When we die to self our spirit is released. That is, ..this is why the sacrifice is so important. And the sacrifice is initiated in the circumcision of the heart, it is in the cutting of the fleshly foreskin from the heart, so that our heart is clean, spiritually pure. What God initially requires is a "cut"-heart. "... and (you) shalt obey his voice according to all that I command thee this day, thou and thy children, with all thine heart, and with all thine soul." "And the Lord thy God will circumcise thine heart, and the heart of thy seed (children), to love the Lord thy God with all thine heart, and with all thy soul, that thou mayest live." "Jesus said unto him, Thou shalt love the Lord thy God with all thy heart.." Matthew 22:37. "So circumcise your heart, and stiffen your neck no longer", Deut.10:14-16. "Circumcise yourselves to the Lord and remove the foreskins of your heart, Jeremiah 4:4.

This is why circumcision of heart is stressed by Paul. Not of fleshly foreskin- the heart-, not a holy day- the heart-, not meats- the heart-, not the commandments- the heart-, and yet the commandments- the heart-, and yet meats- the heart-, and yet the holy days- the heart-, and yet the foreskin-the heart, (Col.2:8-23; Deut. 3:6; Romans 2:28-29).

Our outward actions should reflect our inward condition. We cut the foreskin because our hearts are cut. We keep the holy day because our hearts are wholly separate from evil and idolatry. We keep the command-ments because our hearts love God and our brother. We eat clean meats because our hearts are not defiled nor polluted with other gods. The stat-utes and commands are not a badge of righteousness. The cut heart is the righteousness, and it's reflection is displayed in the keeping of the statutes and commands. The outward keeping of the statutes and commands become a reflection of the spiritual in-keeping of them in our hearts, Romans 4:9-12. "..he (Abraham) received the sign of circumcision, a seal of the righ-teousness of the faith which he had while uncircumcised, so that he might be the father of all who believe without being circumcised, so that he might be so that righteousness might be credited to them..."

We as a nation of priest (Exodus 19:6) must thusly continue the sacri-fices that Our Savior came to end in the flesh once and for all, but the sacrifices we are to now perform are in the "spirit", the same way He laid down His life for us, we are to lay down our own life for our brethren. After all, aren't our human lives more valuable to God than are the animal lives of sheep, oxen and goats?

The cut heart makes us serve the homeless, the widow, the needy, it makes us fight to rehabilitate and free the prisoners, the oppressed strang-ers in our land, to feed the hungry, and get aid and support to the sick and dying. The circumcised heart gives freely to the poor. It is a heart of compassion for the weak, the feeble and marginal who live on the fringes of life. It exalts the elderly and supports the fatherless. It accepts being the servant to all and takes the low humble position. It is a heart of sacrifice and giving. It is the comforter on earth. It in this way acts as the spirit of God for all to benefit.

Josephus vs The Bible

According to the Josephus historical record, Israel paid not only a 1st, but a 2nd and 3rd tithe also. What's its origin?

Let's notice the wording in the Josephus account, Book IV, chapter 8, section 22: "Besides those two tithes, which I have already said you are to pay every year, the one for the Levites, the other for the festivals, you are to bring every third-year a third tithe to be distributed to those that want; to women also that are widows and to the children that are orphans."

Discrepancies with the Biblical account abound, not the least being the inclusion of an annual Levitical tithe. But more importantly, the Josephus account cleverly omits elements of the third-year tithe the Bible account expressly and repeatedly includes. First of all, the Bible does not say "orphans" but it says "fatherless". A child could have a mother but if he is without father, God has a great concern for him.

Secondly the Levite and the stranger are excluded. This is a major exclusion treated as insignificant.

The Biblical account consistently includes the Levite and the stranger each and every time this third-year tithe is described (Deut.14:28-29, 16:13-15, 26:12-16), why?

Obviously, God wanted them included in the third-year tithe, He is concerned for the financial welfare of all. Had the Levite been assigned a yearly 'priestly' tithe, the full significance of their inclusion in the third-year tithe would've been lost.

A problem with the Josephus account is that if you include the Levite in the receiving of the 3rd year tithe, then every 3rd year he would receive nearly 20% of the tithes of the people in addition to receiving a portion of the 2nd or festival tithe, along with the tremendous bounty of first fruit and other offerings.

Regarding the concept of a 'Levitical priestly tithe' which is termed by Josephus the "first tithe", J. Hastings writes, "Against this the following considerations are decisive. No hint is given in Deuteronomy that (a second) tithe is spoken of nor can such an interpretation be fairly put on the passage, for a reference to the assumed first tithe would have one-fifth (20%) of the whole produce should be imposed on the farmers.

Nor is it credible that the Levites should participate in the second tithe because, like the poor and defenseless, they were dependent on charity, if they were in possession of a tithe already made over to them" (J Hastings, D.D.: "tithe").

And so it is, that upon establishing the Levitical first tithe, a yearly enhancement without the inclusion of others; the Levites dismissed themselves from inclusion in all other tithes. They did this without God's permission; an act which violates God's commandments.

What would then be the biblical significance for the inclusion of the Levite and the stranger in the third-year tithe?

Apparently, God wanted the Levite not to forget that he was also a stranger, a slave, afflicted in Egypt, and that God has brought him forth after signs and wonders great and terrible, and with an outstretched hand given him to a land flowing with milk and honey (Deut.1:17-20; 26:5-9). You see the stranger is a part of the third-year tithe because God wanted the Levite to love the stranger and to remember an immigrant's plight (Deut.1:18,19; Ex.23:9). God wanted to remind the Levite of what
   should be his true attitude.

The Levite, however, removed himself from this third-year tithe, and while forsaking inclusion with the class that included the foreigner, fatherless and widow, deprived them of their right to receive the tithe as he enhanced his own position by demanding the tithe be paid to him year to year as a source of extra personal income. This was clearly disobedient to what God had commanded.

Against the backdrop of the Biblical record, the Josephus record indicts the Levite and the manipulations perpetrated.

We should understand some background to Josephus (approx. A.D. 37-1) whose birth name is Josephus Ben Matthias. In the foreword to "Josephus, Complete Works", William Sanford La Sor states, that after sampling the two other sects of the Jews "at the age of nineteen, Josephus joined the Pharisees, and remained in that sect for the rest of his life" (pg. VII).

Rev. Henry Stebbing, D.D. in the introductory Essay to the same book states, "The writings of Josephus may be classed under the two headings of historical and controversial". In suggesting Josephus was "anxious" to inspire Gentile readers, Stebbing writes, "Such, at least, is one of the supposed reasons of those 'discrepancies' which exist between the history of Josephus and that of Scripture" (pg. XIII. pp. 22, pg. XIV. pp.2).

Rev. Stebbing adds, "He (Josephus) was intimately acquainted with whatever had been taught by the learned of his nation...though from his pages, therefore, it is not often that we can add to our stock of positive knowledge, we may in many cases trace by their help the progress of error, discover its origin, and estimate the relative force of those deplorable corruptions whereby it became at last so indissolubly bound up with the national constitution" (pg. XX. pp. 1).

Perhaps Josephus best explains the contradictions, errors and discrepancies when he states in his own words, "What I would explain is this, that the Pharisees have delivered to the people a great many observances by succession from their fathers, which are not written in the law of Moses;" (Bk XIII, chpt. X sec. 6). In other words, the year to year tithe doctrine was not written in the law of Moses.

The Indictment Against the Priests

The Pharisees believed in what is called the "oral traditions", or 'sayings, passed down from the fathers. Christ was accused of trying to undermine Moses because He opposed these oral laws attributed to Moses (John 5:43-47; 9:28, 29).

Our Savior was for the law and the prophets, which He came to fulfill (Matt. 5:17). It was the "oral laws" equated equal to, but having subtle discrepancies with scripture, he opposed.

Christ states, "In vain do they worship me, 'teaching for doctrines' the commandments of men" (Mark 7:7). Christ warned, "Beware of the leaven (spins) of the Pharisees", which is the "doctrine of the Pharisees and the Sadducees" (Mat.16:11-12). The discrepancies in the tithe laws, as described by Josephus were also passed down by the forefathers in this regard.

Even back in Malachi's day the fact is that subtle changes to God's commands upset God very greatly. Notice what He says to the Levites through the prophet Malachi... "Unto you O priests that despise my name"... "And now, O Priests, this commandment is for YOU" (Mal.1:6; 2:1).

God warns them (Mal. 3:1-16), that the messenger of His covenant is coming, to refine and purify with a refiner's fire the SONS OF LEVI (the priests/preachers), to purge them like gold and silver is purged, that they may offer to the Lord an offering in righteousness, as in the former day, to be a swift witness against those (priests) who, oppress, note: "the 'WAGE EARNER' in his wages (tithing was evidently only required of the inherited class).

Notice that the reason the priest was to receive a portion of a tithe at all is because he had no "inheritance". The point is that whoever had no inheritance was not required to tithe. Thus, those who have no inheritance should not be required to tithe specifically the wage earner. Yet the tithe was imposed by the priest upon the wage earner, which God considered oppressing the wage earner.

On top of this they (the priest not the people) defrauded the WIDOW, and the FATHERLESS, and (they) turned aside the STRANGER from his right." "For I am the Lord, I do not change, YET FROM THE DAYS OF YOUR FATHER, YOU HAVE GONE AWAY FROM MY ORDINANCES AND HAVE NOT KEPT THEM, return to me and I will return to you..." (Mal. 3:6, 7, NKJV).

"But you said in what shall we return?" Notice God's answer, "Will a man rob God? Yet you have robbed me", he tells the priests. "But you say, in what way have we robbed you?" they state they aren't aware!... and God replies, "In tithes and offerings".

Men of "tradition" state this robbery was a sin of "withholding tithes" and that the nation of Israel failed to pay the tithes and offerings because of a weak priesthood (Halley's, pg. 385).

It is however obvious that God is not condemning the people, but the priests the sons of Levi, and the priests did offer offerings, and were condemned for offering "lame", "blind" and "sick" animals, apparently keeping the healthy ones for themselves (Mal. 1:6-8,12-14). The robbery was not that the priests were neglecting to pay the tithe, the robbery was that they failed to distribute it to the widow, fatherless and stranger.

What the priests committed was an act of fraud. The priests failed to administer the third-year tithe, keeping it for themselves. Collected a portion from the wage earner, and defrauded the fatherless, and the widow. The act of omitting or turning aside the 'stranger' or immigrant from his "right" to the tithe (v.15), is an egregious violation of God's law.

Those whose right it is to receive the holy tithe must thereby be considered a holy group in God's sight. They're a sacred class of individuals whom God is supporting. The priests were defrauding this very group.

These acts constituted robbing God! And so, if we are stealing from this class of people we are stealing from God. If they back then would steal from God Himself, what makes us think that the priests today would not steal from God Himself?

Also notice they had not only robbed God, but "even the whole nation" (v. 9). It wasn't the nation that was accused of robbery, but the priests, to whom this is all addressed. (The italicized word "even" replaced with the word "and", would read, "You have robbed me, 'and' the whole nation" (v.9)). You see, they stole from the people, and as a result the most High. These were crimes of embezzlement, for which they will be prosecuted (punished) as sorcerers, adulterers, and perjurers (v.5).

Essentially the priests resented suffering as poor people. The priest felt that suffering as mourners for the work of the Lord was shameful and beneath them. They felt that impoverishing oneself so that others may be enriched and relieved of some of their suffering was a horror and thus it made them sorrowful. The priests looked up to the wealthier well-to-do folks who rather than share their wealth defrauded the needy, as ones to be envied, and those who lived a life of poverty, who shared their food and whatever they have with others as being fools to be despised. Is that not how we're programmed to feel today?

The priest did not see the temporariness of this vain life. Those priests are now all dead and what attainment did their robberies for financial gain accord them except punishment from God?

Keeping the tithes the nation gave them, to themselves, and failing to distribute to the widow, fatherless and immigrant was an act of robbing the nation of their tithes. This is since the tithes were misappropriated, much as officials, public and private misappropriate money today. So, we see that by ingratiating themselves with one hundred per cent of the tithes, that should've been shared with the widow, fatherless and stranger, the widow, fatherless and stranger were deprived of what was rightfully theirs and were caused to remain mourners and sufferers. And what is the priest's (preacher's) response? "It is vain to serve God: WHAT PROFIT IS IT that we have kept His ordinances and that we have walked as MOURNERS. The idea of doing it God's way stunned and amazed them, it made them sorrowful. Those who God sees as proud, the priest call blessed, those who God calls wicked, the priest consider should be looked up to, those who tempt God, the priest consider are getting away with something, "So now we call the proud blessed, those who do wickedness are raised up; yes, those who tempt God escape" (Mal.3:14-15, NKJV).

The priest were believing the rich and well-to-do were getting away with their selfish lifestyles, even though they were wicked. And so, the priest were trying to emulate that wickedness as something good. The priest did not want to suffer and thus mourn as the poor whom they despised.

God wanted the Levites to prove Him for the blessings He would pour out (v. 1), but they obviously lacked the fear and awe of Him to do so (v. 5, 16-18). God was essentially saying, sit on your hands and wait on me. They should've been trying to figure out how to distribute the money to those in the most need but instead they were bent on devising ways to obtain the money for themselves.

God curses with a curse the ministry (v.9), indicting them for a pattern of wrongful what he calls atrocities, which the "Elijah" will have to rectify (and it won't be pleasant) before the day of the Lord's return (Mal. 4:15; 4:4-6). This is a warning!

God doesn't say these are not His priests, and He doesn't say that these are not His ordained and anointed leaders, but God does hold them accountable for leading His sheep rightly, and the correction He will have to bring to them if they don't straighten themselves out on their own, will be quite severe. Along with other changes, God plainly wanted the third-year tithes, in the storehouse so that all to whom the produce was rightfully designated could have access (v. 1), and for the unauthorized self-aggrandizement of the tithes by His priests to cease. They were giving God a bad name, and this was an affront to Him.

Doing it God's way put them in a state of poverty which left them pretty much penniless. And in truth it may be very difficult to be impoverished. It may also be very advantageous to be impoverished for by this we live in empathy with the impoverished, the poor and the needy. In such a position, it is our duty to summon help for those our neighbors who are in need. Remember Our Savior said, "blessed are you who are poor, for yours is the Kingdom of Heaven" (Luke 6:2).

Wealth means nothing to Our Savior. He has all the wealth there is. All of our wealth is His wealth on loan to us. What was important to Him was dying for people so they through Him could live for eternity.

Giving His life so others could live is what counted to Him. The wealth means nothing. What counts is Life Eternal. Laying down our wealth so others can live is a symbolism of what He did for us. When the devil offered Him the kingdoms of this world, He despised the wealth of these kingdoms and chose to suffer that we all might live eternally.

So it is, that we also must imitate The Lamb and lay down the riches of this world, walk sorrowful as mourners so that our brothers and sisters may live, live in this life and in the life hereafter. The purpose for all of us is to serve. He that is willing to lose his life in this world will live (Matthew 16:25). We must lose to win. This is what the apostle Paul meant when he said get rid of all covetousness which is idolatry (Colossians 3:5). Be content with what we have (Hebrews 13:5).

All of us are "the rich" compared to those who have less than we do. Like all those who have more than we do are to us, "the rich". That whole thing is actually an illusion. Rich and poor is a potential stumbling block to trip us up. The only real rich are those who've given it all away and followed Christ. I mean, how much are we willing to risk holding on to and lose the Kingdom? This is the way Paul, Silas, Barnabas, Stephen, James, Timothy, Titus, Peter, John, Luke, Matthew and the others lived, they lived more or less as financial mourners. Their joy was in suffering for the spreading of the Kingdom. In terms of eternity this brief life is but several seconds in time. As eternity continues to unfold these brief seconds become macro, micro, then nano-seconds unto the point they are completely forgotten.

In terms of eternity this time will not have occurred. So, this suffering is but "no time" equal to "no suffering" compared to eternity. If our minds are on 'this', then we are suffering, but if our minds are on 'that', we are rejoicing!

There Is No Year To Year Tithe

So, we have just seen that while God clearly lays out the pattern by which we should live financially, whether in offerings, tithes, etc., when we look further into the subject, we find that a biblical directive to pay a "year to year" tithe to the Levite priests (or to the church) is missing.

And while it is widely assumed based upon the historical accounts of Josephus, and others that the Jews tithed properly according to scripture, and that they paid a year to year tithe to the Levites, in addition to a second and third tithe, this change in the ordinance is soundly condemned.

The Wycliffe Bible Commentary states, "Because of variants between the Deuteronomic and the earlier tithe stipulations, the erroneous view was developed by the Jews (and has been accepted by many Christian holy exegetes) that Deuteronomy prescribes a 2nd tithe and some would say, even a 3rd tithe (cf Deut.14:28 ff; 26:12-15). Deuteronomy 14 does not, however, necessarily involve any drastic modification of the earlier tithe law" pg. 174, section 22-29.22.

God in His Word does not condone the idea of a tier of tithes; therefore, if you openly view the subject, you realize that today the two tithes that are God commanded have been eliminated, and the tithe the church does request of us, is not biblical.

Following the guideline that we should not say what the Bible does not say, neither adding to it nor taking away from it, the evidence leaves us to conclude that the "most important" tithe is the third-year tithe, into which the stranger, fatherless, and widow were significantly included. This tithe is left to be also the priestly tithe, the tithe to the Levite because he is not a landowner, he has no inheritance (Num.18:21).

Remember the tithes which the people offer are looked upon by God as 'heave' offerings (v. 24), which are special high or lofty exalted gifts unto the Lord (Strong's, Heb. Ref. 8641).

Also remember this holy tithe occurs every 3rd year, which is titled "The Year of Tithing", (Deut.14:29) by which we can say we have kept the commandments of the Lord; it is also the tithe that generates 'blessings'. (Deut.26:12-15). If this tithe occurs in "The Year of Tithing", and is the holy tithe which will bless all the work of our hands, why would we look for another tithe?

So how would this look in real life? At the end of the third year the church would collect the tithe from the wealthy members, those who are landowners, real estate moguls, corporate heads, stock investors, independently wealthy, entrepreneurs and the like. The church would then turn it into produce and store it for redistribution to the fatherless children, widows and to needy strangers.

The holy tithe is not collected from the fatherless, widow and foreigners but is conversely distributed to them. The tithes would not be demanded from wage earners who have no land or inheritance. God promises blessings if we do it His way. Blessings we would not be able to receive for their overwhelming abundance.

So let's review: The offerings are to be presented three times in a festival season and are offered for the sustenance of the priests.

The entire purpose for the tithe however is to provide an abundance of funds with which the congregation can celebrate the Feast of Tabernacles each year. That tithe is to be saved the entire year for one event, and that is the seven-day festival of tabernacles. Of course the Levite, widow, fatherless and stranger are not to be neglected.

However, in the third year, in "The Year of Tithing", the entire tithe amount is to be given to the Levite, widow, fatherless and stranger, exclusively.

Also, it appears that in that year, the Feast of Tabernacles would be kept within our "gates", or at home, as they did in Nehemiah 8:13-18, when they made booths and set them on their rooftops, in the courtyards and the like.

So it is that Deuteronomy 14:28 says, we are to lay up the tithe within our gates for the Levite, widow, stranger and fatherless every third year. It is very likely that this tithe laid up within our gates would be the tithe referred to as the 'storehouse' tithe mentioned in Malachi 3:10. "Bring ye all the tithes into the store-house, that there may be meat in mine house..."

Let's imagine that all Israel saved-up their tithe and stayed at home, the third year. If all the families and tribes pooled their combined tenth together to provide a tenth of their produce for the designated group spoken of in the Bible, the bounty could add up to be enough for the entire year and possibly two years.

This is the commandment that is missing in our financial economy today. A tithe exclusively for the widow, fatherless and stranger. The Levite's participation in this tithe appears to be contingent on whether he has an inheritance such as lands, production centers, and so forth.

It is obvious that if a Levite is not serving as a priest today, then he would not participate in this third-year tithe. In the case of Barnabus, a Levite of the country of Cyprus, "having land, sold it, and brought the money, and laid it at the Apostles feet." Acts 4:37. Barnabus, a Levite, because he had an inheritance of land, sold what he had, and contributed it to the needs of the brethren.

All things being equal, it appears that the teachers of Israel today who perform the extra labor of serving the congregation, presenting lessons, counseling, baptisms, anointings, weddings, funerals and the like, could be accorded a portion of the third-year tithe for their extra service.

However, it is not for their exclusive use, but to be shared with the others. Neither does the scripture command that the leaders are to be the collectors of the tithe, as tradition appears to dictate.

To prevent the Malachi 3 'robbery' problem, wisdom seems to dictate that a committee be formed to effect righteous distribution of the third-year tithe proceeds. This committee would oversee the righteous and equitable distribution of the storehouse tithe to the widow, stranger and fatherless, so that the desired blessings the most High promised, could be had by each family that obeys this commandment.

New Covenant Changes

THE TITHES MENTIONED IN THE BOOKS OF DEUTERONOMY, Amos, Malachi and such scriptures are commands under old covenant law. Then upon Our Savior's death and resurrection that old covenant was voided, and a new covenant began. The old covenant promised a Savior. So, when the giver of the old covenant died, the Savior arose, and is the resurrected Lamb of God. The Lamb became our new covenant sacrifice by whose blood we receive the forgiveness of sins. It is through Him and not by sheep or goats, that we receive Eternal Life.

But what happened to the cherished old covenant laws now that there is ushered in a new covenant of faith? Our Redeemer said He did not come to destroy the law and the prophets, but He came to fulfill them (Matthew 5:17), but what does that mean?

Well, in the old covenant if we broke a law, we had to offer a blood sacrifice, usually an animal. So, in the new covenant, Christ became that blood sacrifice, (John 1:7).

Now we can ask forgiveness for our covenant transgressions and repent from our sins. It means Christ is no longer as concerned with the literal killing of our brother as He is with the figurative killing of him in our heart. For if we hate our brother or wish to see harm and destruction come upon him, or if we simply neglect to help our brother when he needs help, we murder him figuratively and spiritually, though we never literally, physically lay a hand upon him.

For example, to literally, physically have intercourse with a woman who is not our wife, is to literally, physically violate the law of God. However, in the new covenant if our imagination catches a spirit of sensuous heightened lust for her, and we picture the scenario of seducing her sexually, we have figuratively defiled her in our spirit, even though we literally, physically never touch her.

Unless our wife commits fornication, if we put her away or divorce her, and we subsequently have sex with another or remarry, we are guilty of adultery. If she has intercourse with another, that adultery is on our heads as well. The man is responsible for the marriage. However, if she leaves on her own, only then can the man remarry without it being adultery, (Mark 1:12).

In the spirit of the new covenant there is no more eye for eye, nor tooth for tooth, but there is the turning of the other cheek. It is okay that the brother who knocked out our tooth, keeps his, even though he caused us to lose our own. It's no longer, tit for tat.

In fact, we are to demonstrate love to those who hate us, and we're not to resent those who treat us unkindly. If we get the short end of the stick in any transaction, we are to count it all joy.

We are to literally love our enemies, emotionally, in our heart, in our spirit, in our mind. We are to accept adversity that comes from another and turn it into an advantage.

We rarely have fore-giveness, or be-fore-giveness, in our hearts. That would mean that I am spiritually set-up and ready to give you pardon, prior-to or be-fore, you offend me, be-fore, it happens. It's like saying, I give you pardon, even though you haven't done anything wrong to me yet. So, if you do violate me in some way in the future, you're already pardoned in advance.

A transgression usually incurs a debt. When a trust has been broken there is a natural need for repair. There is a debt-owed. When offended, there is a need for a remedy, repair or a compensation.

A spirit of pre-fore or be-fore-giveness means there is no payment of any type needed. You do not owe me anything, not even an apology.

Most of us habitually reject the opportunity to go an extra mile for our brother. We play-it-off as something that's nice to say, but nearly impossible to do. We rarely break out of our comfort zone, and determine to change our habitual behavior, as to meet the need of going the extra mile though it may cost us something.

We haven't trained ourselves to see the signals. We miss the signals. There is often a signal of a need to "love" someone, but we haven't "re-trained" our senses, re-trained our response system to "notice", and "re-act", to the signals when they "occur".

We may still be calibrated to think that when we win, we win. We haven't yet figured, that very often, in the spirit, when we lose, we win.

The new covenant demands that we actually circumcise our hearts, (Romans 2:29). Remove the "fore-skin", or "fore-flesh", or "fore-self" that gets in the way, of performing the acts of "love" for others, that we would have them-do-for-us.

We need to recalibrate the idea of getting taken advantage of, so that if someone takes something from us, and doesn't return it...we can let it go.

Lending, and hoping not to receive payment in return takes recalibration. But to be repaid by God, it must cost us something in the first place.

Remember, to neglect a brother when he is hungry, or in need of a ride to work, or some other vital thing, is to murder him in our heart. This means, we need to circumcise ourselves in this area of our heart. We must cut-away the fleshly fore-skin, "fore-self", so that we are no longer prevented from availing ourselves to others.

"For if ye love them which love you, what reward have ye? Do not even the publicans the same? And if ye salute your brethren only, what do you more than others? Do not even the Publicans so? Be ye therefore perfect, even as your Father, which is in heaven, is perfect." Matthew 5:46-48. v. 45, "[F]or he maketh his sun to rise on the evil and on the good, and sendeth rain on the just, and on the unjust."

Should we aid a wicked person in their wickedness? No. I REPEAT, DO NOT AID WICKED PEOPLE. Do not aid a wicked person. This would be feeding, empowering and consenting to evil.

But remember Joseph was king under Pharaoh of Egypt, a pagan kingdom, and Daniel ruler under Nebuchadnezzar of Babylon, another pagan kingdom. These men of the most High served these kingdoms and helped the people in them, though they were not people of the most High. We should also be a help to our communities.

The Samaritan helped a man not of his own country. The pious men, the brothers of that man, neglected him. The Samaritan "loved", his "neighbor", someone apart from his own people, who was not of his people, Luke 1:27-35.

So, do all things with prayer.

Under the new covenant, the "circumcised-heart" is even more important. Better to be circumcised in the heart, and not in the flesh, than to be circumcised in the flesh, and not in the heart, Romans 2:25:29.

The Sabbath day which gave us temporary physical rest one day a week has been elevated by Our Redeemer Christ who is our eternal Rest (Hebrews 4:7-10). No longer walking by just the letter of the law, we exercise that eternal Rest, every day of the week, by doing good "Sabbath works", each and every day of our lives.

The new covenant raised the tithe to the higher values of the law which are "judgment, mercy and faith" Matthew 23:23.

The Messiah in Matt.23:23 refers to the exhortation, in Micah, 6:6-8 "with what shall I come before the Lord...with thousands of rams, ten thousand rivers of oil...my firstborn? ..what does the Lord require of you?" Answer: "to act justly to love mercy and to walk humbly with your God." In other words, I don't care how much money you bring to the altar, if you don't fight for the rights of the oppressed, you haven't done nothin'. We're no longer required to just tithe, we are now also required to produce the fruits of a circumcised heart.

Transformation of The Tithe

Here is where evidence of the tithing transformation begins. Under the new covenant the importance of the third-year tithe was superseded with the emphasis given as to the condition of our heart in the form of "justice, mercy and faith."

Was the third tithe done away? Actually, a greater sacrifice was required. "Sell all that thou hast, and distribute unto the poor, and thou shalt have treasure in heaven, and come, follow me." Luke 18:22. "And all that believed were together, and had all things common, And sold their possessions and goods, and parted them to all men, as every man had need" Acts 2:44,45.

To get our heart where it needs to be, (God says) He needs us to surrender our worry about our earthly well-being, how our rudimentary functions will be met, and make us available to the Kingdom one hundred percent. Thus, another action which demonstrates the needed circumcision of the heart can be found right here where Christ says:

"Lay not up for yourselves treasures on earth...
But lay up for yourselves treasures in heaven.
For where your treasure is, there will also be your heart."

There is a qualitative difference in the rewards promised in the new verses the old covenant. The old covenant spoke in terms of temporary earthly benefits. The new covenant speaks in terms of everlasting heavenly benefits "But lay up for yourselves treasures in heaven".

How do we lay up for ourselves treasures in heaven? Well according to the subsequent passages, we do it by serving God, His Kingdom and His righteousness, and so by this we walk in the spirit. We cease from serving our own concerns for our physical survival so that we don't walk in the flesh. Each way is a master. We can have only one master.

"No man can serve two masters:

Ye cannot serve God and mammon" (wealth, treasure)...

And how do we serve God in a way that warrants us the heavenly treasure? It appears we cease from seeking a means to obtain food, drink, clothing and shelter and we seek for His Kingdom and His righteousness.

"Take no thought of your life what ye shall eat...or drink;

Saying; Wherewithal shall we be clothed?

(For after all these things do the [non-believers] seek)

But seek ye first the Kingdom of God, and His righteousness;

...And all these things shall be added unto you."

A corollary chapter to this idea in Matthew 6 can be found in the new covenant book of Hebrews, chapter 4 where it says "there remaineth a Rest to the people of God." Then notice that the Rest refers to us relinquishing our jobs.

Notice Hebrews says, the children of Israel in the wilderness could not enter (the promised rest) because of unbelief. They symbolized being freed from jobs (slavery), baptized through the Red Sea and living dependent (in the wilderness) forty years on God alone. But in that state of dependency, they complained, for it is not natural for us to depend on God for our sustenance, we don't like it. Adam and Eve didn't choose it and neither do we.

So, what was it that was their "unbelief"? What is it they didn't believe that prevented them from receiving their promise-land reward? They didn't believe that God was their savior and that they did not have to save themselves. They didn't believe this even while He was saving them. Let me say it again, they didn't believe that God was their savior and that they did not have to save themselves, even though He was repeatedly in their face in living 'High Definition' color, hands on, saving them.

They asked the question, "did God bring us out here to die?", and the answer was no, God brought them out to save them from death. He is saving us today also, but are we rejecting Him?

When we today believe that God is all we need, and we don't need ourselves, that we are to rest from our own works, the works that would physically sustain us, when we believe He is fully capable and willing to save us, we can then enjoy the Sabbath Rest that He enjoys.

We can't rest until we let God save us. Let me say that again, we can't willingly rest until we let God save us. And what constitutes entering into His Rest? Look at verse 10: "For he that is entered into his rest, he also hath ceased [earthly labors], as God did from His." The job God did was the physical creation of the earth and heavens. Then he entered into His Rest on the seventh day into perpetuity.

We're then exhorted to "labor (work) therefore to enter into that Rest." What is it we must do that constitutes laboring to enter into that Rest? We must pursue His Kingdom and His righteousness. And what constitutes the Kingdom of God and His Righteousness that we are to labor to pursue?

When The Master walked the earth, religious leaders sought to kill Him several times because they claimed He was working on the Sabbath day of rest. What work did He do, that we are to follow in His footsteps doing? Well if you will notice that on that day He healed the sick and infirmed, opened the eyes of the blind and got them and Himself food to eat, which was a violation of Jewish law, Mark 2:23-28, 3:1-7.

The so-called work The Master did on the day of rest which violated Jewish law was to care for God's Kingdom, which embodies caring for the infirmed, maimed, lame, blind, hungry, destitute, fatherless, widow and immigrant.

The biblical story repeatedly shows God's concern for the migrant and the outcast. 'The alien who resides with you shall be to you as the citizen among you; you shall love the alien as yourself, for you were aliens in the land of Egypt: I am the Lord your God' (Leviticus 19:34)." [Jim Wallis, Sojourner] Notice what Rabbi asked His accusers, "Is it lawful to do good on the Sabbath day or to do evil? To save life, or to kill?" The neglect to save life is to kill life. On that Day of Rest, Christ our Savior was administering physical relief and spiritual salvation to those of the Kingdom. This is the same day of Rest we are to "labor therefore to enter into" (Heb. 4:11).

The rest on "To day". This "Day" is to be a Day of rest. Back in that day they rested the seventh day only. "To day" we are to rest perpetually.

Notice that on this day of Rest, Christ lived what he preached to the

Pharisees in Matt.23:23, He walked "Justly" relieving the injured and op-pressed: 'Mercifully' showing acts of compassion to the distressed: and 'Faithfully!', depending on God to be his provider (Gill's Exposition).

The question is, is a Christian to keep the Sabbath today? And the answer is that the new covenant difference is that instead of resting from selfish labors one day each week, we are to rest from selfish labors every day of the week. We are to permanently enter into that Day of Rest as did God in the beginning and perform the salvation works The Prince of Peace performed, every day of our lives.

Let's' say it this way, if we rest from our selfish labors and perform Kingdom works on a particular day, it is literally a Sabbath day to us. Any day we rest from selfish labor is a day of rest, thereby if we cease from labor that materially supports us, we are on Sabbatical. If we then turn and pursue God's redemptive works on these days of rest, restoring hungry, sick, broken and lost souls, our entire day will have been spent as a true Day of Rest. Rest from what? Rest from selfish labor or generating wages for our own sustenance, Matthew 6:33. We are to live in the spirit daily. That Day is our Rest. If we rest only on the physical seventh day, we neglect the spiritual Rest of living, "To Day".

The keeping of the seventh day can be a stumbling block that stunts the indwelling of the holy spirit. We are to live in the spirit "To day", and no longer on just one day. What the keeping of the day could not do for Israel, living in the spirit can do for us, in this new "Day", new Era, new Age.

Another example of Immanuel urging us to rest from our literal jobs is demonstrated when after He had been resurrected and ascended to heaven, Peter and the disciples chose to return to their fishing boats and perform their normal labor. When they got into their boat they labored all night but did not catch any fish. The next morning Immanuel told them to cast their nets on the other side of the boat, and they caught more fish than the nets could hold. Then the Prince of Peace fed them fish and bread and asked Peter if he loved Him. Peter said that yes, he did, and He answered, "feed my lambs" (John 21:15). Subsequently the disciples never went back to their occupation of fishing anymore. Thereby, Peter entered into His Rest.

Peter entered into His perpetual Sabbath. If you don't believe the Savior will sustain you, then you won't enter into His Sabbath, His Sabbatical, His Rest. Peter ceased supporting himself by fishing and entered into a new Day. He entered into "another Day", v.9, "There remaineth therefore a [Sabbath] to the people of God. For he that is entered into His [Sabbath] he also hath ceased from his own works, as God did from his." v.

10-11.

Peter ceased from his own works as God did from His, Hebrews 4:10. His new life occupation was to become fishers of men, (Mark 1:16-17). And after Christ had been resurrected from the dead, the disciples went fishing and couldn't catch anything, and The Christ asked Peter three times, do you love me, and Peter said thou knowest that I love thee, and He Christ then said to Peter, the third time, "Feed my sheep", John 21:17. This interchange signaled a new chapter, a new "Era", a new "Day" in Peter's life.

Is the original seventh day rest negated, No, by no means, rather it is even more important. Christ said, our righteousness must "exceed" that of the Scribes and the Pharisees, (Matt.5:20). How is that done? He states, "it is lawful to do *well* on the Sabbath days." Matthew 12:12.

Should a man work, yes, or he should not eat, but what work should he do? I suggest He should do the Sabbath Day work of Rest. What work is that? It is the Kingdom work of servicing the marginal, charitable work, judicial justice, social justice, health justice, political justice, advocating for the voiceless, lobbying for the disabled, activism for the oppressed and the spiritual discipleship of the gospel.

"The harvest truly is plenteous, but the laborers are few. Pray ye therefore the Lord of the harvest, that he will send forth laborers into his harvest", Matthew 9:37, 38. Ultimately, we must be that sacrificial Lamb.

The New Covenant Difference

Let's see how this works in real life:

If you see that the clear purpose of the old covenant tithe was to aid the non-inherited Levites, the widow, the fatherless and the immigrant, then you understand the transformation that occurred under the new covenant, when the Holy Spirit was poured out on the saints.

"And the multitude of them that believed were of one heart and of one soul: neither said any of them that ought of the things which he possessed was his own; but they had all things common" Acts 4:32-37; 5:1-11. "They had all things in common."

In other words, they didn't just break-off a tenth and give the poor person a temporary thrill, but rather they literally equaled the financial playing field for everyone. It appears they obscured the difference between the rich and the poor brethren. There was no longer an economic distinction. It was 'we' and 'ours', what's yours is mine, and what's mine is yours.

"Discipleship thus means forsaking the seductions and false securities of the debt system for a recommunitized economy of enough for everyone.

In such an economy, which Jesus calls the "kingdom," there are no longer any rich and poor-by definition, therefore, the rich "cannot enter" it (Mark 1:23-25). So, contrary is this vision to our accepted horizons of possibility however, that disciples ancient and modern have difficulty truly believing (1:26)." (Ched Myers 'Sabbath Economics')

This is the new covenant difference, a better covenant, a better promise.

Now notice again The Savior's requirement of us in Luke 18:22, "Now when Jesus heard these things, (the rich ruler wanted to receive the Kingdom of God and stated that he had always kept all the commandments perfectly) he (Jesus) said unto him. Yet lackest thou one thing: sell that thou hast, and distribute unto the poor, and thou shalt have treasure in heaven and come and, follow me." Notice The Savior did not ask for the rich man's money to go to His ministry, but He asked for it to go to the poor. By this example we can see that for us to receive eternity we must give to the poor.

By this example we can see there's not enough room in our heart for two masters, possessions and the holy one of Israel. Giving up earthly security, secures us in heavenly treasures. We have to be willing to suffer today, for an eternal reward tomorrow. Look at what the condition of our heart needs to be as regards to inviting people to our home. Even this is difficult for us to do. Do not invite to supper those who can invite you back, but invite those who cannot return the favor, "the poor the maimed, the lame, the blind and thou shalt be blessed; for they cannot recompense thee: for thou shalt be recompensed at the resurrection of the just", Luke 14:12-14.

Another demonstration of this love as it pertains to the church body can be seen when the Gentile churches (Rom. 15:25-27) contributed to the poor saints in Jerusalem. Should not the wealthier churches extend this service to poorer churches located in impoverished areas even today? (II Cor.8:14-15; II Cor.9:8-9) It is evident that God believes in financial and material equanimity (Exodus 16:18). One thing that is glaringly apparent is that it is not to the ministry the money is to go, but it is to the people. Today's ministries request gifts to themselves but God's word commands that we bless each other, the actual church, with His money.

African-American people would benefit greatly economically if they could understand the principle of communal sharing. If instead of competing as individuals economically they should choose to bond as a group and economically help each other, share all things in common, and help one another in every way.

If they could put down the urges of covetousness, lust and greed and the every-man-for-himself mentality and replace that with, every-man-for-each-other, they could change things.

And a greater movement than that would be if the peoples of the American white churches would choose to even the playing field and economically share with the African American and other poorer peoples. The preachers preach, "give to the church and you will be blessed", when the Bible says the people are the church, and those who are the church who have should give to those who don't have as much…that's to whom the money should go.

Tyranny In The Church World

The book of Malachi depicts the problem the church is having today.

As previously mentioned, the priest were extorting the offerings and the tithes and using it their way, instead of distributing to the less blessed saints as prescribed by God. God called this robbery. The priests were literally defrauding those to whom the tithes were intended.

God told the priest He would bless them Himself if they had the 'faith' to obey Him and do it His way. Instead, the priest bitterly complained that it wasn't worth being a priest if they had to do with the funds what God wanted them to do. What did God want them to do with the tithe? He wanted them to share it with whom it was intended, the widow, fatherless, foreigner, and to stop ripping off the wage earner.

Credibility as it pertains to finances is where the perception of the church has gotten eschewed through the ages, and today is no different. This is where the church has lost face with the world and a large caucus of its' own believers.

It is the appearance of hoarding wealth rather than giving wealth, of greed instead of need, of "me" instead of "we". There are too many preachers sporting autos, houses and clothing, well above the level of their average parishioner.

The Word warns religious leaders, "Woe unto you, hypocrites! For ye devour widows' houses, and for pretense make long prayer..." Matt.23:14, this the church has done and is still doing today.

And in the building of edifices there appears to be no end. We look to Europe for the largest most breathtaking edifices. But to whose glory, the Lord's or to the men that had them built?

What did the rich man do wrong in Luke 12:18? "This will I do: I will pull down my barns, and build greater; But God said unto him, thou fool, this night thy soul shall be required of thee: then whose shall those things be, which thou hast provided? So is he that layeth up treasure for himself...and is not rich toward God."

Essentially do we have buildings sitting empty practically six days per week on average or is there rich use for the Kingdom? A hungry person cannot eat a building. Too many people have been alienated, deceived, not by the devil, but by the "Lord's" own priests. More people would worship at a church but are tired of the robbery; their own lives are enough of a struggle. The priests blame the people, but God blames the priests, the leaders.

God tells the priests in Malachi 3:9 "you've robbed me, even this whole nation." The obvious message is a church should be about the welfare of the poor.

Corruption and false teaching regarding tithing is a discredit to the Kingdom and a stumbling block to the 'would be' believer. It is killing the message of Christ to the world.

But what is the origin of this false teaching and corruption? What makes men act the wrong way whereas the church looks like division, hypocrisy, iniquity, fighting, and wars? James 4:1-8 says that this all stems from the "lust that wars in our members."

Too often churches, good churches teach one thing, yet model another. We teach love, but model lust, the same lust we see in non-believers.

Lust is essentially a lack of faith that God will provide for us, in this life and in the Kingdom to come.

We must eliminate the 'Hypocrisy of the Gospel' where we say one thing but model another. This is the essence of the cause of ills in the world today and especially among our youth. Hypocrisy perverts rather than converts our youth to coming to Christ.

"The Hebrew Bible's vision of Sabbath economics contends that a theology of abundant grace and a communal ethic of redistribution is the only way out of our slavery to the debt system, with its theology of meritocracy and private ethic of wealth concentration. The contemporary church, however, has difficulty hearing this as good news since our theological imaginations have long been captive to the market-driven orthodoxies of modern capitalism." (Ched Myers, 'Sabbath Economics')

More than likely this lust begins with our internal view of the most crucial question of our existence which is, how will 'I' survive? The problem is we usually want to take care of our survival our own way, as did Adam and Eve in the garden in the beginning. Then we teach newcomers as we were wrongly taught and they become twice as bad in this iniquity as we ourselves (Matt.23:15; II Peter 2:2).

Note what James says in chapter 5:1-6, in regard to the condition of lust in the rich which includes preachers, "Go to now, ye rich men, weep and howl for your miseries that shall come upon you. Your riches are corrupted, and your garments are moth-eaten. Ye have nourished your hearts, as in a day of slaughter.

Behold the hire of the laborers who have reaped down your fields, which is of you kept back by fraud, crieth: Ye have condemned and killed the just; and he doth not resist you."

This is obviously not the transcendent attitude God called Christians to display. The Word said we have to lose our life, in order to gain it, Matt. 16:25 and in Matt.5:40, if a brother ask you to go a mile go two, if he ask for your coat give him your cloak also. Our entire life is to be a Sabbath day of helping poor, widows, fatherless, foreigners and thus our whole contribution is to be not a 10% monetary tithe but a 100% living tithe. Sell out, sell all, give it to the poor, and gain treasure in heaven. "Change the way you are living and stop doing the things you are doing. Be fair in your treatment of one another. Stop taking advantage of aliens, fatherless, and widows. Stop killing innocent people (unarmed black males) in this land. Stop worshipping other gods, for that will destroy you" (stop coupling Christian holy days with pagan holidays) (Jeremiah 7:5-7 GNB).

Is Fasting, Obsolete?

Christians get fixed on one thing and completely miss what else is being said, especially in matters of the heart.

The scripture in Isaiah speaks of how God hates all the religiosity we perform in His name when we leave out the most important matter:

"[Rather] is not this the fast that I have chosen; to loose the bonds of wickedness, to undo the bands of the yoke, to let the oppressed go free, and that you break every [enslaving] yoke? Is it not to divide your bread with the hungry and bring the homeless poor into your house-when you see the naked, that you cover him, and that you hide not yourself from [the needs of] your own flesh and blood (elderly parents, in particular)."

We don't want our nice places messed up by dirty homeless people. The wealthier of us can't do this because we have too many things that can be stolen. Better said, we are worried about what the homeless might take from us or what might get broken or damaged. This may be because our hearts are so affixed on the enslaving yoke of our own "niceties". The coffee table, the lamp, the finer china, the expensive rug, the high-end chairs and the like. Our emotional enslavement to all this stuff in our home can prevent us from entering heaven.

We fail to understand the level we need to sink to adequately serve God's most sensitive concerns, the homeless and the poor, the crippled, blind and halt. It is necessary that we the rich, the haughty, well healed get down into their shoes to provide for them. We must suffer a broken cherished favorite and expensive television monitor, cell phone or piece of crystal. The bathroom toilet may get clogged and run over. We may lose cutlery or money might be lost, to serve the Kingdom of God. Remember it is not service if it doesn't considerably cost us something, demean us and set us back. This is the giving God wants. We must sully ourselves for others if need be. We must lose in order to win. It's all about eternity. It's about the Kingdom. That is why if we're seeking Life, real Life, none of these material things have value. Real Life is a treasure above all things!

I don't think we should put women and children in harm's way, because our society is filled with drug addiction, perverted violent types, and predators. But if we have the poor or homeless for supper and do it as a group with other families hosting together, it may bring a measure of safety. Don't do it alone. If need be, notify the local authorities whom you've befriended. Some of us may focus on inviting just women and children, or widows, elderly and orphaned, some may focus on foreigners, some on the lame, maimed or challenged individuals.

Many of us would be uncomfortable and without a conversation around such people. But we might invite friends over who are more comfortable, to assist us. If we don't have friends or family who will fit the bill perhaps we need to study the subject like we would a foreign language and learn.

"If you take away from your midst yokes of oppression, the finger pointed in scorn [toward the oppressed] and every form of false, harsh, unjust and wicked speaking and if you pour out that with which you sustain your own life for the hungry and satisfy the need of the afflicted, then shall your light rise in darkness, and your obscurity and gloom become like the noonday", Isaiah 58:6-10.

God is saying here is the new way I want you to fast. As many of us know, fasting is an affliction of the flesh. It is denying the body food for a designated period of time on purpose. Christians look at fasting as an amazing effort to draw closer to God, a step up from prayer and Bible study, fasting is a tool to seek God more intimately.

So, we Christians see the word "fast" in this scripture but we miss the intent of the scripture, we miss what is really going on here. God here is ordaining a "New Way to Fast".

What is that "New Way to Fast"? What is the new way to deny the self, and afflict the flesh in an amazing effort to draw closer to God? It is to bring a hungry person into our house!

The scriptures say, it is that we should not point the finger at a hungry person, or a naked person and accuse him of being responsible for his own demise and tell him he must pull himself up by his own bootstraps!... bootstraps, bootstraps, the Bible says, we are to pull up our brother by his bootstraps... "it is rather to loose the bands of wickedness, to 'undo the bands' of the yoke, to let the oppressed go free, and that we break every [enslaving] yoke."

It is not to quote the scripture, "the poor we will always have with us", and then sigh, 'so why bother?' Deuteronomy 15:11 says, give to the poor, that we always have with us.

God doesn't need our physical fasting anymore, but rather what He needs from us is for us to divide our bread with the hungry and bring the homeless (with adequate prayer and discretion) into our home.

You see, we are quite capable that even after fasting for forty days and forty nights, of condemning those who are living in tents, sleeping under bridges, in alleys and think that it is somehow their fault.

This is not the sophisticated or political reasoning God is saying He wants from us. God is saying, that the NEW FAST or NEW DENIAL He wants from us is for us to put ourselves on the line, deny ourselves, cause ourselves to suffer for the need of another and share our bread, our precious time, our space, our things and help break the bonds of oppression, the cycle of poverty and deliberate wickedness that has been precipitated AGAINST THEM. This is how God looks at it.

He holds those who are blessed accountable for the condition of those who find themselves less blessed.

Once again He says, stop all your vain [empty] self-serving fasting, and begin to care for the needs of the oppressed, hungry, naked, homeless, deaf, maimed, blind and lame.

Somehow though, we the Christian world miss these key scriptures in our own Bible. We do not have eyes to see this. We do not have the heart to believe this. The evidence is that so many of us still take stock in our fasting but are remiss in repositioning our rhetoric when it comes to doing what God requests in this scripture. The preachers will not preach this to us.

For this we're all guilty.

Just like those who preach tithing, God is no longer concerned with do we tithe or not, but He is concerned with do we give one hundred percent of our lives to Him. He wants to know will we permit Him to care for us while we do His work of faith on behalf of others..

And just what is His work of faith that He requires? He requires we loose the bonds of oppression from those who are our very own flesh, and free them from the affliction perpetrated upon them by their oppressors, those in a position of wealth and rulership.

Is Tithing Obsolete?

The tithe was for Israel. The law was given to Israel and not the Gentiles. When God called the Gentiles, He did not place the burden of Israel's law which Israel could not even keep, upon the Gentiles. He did not place upon the Gentiles the burden of a law which could not save them anyway.

Paul's point was that if we live by the sacrificial law, we die by the sacrificial law. If we do the things required by the sacrificial law, we become obligated to do the whole law and thus deny the sacrificial offering The Lamb made of Himself for us on the cross. What offering? The sacrificial offering. What law? The law of sacrifices of sheep and goats, meats and drinks Colossians 2:8-23; Numbers 28:7-11. If we choose to live by the law of sacrifices, then we reject living under God's grace. It is only by His grace toward us we are saved and not by animal sacrifices. By His sacrifice we now have the faith that our sins are blotted out and it's no longer by the sacrifice of sheep and goats. Paul says the law of sacrifices was too weak and could not save us. Romans 14:6-12; 14:13-23. I Corinthians 8:7-13; I Corinthians 9:1-2.

The Ten Commandments written by God's own finger are considered God's law under Moses. Are the Ten Commandments done away? No, the reality is that the Ten Commandments are to be fulfilled in the spirit. If you simply look at a woman to lust in your heart you've committed adultery in your heart. If you are angry at your brother, without a cause, you've already murdered him in your heart (Matthew 5:28). The Ten Commandments are hung upon two basic commands, 1) love God with all our heart, mind and soul (Deut. 6:5), and, 2) love neighbor equal to self. (Lev.19:18). With these two commandments as our foundation, we then add upon them the Ten Commandments which are to be spiritually written in our hearts and minds. Paul states clearly, we need to obey these commandments in, Romans 13:8-9.

Note that even though circumcision was required as per Abraham's time which was an extremely painful act especially for adult men, which signified the obedience God was looking for down to the reproductive private parts, now the circumcision sacrifice is only profitable if you keep the Law. God is looking for the circumcision of the heart. God wants the extra flesh of our hearts removed and for our hearts to be spiritual and to trust Him. The extra flesh appears to have represented sin and hardness of the heart, Jeremiah 4:4; Deuteronomy 10:16.

Abraham kept the righteousness of the law faithfully, he carried his cross, he crucified the flesh, that is why he wore the badge of circumcision. The spiritual circumcision of having crucified or severed ourselves from the world and the world from us, is what is utmost important, Gal.6:14. In our hearts is the spiritual hygienic cleanliness He seeks of us today and what determines holiness. Circumcision today should be as an outward emblem of the inward circumcision of the heart.

I give my life to benefitting others in the helping work I do so that for me each and every day is a Sabbath day of rest from my selfish labors. I work to enter His rest. It is in fact commanded that we keep this day, Isaiah 58:13-14. And so, in our walk we must be doing the Sabbath works of helping people every day. Is it possible we could be counted as breaking the Sabbath day if we fail each and every day of our lives, to work and advocate for the helpless? Is it important that our own interests are subjugated to the interests of others Every day? Is it not these activities which makes the Sabbath a daily observance in our lives?

In the beginning God created the heavens and the earth and on the Sabbath day rested from all His works. We are to work to enter that Sabbath Day Rest, Hebrews 4:4-11. We must work and find the joy in serving Him by serving needy people and sacrificing our own preferred comforts, v.14, for their needs. The anointed one of Israel Himself said. "Wherefore it is lawful to do well on the Sabbath days." Matthew 12:12.

The Apostles don't command tithing anywhere in the New Testament, however because they kept the feasts, Acts 12:3; 18:21; 20:16, including tabernacles, they may have tithed for that purpose.

"So, Christ has now become the High Priest over all the good things that have come. He has entered that greater more perfect Tabernacle in heaven, which was not made by human hands and is not part of the created world. With His own blood-not the blood of goats and calves-he entered the Most Holy Place once for all time and secured our redemption forever." Hebrews 9:11-12.

The Christian Church Owes An Apology

THE CRUSADES are the most damning evidence of a church run-a-mock, acting in dominance. The results are clear; the church was stupid, destructive, infantile, self-indulgent, greedy, barbaric and heathenistic all in the name of "Jesus".

The church served as the devil in the world. Then in the period preceding the Renaissance the church further screwed up when it met its match against science. The true God showed up and enlightened the world of that day to prove that science was real and religious superstition was false. More importantly He showed up to break the hold that the church had on the world so that it might cease to abuse its' authority on oppressed peoples in the name of "Jesus".

We the church tried to punish science and preached superstition. But it was proven our superstitions were unfounded fallacy, whether it was that the earth was flat or that the earth is the center of the universe or that the sun and the moon rise and fall each day. We killed thousands and tens of thousands in "Jesus" name over these arguments.

We used our authority to ruin homes and families and peoples. We forbid sex except for procreation and forbid priest and nuns from marrying which sparked the advent of abortions, the numbers exceeding what we can imagine.

We repressed the world in the fields of health and sanitation and thousands more died due to other superstitious beliefs and rituals. We went down to Africa to free the natives from their superstitions and impaled them with our own. We essentially wrecked the world during our period of dominance, and now the world wants no part of us. (Simply look up the Czars of Russia and read about how these "Christian" rulers abused their nation.)

Atheism is pursued by a great number of educated people because of us, because of the perversions we've propagated on the people. Christianity once ruled the day, but it was found perverted and perverse, why?

Could it be that the aspirations of greed, lust, hate, power and control blended themselves in with the righteousness of Christ's teachings? Could it be that people filled with hate in the name of Jesus got the chance to oppress the weak? Maybe the saying should apply that people use to describe what happens to people when they receive a great sum of money: Jesus [money] doesn't change who you are, He[it] just makes whoever you are good or bad, come out more so.

Much of what we're seeing in the world today is a simple response of repulsion from the perverse history the church has propagated on this planet.

Our misguided superstitions have destroyed the integrity of the Christian religion. Christianity has put itself out of the schools, the community, and society at large.

Therefore we must get back to the basics, care for the weak, the downtrodden, the oppressed, "in a heart of love" in a spirit of humility, for to do it in 'pride' is ever more horrible. We are also instructed to esteem others better than we esteem our self.

Even in institutions where there were efforts to heal the sick, feed the poor, or take care of orphans, there was often displayed cruel authoritarian oppression and acts of sabotage. Many of those who were disadvantaged were treated in a spirit of cruelty, with excessive punitive abuse and disdain in the name of charity.

Many things the Christians oppose are in fact harmful to the world such as abortion but note that it is the upstanding Christians whose girls are obtaining the abortions to save face. It is the priests and nuns who led the world in the abortions they perpetrated in their own convents and yet hypocritically punitively preach against it in public.

The Christian world is in derision today and the Muslim religion gaining far more converts because of the Christians' own arrogance and barbaric abuses.

Add to that the "dog-n-pony" healing shows that are displayed even on public television today but were once restricted to tent revivals, where a feeble person is sat down into a wheelchair and rolled up on stage, prayed over fervently by a huckster whose henchmen then pull the wheelchair from under the person and the person stands up as if they were healed from being lame.

Clowns are for circuses and there is as Barnum used to say, "a sucker born every day". The more suckers, the more and bigger the shows; more money. Many purport to help people out of the messes they initially set up for people to fall into.

The church supported slave system in the U.S. of A, of itself is not anti-biblical in principle. But it is the cruelty of the whips, beatings, castrations, decapitations, bludgeoning, molestations, maiming, blinding, cutting off noses, fingers, toes, ears, private parts, bashing babies' heads against rocks, starvations, rapes, gang rapes, sodomy, breeding, family break ups, auction blocks, flesh peelings, burnings, drownings, live burials, burnings, pins, needles and nails while preaching "Jesus" and his love on Sunday, then reverting back to this same pattern of horror and cruelty on Monday, that makes the world, the reasonable world despise "Christians".

The American church ought to apologize so that we are sure it has gotten out of its genetic DNA this mentality of cruelty. It needs to be made one hundred percent clear that it has repented of its' culture of oppression and abuse. Such horrors and such brutality perpetrated on people demonstrate the extreme antithesis of what is supposed to be a love that Christ showed the world in giving His life for her sins.

And in this modern world in the year of 2000 plus, the U.S. congress approves a bill which permits the "Christian" nation of the United States of America to do what Christians have been doing throughout the centuries; torture people; how barbaric; how evil.

And the church says nothing...

Have Christians preached one thing which veiled another; an evil debauchery?

Religious control being the opium of the masses is what has been accomplished through the "Christian" church through time and is still being accomplished today. We the people are duped under the banner of the Lord Jesus Christ, which is a cruel joke played on dumb sheep.

The kings, prime ministers, presidents, military advisors, bankers, corporate heads and other great men have decided the propaganda pill they want to drop into our drinks through our education system and media outlets, and we've been drinking that Kool-aide from Constantine till today. King James is good version of the Bible. As real as it may be, not everything in it is a perfect translation. And to compound the matter, wolves have crept in to give that version a slant that is not true to the spirit originally intended. This is why we have to be so careful to not let others feed us their opinion of what we're reading without us checking in with the spirit of God to get His opinion on what the scriptures actually say, (Colossians 2:8) ...

However, due to the botched job Christians made of their authority when they did exercise dominance, the world will no longer listen to what Christianity has to say. Christianity had its' chance and blew it! Christianity contributed deeply to the demise we see in the world today. Christianity continues to contribute to that demise. It is interested in itself and not in oppressed people. The interest it does generally show toward oppressed people is usually latent with a heart filled with disdain and arrogance. This does not represent Our Savior!

It does not demonstrate the love The Savior intended, and men and traditions continue to pervert the scripture as it pertains to money, politics, sex and even charity.

The wealth of the Vatican is a testament to poor people giving to a church their widow's mite and the church giving nothing back in return. The poor people remain poor. The one wealthiest entity in the world as quiet as it's kept for centuries has been and is the Vatican.

Christians forget these things while so called "defending the faith", and fail to look into the mirror of introspection and forget that we need to get the grime off that has caked on our story. How dare a preacher say to a poor person, we ought to give our widow's mite to the church, when The Savior clearly says when we give to the poor we've given to Him. How dare a preacher say that if we haven't been paying our tithes the church can't help us with our food or our rent. Might this not be a huckster spirit attempting to divert monies for their own personal version or perversion of the gospel? (Proverbs 19:17; Matt. 25:4)

The Church's Secret War

There is in fact more than one Christian church within the body called Christianity. There are in fact several. However, I want to isolate two genres that are the antithesis of each other and cannot co-exist and actually be in the same body of Christ. Jim Wallis' book "America's Original Sin", goes into this in detail.

There was the pro-slave church we would call right wing or neo conservative today, and then there was the church of the abolitionists who hated slavery, we would call left-wing or liberals today. The one church baptizes the slaves and yet retains them as 3/5th humans, while the other is empathetic to the slave's position and tried to help free them.

The pro-slave church is the majority church even today. It condoned the cruelty of slavery and sanctioned it. The anti-slave church is a relatively small portion which worked hard to avoid persecution and even death in efforts to free the slaves. Politically today there are the Republican and Democratic parties. Each party has a different philosophy in how to deal with minorities. Both sides' true goals are to exploit the minorities for their own self-aggrandizement. The love of money is the seductress of both sides conservatives and liberals. So, either side the church sides with is flawed. Its' the churches' commission to side with The Savior Christ and Him only.

There is also a war that goes on between those who are for religion and those who are for The Savior. Clearly The Savior came to free the oppressed, to free the prisoners, whereas the majority church today comes to oppress the oppressed and to further confine the prisoners.

The Savior came to even the playing field between the rich and the poor, the church comes to exploit the poor for its own self-aggrandizement. These two polarities were at work when The Savior confronted the children of Abraham keepers of the law of Moses.

The Savior made a clear distinction as to what is a real and what is an "Americanized" church. The Savior accused those who claimed Abraham as their father, the Pharisees, of being sons of snakes, scorpions and the devil. The Sadducees did not fare any better. Many of us today claim Christ to be our Saviour as they claimed Abraham to be their father in times past. But if our hearts are corrupted because we hate any group of people, or any segment of the population of mankind, then brother we are liars. There is a real danger of being in this camp. There is a danger that the camp that is "religious", cannot be preached to, and cannot be turned around. They are not reading this book.

Those who follow the true Christ, the Anointed One, can read this book and divest themselves of erroneous impurities in their own walk with Him.

The Pharisees practiced "religion", or today what is called "Christianity". Those who follow Christ practice what He taught. Face it, He was pro fatherless, He was pro homeless, He was pro illegal immigrant, He was pro poor. Yet, these are the distasteful unseemly parts of the competitive upwardly mobile Christian ministries.

These are the parts of the body that the prouder Christians don't seem to be able to continence and maintain their sense of self-esteem. It's like having to clean the toilet every time you go to church, it's just not going to fly with a competitive capitalistic upwardly mobile type of church-folk. Flashy Armani, Gucci, Benz type Christians have little tolerance for smelly homeless people. People with two legs and a head like theirs, "Who If They'd Just Put Some Effort Forth And Work Hard Wouldn't Need A Hand Out From Me!", type Christians.

The Savior did not come to destroy but save people. The Savior did not protect Himself by destroying people, and while He could've called down legions of angels, The Savior permitted Himself to be harmed in order to save people.

The Savior fellowshipped with sinners and low-lifes. Apparently The Savior felt more comfortable with people who were admittedly sinners. The disciples were uneducated and except for a few, they were backward men. They were the runts of the earth. They were not religious men.

The tension between the two ideologies is so enormous, yet over-looked, that it tears the church apart, and yet it first must be addressed and cleaned up before any real salvation of the world can take place. I won't then get into the further riff in the church caused by divisions named denominations. Can we imagine that the original church of the apostles began to split into denominations? I think not. Why are we not all the Church of God? Why would anyone of us call ourselves any title less than that?

Is to be one denomination or another a form of idol worship? Paul says that this type of thing proves we belong to this world, living by its standards, I Corinthians 3:3-4.

Denomination fights are the antithesis of love, harmony and joy. The church appears to be a battle ground safer to be away from than to be a part of. The reason for this pot-marked mapping of factional oppositions is because the church won't come together on the common denominator of love. How do we invite a non-believer into such a factional family? "We're evangelicals", as opposed to what?! Baptist! Well who are they?! Well they're better than, Catholics! Well who are they?! On and on! Over thirty-four thousand divisions and subdivisions signal a church that is running off the rails.

Let's go back to square one, "Whosoever hath the world's goods, and seeth his brother have need, and shutteth up his bowels of compassion from him, how dwelleth the love of God in him?" I John 3:17. The church instead has a hostile take-over proclivity which is, "if I am stronger and I can take it from you and you can't stop me, then it must be "God's will" mentality. We live by the same standards of sinners.

Thus, instead of the denominator of love has been born the divisions of hate and strife. The feeling of lowliness causes anathema, flight, and Christianity just wouldn't be very sexy if it centered on cleaning toilet bowls every time we met for church.

Back to the two extremes, conservative versus liberals, often one side rails against the other's true validity. This internal struggle causes confusion in the hearts and minds of non-believers and new converts who struggle to identify their own personal beliefs weighed in the balances of what The Savior thinks or would do.

Deeper investigation by the individual Christian has to take place. There have to be serious moments of true introspection and a divorce from the shared human tendency of just following the crowd.

How Does A Kingdom Economic Church Look?

"By this shall all men know that ye are my disciples if ye have love one to another" John 13:35. Outsiders will know The Savior's followers by how we love one another. How we suffer for one another.

Sharing all things in common and distributing to the necessities of the saints, and the less blessed would demonstrate the love the lost need to see in God's true church.

A different kingdom would be on display and it could attract many. It would be more communal in nature. Prominent acts of true loving would be the best witness to the unsaved. If we speak salvation but are not acting salvation then we speak in vain and hurt the cause of the Kingdom, turning more people off than on.

The pinnacle question which The Savior had to answer after His baptism when He met Satan in the wilderness after fasting forty (40) days was, will I take my survival into my hands or will I trust God for my survival?

It appears that after this epic battle against the devil that Christ was then imbued with power and so we see a demonstration of this power in His first miracle as recorded in John 2:9-11.

Acting on the kind of faith Christ acted on, the church would also receive Power! Acts 1:8, "but ye shall receive power," said Christ, "the works that I do shall (you) do also; greater works than these shall (you) do", John 14:12...but today we're confused.

We talk of wealth, when what we need is power, power to heal, power to cast out devils, power to raise the dead, power to calm a storm, power to do the impossible. But why is there so little power? Because we refuse to totally let go and totally let God. We're focused on wealth and not faith. As individuals and as church organizations we still own our own survival. The mentality of owning our own survival then takes us down the road of wealth consciousness. Slight corruption as to whom we serve (mammon or God) can take us off the road that really counts, the consciousness that brings us His POWER!

Society today has fed us the propaganda that having enough money gives us power to get what we want. This is only a half truth. For if we have power, the power from the living God, we can have what money can't buy! Peter with John said to the lame beggar "silver and gold have I none but such as I have I give to thee: in the name of Jesus Christ of Nazareth rise up and walk" Acts 5:6...Power!

The scripture says, (we) can do all things through Christ who strengthens (us) and there's nothing impossible with God. So the church needs to operate in power and power comes from operating in the gifts of love.

Love is seeking His Kingdom as our sole means of survival.

... No love... No power.

A true church demonstrates love and is rewarded with power!

The eight (8) hours that we work each day not including travel and preparation to travel, could've been spent:

1. Visiting a prisoner and sharing the gospel.
2. Looking in on a hospital patient or/and
3. Feeding a hungry child, a widow who needs help.
4. Supporting and participating in social justice causes.

Multiply any three of these four acts by five days a week and we would have fifteen acts of service accomplished for fifteen people.

We either spend 70 to 80% of our time supporting self or we spend 70 to 80% of our time supporting others. This is why we have so many immobilized people sitting in church pews today who hear what we're saying about the need to save souls, but consumed by their own lusts, they haven't the wherewithal to comply.

Rather than doing our own jobs, God urges us to put off our own works, and enter into His Rest, as He ceased from doing his works in the beginning. Christ says to us "Come ye blessed of my father, inherit the Kingdom I have prepared for you... when I was hungry ye gave me food, when thirsty ye gave me drink, sick and ye visited me", Matt.25:34, 35.

The righteous will reply because they were already saved and were naturally doing these things, "when did we do these things?" These are the things the saved would do, not to get saved, but because they are saved. Again, "because they are saved."

Christ gave all of us salvation, but that salvation doesn't work in all of us unless we accept it, and we demonstrate we accept it by obeying His commandments. They wanted to know when they had done all of that...Jesus' reply was, "Truly I say unto you inasmuch as ye have done it unto one of the least of these my brethren ye have done it unto me." These are the brethren that embody the

Kingdom Christ says we are to exclusively pursue.

To pursue Christ this way would cause us to wonder what if I can't support myself? So we reason we need to work for enough money to support ourselves first, so we can have food, homes, clothes and transportation to better help the less blessed.

But The Savior told the young ruler to get rid of all that stuff, before you even follow me. Why? Because we can't serve two masters. Because we can't have a heart for God and a dependence on material riches at the same time, they oppose one another. If we value money we may like God and like knowing of God, He may even be our friend, but He won't be our lover and so our heart won't be fully into Him.

"For where your treasure is, there will also be your heart", Matt. 6:21. God knows the heart, and so how can He determine our heart? He watches how we spend our time and our money, whether it's for His Kingdom or whether it's for self. He watches what we treasure, whether it's His Kingdom or money, whether we're for His Kingdom or for the world, whether for the poor or the rich. To avoid the deception of getting sucked into the "rat race" God says pursue His Kingdom first.

"And He (Jesus) said unto another. Follow me. But he said, Lord, suffer me first to go and bury my father. And another also said. Lord I will follow thee; but let me first go bid them farewell, And Jesus said, No man having put his hand to the plow and looking back, is fit for the kingdom of God" Luke 9:58-62. We can't hesitate, we can't stumble, we must not stutter.

We may ask, "how can I give if I have nothing to give?" God might answer, "give yourself, follow me, give your heart your mind, your talent and your intelligence for you can do all things through Christ who strengthens you". God also says, He would supply all our needs.

"And (Jesus) commanded them (the disciples) that they should take nothing for their journey, save a staff only; no scrip, no bread no money in their purse" Mark 6:7,8.

But what about medical insurance for me and my family? God knows our needs; "For your heavenly Father knoweth you have need of all these things" Matt.6:32, "Beloved, I wish above all things that thou mayest prosper and be in health, even as thy soul prospereth" III John 1:2.

We might reason that if we don't pay the rent, we'll be evicted from our house, and we'll be the homeless, and God might say "your heavenly Father knows you have need... Take no thought for tomorrow". We are to take no thought for tomorrow so we won't be distracted and thereby hindered in our effort to freely and fully help others today, no matter the consequences.

But, but, but... "If I have no source of income how will I eat?" and God may say, "Behold the fowls of the air: for they sow not, neither do they reap, nor gather into barns; yet your heavenly Father feedeth them. Are ye not much better than they?" Matt.6:28.

After the disciples returned having taken nothing for their journey, The Prince of Peace asked in retrospect, "And he said unto them, when I sent you without purse, and scrip, and shoes, lacked ye anything? And they said Nothing", Luke 22:35. We're not required to give just a tenth anymore but all that we have, one hundred percent, all that we are, our whole life to the Kingdom.

And what shall we receive in return? Matt.19:28, 29, "Verily I say unto you, that ye which have followed me, in the (re-creation) when the Son of man shall sit on the throne of his glory, ye also shall sit upon twelve thrones... I believe the point is that to be rulers with the Father we have to have a heart like the heart He has which is to care for the least of us humans.

In Acts 20:20, the scriptures witness that they traveled far and wide preaching the gospel and ministering to the needy. They stayed in one house at a time, supported by the hosts. Christ stated that the laborer is worthy of his hire, Luke 10:7. The Levites were supported by the congregation of Israel of old, and so should those who labor amongst us.

The church folk's funds should support this activity. That is true ministry.

"And everyone that hath forsaken houses, or brethren, or sister, or father, or mother, or wife, or children, or lands, for my name's sake, shall receive a hundredfold, and shall receive everlasting life."

What's at stake here? At stake here is eternal, everlasting life. We can't allow even family members be an excuse to stop us from doing what we must do. Eternal Life is greater than anything!

WhataChurchNeeds to LookMoreLike

I.   A CHURCH SHOULD HAVE A CAUCUS OF BELIEVERS who live in this faith preached by The Savior, who've given it all up and work solely in the trenches for the Kingdom.

II. A church's other members should literally share all things in common. Members provide for members, especially for those who work solely in the trenches for the Kingdom. Church folks must put up church folks who are in the field preaching the good news and healing the sick. Acts 20:20; 5:42, "And daily in the temple, and in every house, they ceased not to teach and preach Jesus Christ."

III. A church should cater to the lame, wheelchair victims, blind, mentally and/or physically challenged, unemployed, homeless, fatherless, widows, victims of addiction, weak, stupid, ugly, hungry, foreigners, filthy, naked and the brokenhearted.

IV. A church should support poorer churches, especially churches located in areas of poverty and despair who are trying to enrich that community through social justice, activism and feeding ministries.

V.   A church should be a supporter physically and financially of one or more organizations that are charitable, and one or more organizations that fight for social justice.

I Cor. 9:9-11; I Timothy 5:8, if church members are quitting their jobs and serving those in need, visiting the sick, feeding the hungry, ministering to the prisoners, they must be supported by the other members of the church. The other members of the church must also provide the food stock with which to feed the poor. Provide housing to house the homeless. Clothing to clothe the naked. Preach the gospel of the Kingdom of the most High. This is what it means when the scripture says: "Do not muzzle the ox that treadeth out the corn." And, "The labourer is worthy of his reward." I Timothy 5:18.

Lodge strangers, wash saints' feet, relieve the afflicted, diligently follow every good work.

If we are children of our Father God in heaven then, "wist [we] not that [we] must be about [our] Father's business?" (Luke 2:49). "The harvest truly is plenteous, but the labourers are few." Matthew 9:37. There needs to be more laborers.

Is there a nobler cause, a better purpose for our 'earth' lives? Fight for the disenfranchised of every stripe. If the church isn't straightened, society won't be straightened. But if we can get squads, regiments, battalions and armies from the church or churches to intervene, we can change things. The church is to obviously be activist.

"People are dying that could be saved. We need to discover our humanity. Give up our life for the people, or generations more will die or live poor butchered half-lives.

We must display uncompromising resistance to wrong, we must have a commitment to identify and fight injustice at every turn" (George Jackson). It is in this way that we must "do justly, love mercy and walk humbly with [our] God", Micah" 6:6-8. These are the most important matters.

Do we realize the level of worship that will go on in our church services with a congregation of people who've devoted themselves on this level? When they come out of the field each week to be recharged at church... When they come to church to cater to the lost and despondent that they've brought to church from the field? How different this looks from many of the spectacular television ministries we see on the air?

The level of praising, testifying, worshiping, miracles and power displayed would be exceptional.

What church people fail to realize is that our worship is in vain, no matter how many prayers, no matter how earth and heaven shakingly powerful the prayers, no matter how earnest and passionately we lift up our hands to Him in praise and surrender, no matter how many church services we schedule and religiously attend, no matter how much money we raise and put into the offering plate, if we neglect to do what God specifically wants of us, we are likened to bloody murderers and the perverts and homosexuals of Sodom and Gomorrah, Isaiah 1:10-15; (Ezekiel 16:49). What is it that we neglect to do that makes all our religious activities vile and hypocritical in God's sight? Here's what God says we neglect to do. Verse 17: "Learn to do well: seek judgment (fight against injustices, speak truth to power), relieve the oppressed (black folks, handicapped, elderly, poor white folks, illegal immigrants, children), judge the fatherless (do justice to fatherless, foster kids), plead for the widow (she who has been left without inheritance, even single moms)."

If we do not actively and vociferously in majority fight against the injustices, oppressions and murders, whether by gangbangers, the police or politicians, that are taking place in our streets, and by our, or another's military, then our hands are bloodied with the very blood we let be shed due to our inaction.

Amos 5:21 "I hate all your show and pretense-the hypocrisy of your religious festivals and solemn assemblies. 22. I will not accept your burnt offerings and grain offerings. I won't even notice all your choice peace offerings. 23. Away with your noisy hymns of praise! I will not listen to the music of your [guitars and keyboards]. 24. Instead, I want to see a mighty flood of justice, (notice that this isn't a side issue, it is the main thing in God's eyes. He wants justice to flow like torrents of water) an endless river of righteous living."

Are our pastors preaching this from our pulpits each church service? Are pastors making the effort to publicize the efforts being made to support various causes? Are they telling the people they need to stop sitting on their hands and get into action? Is he warning them? Are our pastors publicly speaking up for the causes for which they're fighting, and reporting the progress? Are the pastors hammering out the urgency as to why people must pick up their crosses? Are the pastors regularly training the people to become true sacrificial servants of the most High?

Are they taking up the banner against injustice, or are they dancing around the subject to protect their 501(c)3 status? Where are the churches that are supporting the civil and human rights organizations that are already in existence? Where are the churches who are taking up the causes of those who are already lobbyist in the White House, who fight to protect the rights of the weak and disadvantaged? Where are the churches who are doing these things? Why can't we identify them?

Why are the churches ignoring the plight of the Native American, (who would be classified a foreigner in this his own land) commonly mis-known as Indians? Why do churches fail to point out that it is at the hands of their devastation, that we even celebrate Thanksgiving? Why do we not recognize the mass amount of bloodshed they suffered at the hands of those of us who give thanks? Do we actually think that God hears our thanksgiving when He says, "I hate all your show and pretense-the hypocrisy of your religious festivals and solemn assemblies"? Why do our churches side with the oppressors? Why do we fail to have the true attitude of Christ who did not come to destroy, but to save?

If we do not concern ourselves first and foremost with those in our world who are the weak, the poor, the vulnerable, the children, then we are guilty of the sins that led to the homosexual perversions of Sodom and Gomorrah. It is not the job of the government or better said we are the government, government of and by the people. It is the job of those of us who claim to be members of the Kingdom of Heaven, to exercise our governmental rights and impose righteousness upon our nation. We must stay clear of the subversive propaganda of the "wolves", who are in power, and know what the message of Christ really is, that it is Christ who said clearly to love your neighbor as yourself, and pointed out specifically that the foreigner, or those who are not like us, is our neighbor, whom we are to love. We are supposed to be the gatekeepers of the earth, the salt, the light, the standard bearers of the Kingdom of Heaven. But instead of fighting for the rights of the weak and the most vulnerable, we're busy fighting for "a piece of the pie".

We're thus off our post, we're missing the mark, and thereby "Americanizing God". Are we hearing what God Himself is saying here when he says, "Then shall he say unto them on the left hand. Depart from me, ye cursed, into everlasting fire, prepared for the devil and his angels:" (Matt. 25:41)? "In light of [our] biblical understanding of the poor, what does this mean for Christians and the Church? What are [our] respective responsibilities? It can be said in two words: Imitate God. When God's people care for the poor, they imitate God and those who neglect the poor and oppressed are really not God's people at all-no matter how frequent their religious ritual or how orthodox their creeds and confessions." (Cain Hope Felder, PhD)

The 'Americanized Christians' emphasize this scripture, "Blessed be the Lord, who daily loadeth us with benefits, even the God of our salvation. Selah." Psa. 68:27. However the REAL church never fails to act on this scripture, "A father of the fatherless, and a judge of the widows, is God in his holy habitation." Psalms 68:5. Let us first imitate him, and then I'm sure he'll 'load us up with benefits'.

We see this part of the scripture, "And whatsoever we ask, we receive of him because we keep his commandments, and do the things that are pleasing in his sight" I John 3:22. But what are the things that are pleasing in his sight? What are these commandments we are commanded to keep? Read: "But whoso hath this world's good, and seeth his brother have need, and shutteth up his bowels of compassion from him, how dwelleth the love of God in him?"

On the contrary churches are preaching that He is our risen Lord and Saviour and how we must give our hearts to Him and "plead the blood", but the people in the congregation are manifesting the dysfunctional traits mentioned as follows:

"People will be selfish, greedy, boastful, and conceited; they will be insulting, disobedient to their parents, ungrateful, and irreligious; they will be unkind, merciless, slanderers, violent, and fierce; they will hate good; they will be treacherous, reckless, and swollen with pride; they will love pleasure rather than God; they will hold to the outward form of our religion, but reject its real power" (2 Timothy 3:2-5, GNB).

We are many of us, immobile Christians, making no real efforts in the world to help anyone or do anything more than would the average person. We are anesthetized, caught-up in concerns of everyday living, work, family, friends, bills, health, aches and pains, but manifesting no real intention, no real outside efforts. No sacrifice, no loss of life, pleasure or comforts. We practice a form of godliness, hearing, reading, teaching even studying the word but doing no real work, bearing no real fruit (John 15:8). Otherwise failing to forward the Kingdom on this earth (James 2:14-15).

On Activism

When Martin Luther King had come to a point where the momentum for Jim Crow to be defeated had finally taken a life form of its own and Congress began to pass legislation to ensure that the critical discrimination in the South would be defeated he began to challenge the racism in the North.

He picked Chicago for starters. But notice he also joined his voice in the garbage workers' strike in Memphis Tennessee. He also spoke out boldly against the war in Vietnam. He began to speak against man's inhumanity to man. And I personally believe it is for these sentiments he was assassinated. But then who are the real Christians, is it we who seek to avoid issues that will get us assassinated, is it we who struggle each day to find that elusive "pot of gold"? Is it we who get out in the battlefield of activism and fight for the rights of the poor, helpless, oppressed, imprisoned, the widow, the fatherless and the foreigner at all cost?

Beyond Vietnam: A Time To Break Silence
(Speech by Martin Luther King,1964)

"I come to this magnificent house of worship tonight because my conscience leaves me no other choice. I join with you in this meeting because I am in deepest agreement with the aims and work of the organization which has brought us together: Clergy and Laymen Concerned about Vietnam. The recent statement of your executive committee are the sentiments of my own heart and I found myself in full accord when I read its opening lines: "A time comes when silence is betrayal." That time has come for us in relation to Vietnam.

The truth of these words is beyond doubt but the mission to which they call us is a most difficult one. Even when pressed by the demands of inner truth, men do not easily assume the task of opposing their government's policy, especially in time of war. Nor does the human spirit move without great difficulty against all the apathy of conformist thought with- in one's own bosom and in the surrounding world. Moreover when the issues at hand seem as perplexed as they often do in the case of this dreadful conflict we are always on the verge of being mesmerized by uncertainty; but we must move on.

Some of us who have already begun to break the silence of the night have found that the calling to speak is often a vocation of agony, but we must speak. We must speak with all the humility that is appropriate to our limited vision, but we must speak. And we must rejoice as well, for surely this is the first time in our nation's history that a significant number of its religious leaders have chosen to move beyond the prophesying of smooth patriotism to the high grounds of a firm dissent based upon the mandates of conscience and the reading of history. Perhaps a new spirit is rising among us. If it is, let us trace its movement well and pray that our own inner being may be sensitive to its guidance, for we are deeply in need of a new way beyond the darkness that seems so close around us.

Over the past two years, as I have moved to break the betrayal of my own silences and to speak from the burnings of my own heart, as

I have called for radical departures from the destruction of Vietnam, many persons have questioned me about the wisdom of my path. At the heart of their concerns this query has often loomed large and loud: Why are you speaking about war. Dr. King? Why are you joining the voices of dissent? Peace and civil rights don't mix, they say. Aren't you hurting the cause of your people, they ask? And when I hear them, though I often understand the source of their concern, I am nevertheless greatly saddened, for such questions mean that the inquirers have not really known me, my commitment or my calling. Indeed, their questions suggest that they do not know the world in which they live.

In the light of such tragic misunderstandings, I deem it of signal importance to try to state clearly, and I trust concisely, why I believe that the path from Dexter Avenue Baptist Church — the church in Montgomery, Alabama, where I began my pastorate — leads clearly to this sanctuary tonight.

I come to this platform tonight to make a passionate plea to my beloved nation. This speech is not addressed to Hanoi or to the National Liberation Front. It is not addressed to China or to Russia.

Nor is it an attempt to overlook the ambiguity of the total situation and the need for a collective solution to the tragedy of Vietnam. Neither is it an attempt to make North Vietnam or the National Liberation Front paragons of virtue, nor to overlook the role they can play in a successful resolution of the problem. While they both may have justifiable reason to be suspicious of the good faith of the United States, life and history give eloquent testimony to the fact that conflicts are never resolved without trustful give and take on both sides.

Tonight, however, I wish not to speak with Hanoi and the NLF, but rather to my fellow Americans, who, with me, bear the greatest responsibility in ending a conflict that has exacted a heavy price on both continents."

The Importance Of Vietnam

"Since I am a preacher by trade, I suppose it is not surprising that I have seven major reasons for bringing Vietnam into the field of my moral vision. There is at the outset a very obvious and almost facile connection between the war in Vietnam and the struggle I, and others, have been waging in America. A few years ago there was a shining moment in that struggle. It seemed as if there was a real promise of hope for the poor — both black and white — through the poverty program. There were experiments, hopes, new beginnings. Then came the buildup in Vietnam and I watched the program broken and eviscerated as if it were some idle political plaything of a society gone mad on war, and I knew that America would never invest the necessary funds or energies in rehabilitation of its poor so long as adventures like Vietnam continued to draw men and skills and money like some demonic destructive suction tube. So I was increasingly compelled to see the war as an enemy of the poor and to attack it as such.

Perhaps the more tragic recognition of reality took place when it became clear to me that the war was doing far more than devastating the hopes of the poor at home. It was sending their sons and their brothers and their husbands to fight and to die in extraordinarily high proportions relative to the rest of the population. We were taking the black young men who had been crippled by our society and sending them eight thousand miles away to guarantee liberties in Southeast Asia which they had not found in southwest Georgia and East Harlem. So we have been repeatedly faced with the cruel irony of watching negro and white boys on TV screens as they kill and die together for a nation that has been unable to seat them together in the same schools. So we watch them in brutal solidarity burning the huts of a poor village, but we realize that they would never live on the same block in Detroit. I could not be silent in the face of such cruel manipulation of the poor.

My third reason moves to an even deeper level of awareness, for it grows out of my experience in the ghettos of the North over the last three years — especially the last three summers. As I have walked among the desperate, rejected and angry young men I have told them that Molotov cocktails and rifles would not solve their problems. I have tried to offer them my deepest compassion while maintaining my conviction

97

that social change comes most meaningfully through nonviolent action. But they asked - and rightly so — what about Vietnam? They asked if our own nation wasn't using massive doses of violence to solve its problems, to bring about the changes it wanted. Their questions hit home, and I knew that I could never again raise my voice against the violence of the oppressed in the ghettos without having first spoken clearly to the greatest purveyor of violence in the world today — my own government. For the sake of those boys, for the sake of this government, for the sake of hundreds of thousands trembling under our violence, I cannot be silent. For those who ask the question, "Aren't you a civil rights leader?" and thereby mean to exclude me from the movement for peace, I have this further answer. In 1957 when a group of us formed the Southern Christian Leadership Conference, we chose as our motto: "To save the soul of America." We were convinced that we could not limit our vision to certain rights for black people, but instead affirmed the conviction that America would never be free or saved from itself unless the descendants of its slaves were loosed completely from the shackles they still wear. In a way we were agreeing with Langston Hughes, that black bard of Harlem, who had written earlier:

O, yes,
I say it plain, America never was America to me,
And yet I swear this oath —
America will be!

Now, it should be incandescently clear that no one who has any concern for the integrity and life of America today can ignore the present war. If America's soul becomes totally poisoned, part of the autopsy must read Vietnam. It can never be saved so long as it destroys the deepest hopes of men the world over. So it is that those of us who are yet determined that America will be are led down the path of protest and dissent, working for the health of our land.

As if the weight of such a commitment to the life and health of America were not enough, another burden of responsibility was placed upon me in

1964; and I cannot forget that the Nobel Prize for Peace was also a commission — a commission to work harder than I had ever worked before for "the brotherhood of man." This is a calling that takes me beyond national allegiances, but even if it were not present I would yet have to live with the meaning of my commitment to the ministry of Jesus Christ. To me the relationship of this ministry to the making of peace is so obvious that I sometimes marvel at those who ask me why I am speaking against the war. Could it be that they do not know that the good news was meant for all men -- for Communist and capitalist, for their children and ours, for black and for white, for revolutionary and conservative? Have they forgot- ten that my ministry is in obedience to the one who loved his enemies so fully that he died for them? What then can I say to the "Vietcong" or to Castro or to Mao as a faithful minister of this one? Can I threaten them with death or must! not share with them my life?

Finally, as I try to delineate for you and for myself the road that leads from Montgomery to this place I would have offered all that was most valid if I simply said that I must be true to my conviction that I share with all men the calling to be a son of the living God. Beyond the calling of race or nation or creed is this vocation of sonship and brotherhood, and because I believe that the Father is deeply concerned especially for his suffering and helpless and outcast children, I come tonight to speak for them.

This I believe to be the privilege and the burden of all of us who deem ourselves bound by allegiances and loyalties which are broader and deeper than nationalism and which go beyond our nation's self-defined goals and positions. We are called to speak for the weak, for the voiceless, for victims of our nation and for those it calls enemy, for no document from human hands can make these humans any less our brothers."

Strange Liberators

"And as I ponder the madness of Vietnam and search within myself for ways to understand and respond to compassion my mind goes constantly to the people of that peninsula. I speak now not of the soldiers of each side, not of the junta in Saigon, but simply of the people who have been living under the curse of war for almost three continuous decades now. I think of them too because it is clear to me that there will be no meaningful solution there until some attempt is made to know them and hear their broken cries.

They must see Americans as strange liberators. The Vietnamese people proclaimed their own independence in 1945 after a combined French and Japanese occupation, and before the Communist revolution in China. They were led by Ho Chi Minh. Even though they quoted the American Declaration of Independence in their own document of freedom, we refused to recognize them. Instead, we decided to support France in its reconquest of her former colony.

Our government felt then that the Vietnamese people were not "ready" for independence, and we again fell victim to the deadly Western arrogance that has poisoned the international atmosphere for so long. With that tragic decision we rejected a revolutionary government seeking self-determination, and a government that had been established not by China (for whom the Vietnamese have no great love) but by clearly indigenous forces that included some Communists. For the peasants this new government meant real land reform, one of the most important needs in their lives.

For nine years following 1945 we denied the people of Vietnam the right of independence. For nine years we vigorously supported the French in their abortive effort to recolonize Vietnam.

Before the end of the war we were meeting eighty percent of the French war costs. Even before the French were defeated at Dien Bien Phu, they began to despair of the reckless action, but we did not. We encouraged them with our huge financial and military supplies to continue the war even after they had lost the will. Soon we would be paying almost the full costs of this tragic attempt at recolonization.

After the French were defeated it looked as if independence and land reform would come again through the Geneva agreements. But instead there came the United States, determined that Ho should not unify the temporarily divided nation, and the peasants watched again as we supported one of the most vicious modern dictators—our chosen man. Premier Diem. The peasants watched and cringed as Diem ruthlessly routed out all opposition, supported their extortionist landlords and refused even to discuss reunification with the north.

The peasants watched as all this was presided over by U.S. influence and then by increasing numbers of U.S. troops who came to help quell the insurgency that Diem's methods had aroused. When Diem was overthrown they may have been happy, but the long line of military dictatorships seemed to offer no real change especially in terms of their need for land and peace.

The only change came from America as we increased our troop commitments in support of governments which were singularly corrupt, inept and without popular support. All the while the people read our leaflets and received regular promises of peace and democracy and land reform. Now they languish under our bombs and consider us not their fellow Vietnamese the real enemy. They move sadly and apathetically as we herd them off the land of their fathers into concentration camps where minimal social needs are rarely met. They know they must move or be destroyed by our bombs. So they go primarily women and children and the aged.

They watch as we poison their water, as we kill a million acres of their crops. They must weep as the bulldozers roar through their areas preparing to destroy the precious trees. They wander into the hospitals, with at least twenty casualties from American firepower for one "Vietcong"-inflicted injury. So far we may have killed a million of them mostly children. They wander into the towns and see thousands of the children, homeless, without clothes, running in packs on the streets like animals. They see the children, degraded by our soldiers as they beg for food. They see the children selling their sisters to our soldiers, soliciting for their mothers.

What do the peasants think as we ally ourselves with the landlords and as we refuse to put any action into our many words concerning land reform? What do they think as we test our latest weapons on them, just as the Germans tested out new medicine and new tortures in the concentration camps of Europe? Where are the roots of the independent Vietnam we claim to be building? Is it among these voiceless ones?

We have destroyed their two most cherished institutions: the family and the village. We have destroyed their land and their crops. We have cooperated in the crushing of the nation's only non-Communist revolutionary political force — the unified Buddhist church. We have supported the enemies of the peasants of Saigon, We have corrupted their women and children and killed their men. What liberators?

Now there is little left to build on — save bitterness. Soon the only solid physical foundations remaining will be found at our military bases and in the concrete of the concentration camps we call fortified hamlets. The peasants may well wonder if we plan to build our new Vietnam on such grounds as these? Could we blame them for such thoughts? We must speak for them and raise the questions they cannot raise. These too are our brothers.

Perhaps the more difficult but no less necessary task is to speak for those who have been designated as our enemies. What of the National Liberation Front — that strangely anonymous group we call VC or Communists? What must they think of us in America when they realize that we permitted the repression and cruelty of Diem which helped to bring them into being as a resistance group in the south? What do they think of our condoning the violence which led to their own taking up of arms? How can they believe in our integrity when now we speak of "aggression from the north" as if there were nothing more essential to the war? How can they trust us when now we charge them with violence after the murderous reign of Diem and charge them with violence while we pour every new weapon of death into their land? Surely we must understand their feelings even if we do not condone their actions. Surely we must see that the men we supported pressed them to their violence. Surely we must see that our own computerized plans of destruction simply dwarf their greatest acts.

How do they judge us when our officials know that their membership is less than twenty-five percent Communist and yet insist on giving them the blanket name? What must they be thinking when they know that we are aware of their control of major sections of Vietnam and yet we appear ready to allow national elections in which this highly organized political parallel government will have no part? They ask how we can speak of free elections when the Saigon press is censored and controlled by the military junta. And they are surely right to wonder what kind of new government we plan to help form without them — the only party in real touch with the peasants. They question our political goals and they deny the reality of a peace settlement from which they will be excluded. Their questions are frighteningly relevant. Is our nation planning to build on political myth again and then shore it up with the power of new violence?

Here is the true meaning and value of compassion and nonviolence when it helps us to see the enemy's point of view, to hear his questions, to know his assessment of ourselves. For from his view we may indeed see the basic weaknesses of our own condition, and if we are mature, we may learn and grow and profit from the wisdom of the brothers who are called the opposition.

So, too, with Hanoi. In the north, where our bombs now pummel the land, and our mines endanger the waterways, we are met by a deep but understandable mistrust. To speak for them is to explain this lack of confidence in Western words, and especially their distrust of American intentions now. In Hanoi are the men who led the nation to independence against the Japanese and the French, the men who sought membership in the French commonwealth and were betrayed by the weakness of Paris and the willfulness of the colonial armies. It was they who led a second struggle against French domination at tremendous costs, and then were persuaded to give up the land they controlled between the thirteenth and seventeenth parallel as a temporary measure at Geneva. After 1954 they watched us conspire with Diem to prevent elections which would have surely brought Ho Chi Minh to power over a united Vietnam, and they realized they had been betrayed again.

When we ask why they do not leap to negotiate, these things must be remembered. Also it must be dear that the leaders of Hanoi considered the presence of American troops in support of the Diem regime to have been the initial military breach of the Geneva agreements concerning foreign troops, and they remind us that they did not begin to send in any large number of supplies or men until American forces had moved into the tens of thousands.

Hanoi remembers how our leaders refused to tell us the truth about the earlier North Vietnamese overtures for peace, how the president claimed that none existed when they had clearly been made. Ho Chi Minh has watched as America has spoken of peace and built up its forces, and now he has surely heard of the increasing international rumors of American plans for an invasion of the north. He knows the bombing and shelling and mining we are doing are part of traditional pre-invasion strategy. Perhaps only his sense of humor and of irony can save him when he hears the most powerful nation of the world speaking of aggression as it drops thousands of bombs on a poor weak nation more than eight thousand miles away from its shores.

At this point I should make it clear that while I have tried in these last few minutes to give a voice to the voiceless on Vietnam and to understand the arguments of those who are called enemy; I am as deeply concerned about our troops there as anything else. For it occurs to me that what we are submitting them to in Vietnam is not simply the brutalizing process that goes on in any war where armies face each other and seek to destroy. We are adding cynicism to the process of death, for they must know after a short period there that none of the things we claim to be fighting for are really involved. Before long they must know that their government has sent them into a struggle among Vietnamese, and the more sophisticated surely realize that we are on the side of the wealthy and the secure while we create hell for the poor."

The Madness Must Cease

"Somehow this madness must cease. We must stop now. I speak as a child of God and brother to the suffering poor of Vietnam. I speak for those whose land is being laid waste, whose homes are being destroyed, whose culture is being subverted. I speak for the poor of America who are paying the double price of smashed hopes at home and death and corruption in Vietnam. I speak as a citizen of the world, for the world as it stands aghast at the path we have taken. I speak as an American to the leaders of my own nation. The great initiative in this war is ours. The initiative to stop it must be ours.

This is the message of the great Buddhist leaders of Vietnam. Recently one of them wrote these words:

"Each day the war goes on the hatred increases in the heart of the Vietnamese and in the hearts of those of humanitarian instinct. The Americans are forcing even their friends into becoming their enemies. It is curious that the Americans, who calculate so carefully on the possibilities of military victory, do not realize that in the process they are incurring deep psychological and political defeat. The image of America will never again be the image of revolution, freedom and democracy, but the image of violence and militarism."

If we continue, there will be no doubt in my mind and in the mind of the world that we have no honorable intentions in Vietnam. It will become clear that our minimal expectation is to occupy it as an American colony and men will not refrain from thinking that our maximum hope is to goad China into a war so that we may bomb her nuclear installations. If we do not stop our war against the people of Vietnam immediately the world will be left with no other alternative than to see this as some horribly clumsy and deadly game we have decided to play.

The world now demands a maturity of America that we may not be able to achieve. It demands that we admit that we have been wrong from the beginning of our adventure in Vietnam, that we have been detrimental to the life of the Vietnamese people. The situation is one in which we must be ready to turn sharply from our present ways.

In order to atone for our sins and errors in Vietnam, we should take the initiative in bringing a halt to this tragic war. I would like to suggest five concrete things that our government should do immediately to begin the long and difficult process of extricating ourselves from this nightmarish conflict:

1. End all bombing in North and South Vietnam.
2. Declare a unilateral cease-fire in the hope that such action will create the atmosphere for negotiation.
3. Take immediate steps to prevent other battlegrounds in Southeast Asia by curtailing our military buildup in Thailand and our interference in Laos.
4. Realistically accept the fact that the National Liberation Front has substantial support in South Vietnam and must thereby play a role in any meaningful negotiations and in any future Vietnam government.
5. Set a date that we will remove all foreign troops from Vietnam in accordance with the 1954 Geneva agreement.

Part of our ongoing commitment might well express itself in an offer to grant asylum to any Vietnamese who fears for his life under a new regime which included the Liberation Front. Then we must make what reparations we can for the damage we have done. We must provide the medical aid that is badly needed, making it available in this country if necessary."

Protesting The War
"Meanwhile we in the churches and synagogues have a continuing task while we urge our government to disengage itself from a disgraceful

commitment. We must continue to raise our voices if our nation persists in its perverse ways in Vietnam. We must be prepared to match actions with words by seeking out every creative means of protest possible.

As we counsel young men concerning military service we must clarify for them our nation's role in Vietnam and challenge them with the alternative of conscientious objection. I am pleased to say that this is the path now being chosen by more than seventy students at my own alma mater, Morehouse College, and I recommend it to all who find the American course in Vietnam a dishonorable and unjust one. Moreover I would encourage all ministers of draft age to give up their ministerial exemptions and seek status as conscientious objectors. These are the times for real choices and not false ones. We are at the moment when our lives must be placed on the line if our nation is to survive its own folly. Every man of humane convictions must decide on the protest that best suits his convictions, but we must all protest.

There is something seductively tempting about stopping there and sending us all off on what in some circles has become a popular crusade against the war in Vietnam. I say we must enter the struggle, but I wish to go on now to say something even more disturbing.

The war in Vietnam is but a symptom of a far deeper malady within the American spirit, and if we ignore this sobering reality we will find ourselves organizing clergy- and laymen-concerned committees for the next generation. They will be concerned about Guatemala and Peru. They will be concerned about Thailand and Cambodia. They will be concerned about Mozambique and South Africa. We will be marching for these and a dozen other names and attending rallies without end unless there is a significant and profound change in American life and policy. Such thoughts take us beyond Vietnam, but not beyond our calling as sons of the living God.

In 1957 a sensitive American official overseas said that it seemed to him that our nation was on the wrong side of a world revolution.

During the past ten years we have seen emerge a pattern of suppression which now has justified the presence of U.S. military "advisors" in Venezuela. This need to maintain social stability for our investments accounts for the counter-revolutionary action of American forces in Guatemala. It tells why American helicopters are being used against guerrillas in Colombia and why American napalm and green beret forces have already been active against rebels in Peru. It is with such activity in mind that the words of the late John F. Kennedy come back to haunt us. Five years ago he said, "Those who make peaceful revolution impossible will make violent revolution inevitable."

Increasingly, by choice or by accident, this is the role our nation has taken - the role of those who make peaceful revolution impossible by refusing to give up the privileges and the pleasures that come from the immense profits of overseas investment.

I am convinced that if we are to get on the right side of the world revolution, we as a nation must undergo a radical revolution of values. We must rapidly begin the shift from a "thing-oriented" society to a "person-oriented" society. When machines and computers, profit motives and property rights are considered more important than people, the giant triplets of racism, materialism, and militarism are incapable of being conquered.

A true revolution of values will soon cause us to question the fairness and justice of many of our past and present policies, on the one hand we are called to play the good Samaritan on life's roadside; but that will be only an initial act. One day we must come to see that the whole Jericho road must be transformed so that men and women will not be constantly beaten and robbed as they make their journey on life's highway. True compassion is more than flinging a coin to a beggar; it is not haphazard and superficial. It comes to see that an edifice which produces beggars needs restructuring.

A true revolution of values will soon look uneasily on the glaring contrast of poverty and wealth. With righteous indignation, it will look across the seas and see individual capitalists of the West investing huge sums of money in Asia, Africa and South America, only to take the profits out with no concern for the social betterment of the countries, and say: "This is not just." It will look at our alliance with the landed gentry of Latin America and say: "This is not just." The Western arrogance of feeling that It has everything to teach others and nothing to learn from them is not just. A true revolution of values will lay hands on the world order and say of war; "This way of settling differences is not just." This business of burning human beings with napalm, of filling our nation's homes with orphans and widows, of injecting poisonous drugs of hate into veins of people normally humane, of sending men home from dark and bloody battlefields physically handicapped and psychologically deranged, cannot be reconciled with wisdom, justice and love.

A nation that continues year after year to spend more money on military defense than on programs of social uplift is approaching spiritual death.

America, the richest and most powerful nation in the world, can well lead the way in this revolution of values. There is nothing, except a tragic death wish, to prevent us from reordering our priorities, so that the pursuit of peace will take precedence over the pursuit of war. There is nothing to keep us from molding a recalcitrant status quo with bruised hands until we have fashioned it into a brotherhood.

This kind of positive revolution of values is our best defense against communism. War is not the answer. Communism will never be defeated by the use of atomic bombs or nuclear weapons. Let us not join those who shout war and through their misguided passions urge the United States to relinquish its participation in the United Nations. These are days which demand wise restraint and calm reasonableness.

We must not call everyone a Communist or an appeaser who advocates the seating of Red China in the United Nations and who recognizes that hate and hysteria are not the final answers to the problem of these turbulent days. We must not engage in a negative anticommunism, but rather in a positive thrust for democracy, realizing that our greatest defense against communism is to take offensive action in behalf of justice. We must with positive action seek to remove those conditions of poverty, insecurity and injustice which are the fertile soil in which the seed of communism grows and develops."

The People Are Important

"These are revolutionary times. All over the globe men are revolting against old systems of exploitation and oppression and out of the wombs of a frail world new systems of justice and equality are being born. The shirtless and barefoot people of the land are rising up as never before. "The people who sat in darkness have seen a great light." We in the West must support these revolutions. It is a sad fact that, because of comfort, complacency, a morbid fear of communism, and our proneness to adjust to injustice, the Western nations that initiated so much of the revolutionary spirit of the modern world have now become the arch anti-revolutionaries. This has driven many to feel that only Marxism has the revolutionary spirit. Therefore, communism is a judgement against our failure to make democracy real and follow through on the revolutions we initiated.

Our only hope today lies in our ability to recapture the revolutionary spirit and go out into a sometimes hostile world declaring eternal hostility to poverty, racism, and militarism. With this powerful commitment we shall boldly challenge the status quo and unjust mores and thereby speed the day when "every valley shall be exalted, and every mountain and hill shall be made low, and the crooked shall be made straight and the rough places plain."

A genuine revolution of values means in the final analysis that our loyalties must become ecumenical rather than sectional. Every nation must now develop an overriding loyalty to mankind as a whole in order to preserve the best in their individual societies.

This call for a worldwide fellowship that lifts neighborly concern beyond one's tribe, race, class and nation is in reality a call for an all- embracing and unconditional love for all men. This oft misunderstood and misinterpreted concept so readily dismissed by the Nietzsches of the world as a weak and cowardly force - has now become an absolute necessity for the survival of man. When I speak of love I am not speaking of some sentimental and weak response, I am speaking of that force which all of the great religions have seen as the supreme unifying principle of life. Love is somehow the key that unlocks the door which leads to ultimate reality. This Hindu-Moslem-Christian-Jewish-Buddhist belief about ultimate reality is beautifully summed up in the first epistle of Saint John:

Let us love one another; for love is God and everyone that loveth is born of God and knoweth God. He that loveth not knoweth not God; for God is love. If we love one another God dwelleth in us, and his love is perfected in us.

Let us hope that this spirit will become the order of the day. We can no longer afford to worship the god of hate or bow before the altar of retaliation. The oceans of history are made turbulent by the ever-rising tides of hate. History is cluttered with the wreckage of nations and individuals that pursued this self-defeating path of hate. As Arnold Toynbee says: "Love is the ultimate force that makes for the saving choice of life and good against the damning choice of death and evil. Therefore the first hope in our Inventory must be the hope that love is going to have the last word."

We are now faced with the fact that tomorrow is today. We are confronted with the fierce urgency of now in this unfolding conundrum of life and history there is such a thing as being too late. Procrastination is still the thief of time. Life often leaves us standing bare, naked and dejected with a lost opportunity. The "tide in the affairs of men" does not remain at the flood; it ebbs. We may cry out desperately for time to pause in her passage, but time is deaf to every plea and rushes on. Over the bleached bones and jumbled residue of numerous civilizations are written the pathetic words: "Too late." There is an invisible book of life that faithfully records our vigilance or our neglect. "The moving finger writes, and having writ moves on..." We still have a choice today; nonviolent coexistence or violent co-annihilation.

We must move past indecision to action. We must find new ways to speak for peace in Vietnam and justice throughout the developing world — a world that borders on our doors. If we do not act we shall surely be dragged down the long dark and shameful corridors of time reserved for those who possess power without compassion, might without morality, and strength without sight.

Now let us begin. Now let us rededicate ourselves to the long and bitter — but beautiful — struggle for a new world. This is the calling of the sons of God, and our brothers wait eagerly for our response. Shall we say the odds are too great? Shall we tell them the struggle is too hard?

Will our message be that the forces of American life militate against their arrival as full men, and we send our deepest regrets? Or will there be another message, of longing, of hope, of solidarity with their yearnings, of commitment to their cause, whatever the cost? The choice is ours, and though we might prefer it otherwise we must choose in this crucial moment of human history.

As that noble bard of yesterday, James Russell Lowell, eloquently stated:

> Once to every man and nation
> Comes the moment to decide,
> In the strife of truth and falsehood,
> For the good or evil side;
> Some great cause, God's new Messiah,
> Off'ring each the bloom or blight.
> And the choice goes by forever
> Twixt that darkness and that light.

Though the cause of evil prosper.
Yet 'tis truth alone is strong;
Though her portion be the scaffold,
And upon the throne be wrong:
Yet that scaffold sways the future,
And behind the dim unknown,
Standeth God within the shadow
Keeping watch above his own."

The End

Always Looking For A Bad Guy

Vietnam is an example of what the United States has been doing since World War II. When we discovered the profit that could be made through "The Marshall Plan", we began to go into countries, wreck them and then rebuild them so they are beholden to us. The Korean War is another example of that. We'll spend time and energy pointing out the flaws of another culture and its dictatorial leader as an excuse to bomb their brains out. We kill women and little children and marginalize it as necessary collateral damage. We're simply destroying their infrastructure so that we can insert our own. Our corporations are 'Johnny on the spot' ready to help rebuild these poor miserable nations. We're building our own empire on their soil. And the American churches support this. This is why God says in Isaiah 1, that our "hands are bloody. "The church due to the fact that we also covet wealth will condone the killing of a brother to obtain their wealth. The evidence of our covetous mindset is revealed by our failure to love and support our oppressed brothers and sisters right here at home. We find ourselves supporting America's military exploits of plundering and rebuilding nations under the guise of "bringing democracy to the world". Instead of showing love to our neighbors we destroy our neighbors "for their own good", and use the familiar phrase, "American-Self-Interests".

As Americans, we are fighting wars against new faces and new places, but the same things are going on, the same double standards, the same lies and oppression. To keep an industry thriving the industry must continue to make a profit. In order to continue to make a profit the American Industrial Military Complex must find "new markets". When we find a new market we ignite a controversy in that market in order to make a war. That is why we are always looking for a bad guy. This country thrives on the enslavement and exploitation of others as a means to its' existence, always has and always will, unless we the Christian church snap out of our malaise and unite to stop it.

What does God say the Christian is to do? We are to actively love our brothers, especially the poor.

"My little children, let us not love in word, neither in tongue; but indeed and in truth." 1 John 3:17. The problem is our churches are not built on the foundation of love.

We know the royal law is fulfilled when we obey the command, "Thou shalt love thy neighbor as thyself, ye do well:" But right after that it says, "But if ye have respect to persons, ye commit sin," but then we immediately go and have respect to persons, James 2:6-9. "Hath not God chosen the poor of this world rich in faith, and heirs of the kingdom which he hath promised to them that love him? BUT YE HAVE DESPISED THE POOR."

How? "If a brother or sister be naked, and destitute of daily food, And one of you say unto them. Depart in peace, be ye warmed and filled; notwithstanding ye give them not those things which are needful to the body; what doth it profit? Even so faith, if it hath not works, is dead, being alone." James 2:15-17.

There are multiple millions in this world today who are invisible, hungry and naked and have no voice. If we have, and they have not, then we need to give of what we have, so that they have also.

"Faith, if it hath not works is dead," A true church is doing the feeding and the clothing that God commands us to do.

"For the wicked have been found among my people. It looketh about the covering of snares. They have set up a trap to capture men.

28. They have been fat, they have shone (they're flashy), Yea, they have over passed the acts of the evil. Judgment they have not judged. The judgment of the fatherless and they prosper, And the judgment of the needy they have not judged.

29. For these do not I inspect, an affirmation of Jehovah, On a nation such as this. Doth not my soul avenge itself? An astonishing and horrible thing hath been in the land. The prophets have prophesied falsely. And the priests bear rule by their means. And My people have loved [it] so. And what do they at its latter end?" Jeremiah 5:26-31, Young's Literal Translation.

Many church leaders use the name of the Lord to give authority to their own ideas. "For ye have perverted the words of the living God, of the Lord of hosts our God." Jeremiah 23:36.

I think Jules says it best:
"There's this passage I got memorized. Ezekiel 25:17. The path of the righteous man is beset on all sides by the inequities of the selfish and the tyranny of evil men. Blessed is he who, in the name of charity and good will, shepherds the weak through the valley of darkness, for he is truly his brother's keeper and the finder of lost children. And I will strike down upon thee with great vengeance and furious anger those who attempt to poison and destroy my brothers. And you will know my name is the Lord when I lay my vengeance upon thee."

Some preachers puff up the people, "they make you vain: they speak a vision of their own heart, and not out of the mouth of the Lord." Jeremiah 23:16. Many use the words of life to extract money from believers and to get believers to support the heinous crimes this secular country commits against humanity.

One of the attributes that made Job know that he was righteous was the fact that though he was the richest man in the east, he never trusted riches or took pride in wealth, Job 31:24.

How often is it that we the called-out ones get caught up in the pursuit of wealth? How off track has the church as a whole gotten because of the greed of the clergy? The clergy reasons that if we do not concern ourselves with or pursue wealth then we cannot pay the light or water bills or pay the mortgage on the church building. Jesus however said don't be like the Gentiles who pursue all these things, trust God, pursue His Kingdom and His righteousness and He will supply all our needs (Matt. 6:33).

There are myriads of stories of natural people who know more about stepping out on faith than a whole church load of Christians. There are people who have risked their lives because they have integrity and sacrificed riches for the cause of righteousness, who've gone the extra mile to help others and never complained. There are hookers who know more about how to love a man than does a wife who has too much self-interest, who know how to be a true successful temptress to a husband, how to love him in a way that inspires him to divest upon her all her wildest dreams.

There are thousands of servants who know nothing about God or Christianity or Islam who are in the trenches of the scum of the earth and sacrifice their lives trying to help and aid the helpless.

What will this account for when their lives are evaluated in terms of their sacrifice and contribution to the less blessed?

I know a street urchin who lives amongst homeless and is himself homeless. His name is Elmer. His ministry is to help those that live at that street level of life. His spirit is to serve and lift those fit for destruction from their destruction.

We may not realize that when we were born into this world, this world at the time we entered it was already corrupt and evil, and all righteousness had already gone out of it. So thinking that we're here to salvage some goodness that used to be here is a misconceived thought. There is no good that was here when we arrived on the scene. There is no good that is here now. So our perspectives have no basis for discerning what or who in this world is good or evil. As the scripture says, "there is no one righteous, not even one", there is no one who understands, there is no one who seeks God. All have turned away, they have together become worthless; there's no one who does good, not even one. Their throats are open graves; their tongues practice deceit. The poison of vipers is on their lips...there is no fear of God before their eyes." This prophecy speaks of the church ministries who outwardly appear to call on Him, Romans 3:1-18. (Psalms 14:1-3; 53:1-3 Ecclesiastes 7:2)

So, we must not depend on what we think we know or have known, but we must with God's help, make a fresh start.

For instance, who taught us to hate sinners? The devil. Who taught us to hate ourselves as sinners? The devil and remember he is a liar. He tricked us. We think we are doing well by hating sinners and hating the world, but he tricked us "for God so loved the world" and we're to love the world also. We're told not to lust which is the hate of not having. Lust is a form of covetousness which is to hate what we don't have. We are to love and do good to the world, the world which is opposite of who God is, in order to demonstrate unconditional infinite love which is Eternal Life above all destruction.

We can't say we love God and at the same time talk badly about a fellow human being. If we hate the human being, then we hate God. If we hate the one, we hate the other. If we fear a fellow human being, we cannot say we love God because love casts out all fear. So those fear mongers who preach the destruction of others for our own safety and security are spinning a false gospel of 'hate' toward neighbor, wrapped in the package of fear, a gospel that is the antithesis of love.

Many Christians claim we love on a personal basis, for instance family and friends, but when it comes to a societal or national crisis we are seduced by the hype of those who fan the flames of hate. Neither must we despise self or be disappointed in self and curse self as some church teachers would con us into believing shows righteous piety. Since we're in His likeness and similar to Him, we must love self if we say we love God. God loved us and died for us even as sinners. We can't have both love and hate. If we have true love, we just love.

Even if our enemy does something hateful against us, we can't say we love God and then complain about the negative points that our enemy displays. We cannot speak bad words against anyone, especially anyone who upsets us or is doing negative things, because out of our same mouth cannot come blessings and cursing, James 3:10.

The Savior said, God is kind to the unthankful and to the evil. So, haters are essentially microwaving themselves in their state and need our love, not our condemnation. They need love more than anyone else.

There is a reason the last person most church members would hire to do a job for them would be another Christian. Why is that? The last person that one church member would team up with in a business relationship would be another church member? Why is that?

Carmen the famous Christian songwriter and performer said on an August 15th, 2007, TV broadcast that in his dealings in the music industry, the people who have sued him, ripped him off, and sabotaged him every step of the way were… Christians…not the non-Christians.

Face ourselves; we tend to be the meanest people to a waitress in a restaurant that a waitress has ever experienced… Christians.

By our fruit we are known, and the fruit we're demonstrating to the non-believer is not good. Therefore, we must inspect the tree, at the root.

When a trusted church official can sexually molest a child, and then upon being caught his peers transfer him to another church to hide his guilt, and the congregation supports it, then the devil must be in charge. There is something violently wrong with our Christian culture if we're not outraged for the devastation suffered by the molested child.

The level of love we have for the weak, the helpless, the least, speaks to what is our root motivation in our Christian walk. It is to save our own butts. We tend to want to multi-layer ourselves into deeper and deeper realms of security, comfort and luxury at the expense of the needy. It is important to understand the tricks that cause our dysfunction.

People who hate themselves as poor might do something in hate of their condition to rectify their situation. Some of us will do something illegal and get caught. We'll end up in prison and if we don't change this mental attitude when we get out, the hate we continue to harbor regarding being poor will more than likely land us back in prison. The lesson we must therefore learn is to love our self as poor, or unpopular, or as a failure.

And so, if God loves us at our worst, then we must love ourselves at our worst and thus we can love our brothers at their worst and love without condemnation.

The church in general seeks to avoid the issues of the world, hide from its' challenges, look at the bright side of everything, but that is the opposite of why God has allowed so much evil to exist in the world. His goal is that we become like Him and love the world and give up our lives to help heal the ills we recognize that exist, Matt. 10:39. In doing justice in the world we get to develop and demonstrate the unconditional, infinite and unmeasured love that He has for us.

We are not to be sitting on the sidelines piously pointing out the evils that are going on with "those horrible sinners", while we passively watch the evening news, but rather we must have a heart for saving as many people as possible, because we have the love of God for the people. We must demonstrate God-level love, by dealing with the issues and not ignoring them.

Yes, we must learn to love life's bad guy. Have you ever watched a movie and pulled for the bad guy? In a movie, the bad guy usually ends up paying for his ill-deeds and we wouldn't necessarily follow his example, but we do admire him if he's good at what he does. If he's the best of the bad guys we're sad when he gets caught or suffers his just rewards. This pulling for the bad guy is an example of loving the sinner. We may not agree with his take on living in society the way he has chosen to live, and we wouldn't necessarily become a criminal because we want to emulate him, but we do enjoy watching his devious lifestyle and hold a certain admiration for him through his ups and downs.

We may hate his enemies and hope for their destruction, but if we were to see a book or a movie featuring his enemies, showing us their vast accomplishments and why their ways carried them to the prominence it has, we might admire them as well in the context of their circumstances.

So, the majority script being written in this life experience of ours is the bad guy story. A good portion of our preachers, priests, teachers, politicians, military leaders, kings, judges, police officials do not meet the criteria of good guys.

Is it possible, that the bad guy story that dominates our world reality has a reason for being thus? That there are possible perspectives, we're not perceiving or fully appreciating? Is it possible, the best of the least of these may rise above us all, if we fail to grasp the message in regard to love?

From a certain perspective, if they have loved their enemy, or have helped hundreds of less blessed, and even risked their lives for a hated foe, whereas we haven't, it could put us in a tricky position as to whom God is most pleased.

Considering what one knows, how he's shaped, how he's brought into this world, the timing, circumstances, parental variables, the layers of context, whether born in New York, Paris, Hong Kong or Timbuktu, we know not how God equates people.

From each man's perspective, he is a product of his environment, circumstances, genetics, genre, prevailing perspectives, education and personality traits.

Are all bad contexts thus bad? Can they not invariably serve a positive purpose? A bad guy can reason that if the good guys are crooked, and many are, in fact the whole world is corrupt, what's the problem with him needing to look out for himself and his family, the way that he does?

What Is The True Measure Of Love?
With all the riches of the kingdoms of this world, a rich man who also possesses self-hate is impoverished beyond words.

With nothing, a poor man with self-love has all the necessary values and riches he needs. Whether poor or rich, if you have the intrinsic qualities of self-love, you are beautiful, rich and complete. To demonstrate self-love, we practice loving others. If we love others we love our self. To love others is the best way to have love for self which also loves God.

To demonstrate the infinite scope of His love is it not true that from before the beginning of the world God created us subject to vanity which is the opposite of who He is?

Our God and our creator created us as destined to death, which is opposite of what He is, that He might be forced to die for us to save us from the fate of being opposite of Himself.

Might it be possible that God who is infinitely opposite of us who are born in iniquity, created us who would choose the tree of pride and vanity and thus commit suicide, to save us to show the immeasurable unconditional state of His love?

Is it possible that what The Savior demonstrated is that to love is to help the unlovable who would commit suicide, to love he who would hurt us and not just us, but hurt himself? He who does not love himself?

Have we ever thought that what is being demonstrated in the human drama is that people born in the flesh cannot do well; there is none good, no not one? That flesh works in futile emptiness and makes a headlong bee-line towards death and self-destruction? That man in his best state is altogether vanity which is empty futility?

We must consider that flesh does not favor God. Flesh rather wars against God and revels without means of saving itself. Flesh commits its own destruction. Flesh thus hates itself. Whereas God loves Himself and loves flesh also.

When we stop and ponder that God created in His image, His opposite so that He could demonstrate the infinite measure of His love, it must stagger us. To ponder that God is in the business of demonstrating that love by having mercy on those that seek His destruction is quite astounding.

To be willing to suffer at the hands of those who hate you the most, to take literal torture from those who you created and to lose your own life for these same ones...this is love. To die for the haters, the abusers, the demon possessed, the killers, the perverted, the idolaters, peoples of strange religions, the worst of the worst, your own destroyers, this is love.

Honestly, who loves God? Nobody loves God, but rather some of us hate the adverse results that sin brings, but who amongst us really loves God? To truly love God we'd have to demonstrate that love by growing our love in the field of this evil world. This world which hates God is the testing ground for growing our love. Essentially, God loves Himself through us. We must also love this world if we allow His love to have its' full way in us. To fully assess whether we love God or not, we would first have to admit that we love our evil enemy. Once we can say that we love our evil enemy as well as our friends then we are assured that we can say we love God. If there is anyone or group of people we don't love, then we don't love God. That means as Christians, we are liars. Scripture says liars will not make it into heaven, Revelations 21:8.

Also in reality God to us is our enemy. From our perspective, He is an adversary of everything that our flesh would rather do. Our flesh wars against God, it hates God's righteousness and lusts to do evil.

In our flesh, our true enemy is God, for our flesh constantly wants to do what is evil and disobedient to God. When we can see that we must love our enemy, who is simply anyone opposite of us or who opposes us, then we can realize the surround sound need, to love our enemy also as God.

Consequently, if we love God, we also love our enemy. If we love our enemy, we also love God.

Thereby if we hate our enemy we thus hate God, the natural empirical selfishness of our flesh hates to love our enemies. But the point is that the enemy of the flesh is God and we are to love God, with all our heart, mind and soul.

Loving God that much requires that our flesh, which is also our enemy, love Him, who loves our flesh, God, with all our heart mind and soul. In the same way, we are to love our fleshly enemies, no less than with all our heart mind and soul. And we must also love our own flesh which opposes God as an enemy and is the enemy of God, with all our heart mind and soul.

And we are to love those who oppose us as lovers of God with all our heart mind and soul. Another reason for loving our enemy is that sometimes our enemy can help us more than can our friend. An enemy will tell us the truth about ourselves whereas we and sometimes our friends are blind to see it or afraid to admit it.

Many of us who have low self-esteem are actually in denial of the love that God has for us, thinking that we are worthless we oppose the value of the love God has for us. In effect, we disagree with what God thinks of us (after all He thought enough of us to die for us) thus our position of low self-esteem is opposing God and is thus hating God's attitude toward us. Thus, this state of being can also be an attitude of hating our enemies. Conversely, we who are puffed up with self-confidence and arrogantly profess that yes, we love ourselves, in truth might hate ourselves if we despise ourselves as weak or cowardly. Therefore, we who disdain being in the company of weak and cowardly people may idolize ourselves as confident but may not yet completely love ourselves. I do not speak here of having self-vanity, which tricks us into thinking we love. Loving self is not a feeling of superiority above others, feeling like we have the right to look down on others as inferiors. That attitude is a false love or vanity, an emotion generated from the ignorance of empirical selfishness. Some call it a "diva" complex.

I speak here of genuine self-love which is so secure in itself, it exalts others as being even better than self. It is a love that is humble in spirit and action and seeks to help and serve all. Even if it is thought that we have what appears to be negative traits of being ugly, stupid or poor, if we have the intrinsic qualities of self-love then we are as beautiful, brilliant or wealthy as is possible.

God's love is unlimited. It is standalone infinite love that encompasses all, the weak the strong, the poor the rich, the short the tall, the ugly the beautiful, the sick the well, the stupid the smart, the evil the good, the female the male, the inferior the superior, the child the elderly, the feeble, the talented, the humble the arrogant, the hater the lover, all words and their opposites, it is surround sound, immeasurable love.

We must love ourselves as poor or as rich. We must love ourselves as short or tall. Love ourselves as female or male, as dark or light, as failure or winner, as slow or fast, as foolish or wise, as sinner or saint, as lowly or exalted, oppressed or oppressor.

For in whatsoever state we find ourselves we are to love ourselves, as invalid or whole, as mentally challenged or genius, as obscure or celebrity, as criminal or just, we love ourselves and in loving ourselves in whatever state we find ourselves we love others in whatever state we find them. In that we love ourselves in every way possible, positive or negative, we can love others as ourselves.

If we can love ourselves as homeless or housed, then we can love homeless as we can love ourselves as homeless. When we can love ourselves as rejected by the crowd, then we can love others who are rejected by the crowd. When we can love others as ugly, weak, insufficient, lazy, losers, stupid, strong, smart, arrogant, obnoxious, then we can love others, for The Word instructs us to do unto others as we would have them do unto us.

Many who are fans of sports teams despise the team when it is losing and can't love the team as losers, because we don't love ourselves as losers, only as winners. We who can remain loyal to a team even as losers, have a better grip on loving ourselves as losers because we love ourselves as losers and/or winners, because our 'love' is unconditional.

When we don't love ourselves as beggar, is the reason we despise beggars. When we don't love ourselves as broke is the reason we despise broke people. When we don't love ourselves as mentally or physically challenged is the reason we're uncomfortable around mentally or physically challenged people.

We don't love ourselves as fat, is the reason we despise fat people, we despise handicapped so we're not comfortable around handicapped people.

When we hate ourselves as a virgin, we become motivated toward promiscuity. When we don't love ourselves as having a sexual transmitted disease is the reason we despise people with HIV / AIDS. The reason for this dissertation is to say this, in order to fully serve God, we must love all our enemies and love all the things we hate, even those things fitted for destruction.

We often naturally despise what we hate to see ourselves as. We often despise what we fear might happen to us. But fear is the hate of what might happen to us. We are afraid that the thing we hate most will happen to us. Fear mongers control direct and drive our lives in this country and in this world. They make us behave in ways to assay our hate of self. It is our own hate that often drives us toward what will eventually happen to us. It is through the use of the fear of others and what they might do to us that we as a nation are "motivated" to take certain policy paths that negate freedoms in the name of security.

Religious leaders consciously and unconsciously, use the same tactics in order to keep us on the path of the desired effect. Playing to our fears, the fear or hate of what might happen to us is a debilitating premise from which to control us. If we love, then we do not fear! If we love, then we do not hate what might happen to us because we love our self.

So if we love those who despitefully use us, who would strike us, who would steal our stuff, then we do not fear them because we love them. Put another way, we do not hate what they will do to us because we love those who would take advantage of and misuse us. Thus, we do not fear them or fear what they might do to us because love casts out all fear. I John 4:18 NIV, "Perfect Love casts out [hate]." In hate are the seeds of fear. We even fear what we might do or how we might feel if someone does despitefully misuse us.

My apartment was broken into and robbed awhile ago, and the violation that I felt made me feel I had the right to take their life if I caught them. I felt lower than dirt and so my natural reaction is that they needed to feel what I felt so they could get a taste of their own medicine. But that response is not love but hate. The robber hated me by taking my stuff which did not belong to him, but in return I must not be like him and hate what he did or hate him but love him and offer him more stuff if I could find him. By understanding the proper reaction to what the thief did, I thus learn not to fear what man might do to me, but trust in our God.

The stuff belongs to God. What was expressed was the idolatry I had for it, the attachment, the covetousness in my heart, the hold it had on me. It was my god. The stuff should not come before love. Love gives the stuff away. The only bad thing a person can do to us is to get us to hate. Hurting us, or taking something from us, is immaterial. Cursing, or spitting, demeaning, disrupting or beating the life out of us is their prerogative, but what we must not do is fall into the trap of feeling negatively against them when they do this. "Father forgive them for they know not what they do".

We may even act to curb certain of their behavior, but we do not do this with malice or contempt. We rejoice because it tests our resolve to love unconditionally. We remember this is what enemies are for. This is all about Kingdom business, it's our training course for being a Kingdom of God ruler. To be that ruler we must love, only love. Hateful occurrences are tests to qualify us for rulership. If we give into hate, we lose, if it bounces off us we gain. In training, we have obstacle courses. The courses are set to trip us up. How will we react? Pass or fail?

We must not be our own idol. We must not worship our own wants, fears, feelings or desires. That's why people can insult us and tear us down and that is because we're not more important than is love. Love is God and God is Love. What puts us in prison is our enslavement to anything that is earthly or material, including our own self.

All is nothing, when properly understood. Nothing we own, not things, ideas, positions, likes, talents, gifts, feelings, friends, family members, relationships, nothing is anything. Nothing comes before we love. Nothing stops, nothing blocks, nothing puts love on hold. All is nothing at all in terms of love. If anything prevents love, it is our "prison", that which keeps us bound. True freedom is the love that is active in us. No matter our circumstances, circumstances which appear real but are illusions based on conjured up misconceptions. All needs and goals have an expiration date. They are vapor, smoke, temporary, like the wind.

Be not afraid. All who appear to be in control are not in control. Their time ends too, and swiftly. All is nothing, be not afraid!

We might not like many things to happen to us, but to be like God our love has to be without limits, without condition.

Some are afraid of failure. Notice the word 'afraid'. What we might be saying is we hate ourselves as 'failure'. That might also be admitting we love our self only as successful. As a result, we by default hate people who are content, and only love people who are achievers; this could be a flaw in loving.

Love Does Not, Cannot Fail

In the wilderness, the children of Israel were getting nowhere fast and it did not feel good to them. It was in fact frightening and demeaning in their eyes. Their only resort was to cry out to God for everything. Instead of just crying out, they complained bitterly.

There were hostile nations all about and the children of Israel were not armed. They didn't even know how to fight. They felt demoralized, they complained bitterly.

Upon facing these nations, they watched as God fought their battles for them and defeated their enemies, one by one.

The Promised Land was ultimately theirs for the taking, but that too appeared to be impossible to them. They again failed to see the giant God who could "make a way" for them, against impossible odds.

When God says, He will provide all our needs, how can He prove it if we don't get to enjoy the 'wandering in the wilderness' experience? The children of Israel who were freed from slavery and baptized through the Red Sea were thrust into a desert experience. They were thrust into a situation where there was no water, no food, no heater and no air conditioner. They were homeless.

Instead of self-hate, they needed the self-love that Caleb and Joshua had. They needed to know that their God does not and cannot break His promise. To know that love does not and cannot fail. Heaven and earth may fail, but God's love will not fail. He swore by Himself because there is none greater that He would keep His word, and He made the same promise to us. Oh, how great is this love, how unfathomable? Yes, the Matthew 6 obedience will throw us into a wilderness experience but remember the wilderness experience will take us to a Promised Land if we believe.

When we feel secure with self only when successful, and insecure with self when we fail, we are also saying we hate others as failures and we mainly love all those who appear successful. We are saying our wishes are appeased when our opinions are met, and that we are deeply distraught when they are not. In other words, we love conditionally.

We very often hate the part in someone that we hate in ourselves. "The problem is not the thing we hate, rather the problem is the hate of the thing." (Gordon Harry). We must learn not to hate. "The problem between the races in this nation is not 'racism' but is 'haticism'." (Gordon Harry). The problem between nations is haticism, between church sects is haticism, between neighbors, even family members is haticism.

To prevent a molester from molesting us again loves self and that is good, it also loves the molester, not allowing him/her to add to their self-hate by doing something wrong to us or someone else. We are to love them against their depravity, against that which brings them down. But we must forgive them, and we must no longer hate them. However love is to see that they receive judgment for their transgressions so others are protected from their depravity.

What is love? Love equals loving he that loves you least. I John 4:1, despite what we think, we are all interconnected. What I give out will come back to me. You can't say you love God and at the same time talk badly about a fellow human being. If you hate the human being, you hate God. If you hate the one, you hate the other. Thus, we can't even curse ourselves. We can't be disappointed in ourselves and curse ourselves and say we love God, because we're in His likeness, like Him, He died for us and thus we must love ourselves, if we say we love God. We can't have both love and hate, if we have true love, we just love.

Even if our enemy does something hateful to us, we can't say we love God, then complain against our enemy. We cannot speak bad words against anyone, especially anyone who hates us.

Neither against anyone who upsets us or is doing negative things, because out of our same mouth cannot come blessings and cursings. So, if we do say negative things about the negative things of our brother, then we don't love God.

James says in chapter 3, verse 8 and 9 "But the tongue can no man tame; it is an unruly evil, full of deadly poison. Therewith bless we God, even the Father; and therewith curse we men, which are made after the similitude of God."

If someone hates us realize that it is hurtful to them. Hate devastates and destroys. If someone hates themselves, they are obliterating themselves in the throes of the sorrow of their haticism and it is eating them alive.

It is as if a microwave oven is on inside their bodies, zapping all their interior organs. These people are microwaving themselves; people need love, not condemnation.

The Savior said God is kind to the unthankful and to the evil. They need love more than anyone else. Their state of self-annihilation must become obvious to us.

Because while we hated Him, He loved us, and sent His only begotten Son, to die for us! ... this is love. He by this expects what He put out to come back to Him, that we all of us even the worst most depraved will be redeemed. Christ by His death transformed us, all of us from certain death to life everlasting, for yes love does conquer all. If it is not capable of conquering all, then is it love?

Even hate is not the enemy of love but is rather an agent that proves love... and while we hated him, in our hatred of him, in our sins he loved us and died for us...this is love. By the same reasoning those who oppose us are friends of God for our sakes. For our enemies are working for our good, that we would learn to love God, as God loves us. He loves us with all His heart, mind and soul.

James and John the most pacifist of the disciples asked The Master for permission to call fire out of heaven because the Samaritans wouldn't allow them passage to Jerusalem. And The Master responded with, I came to save, not destroy, Luke 9:51-58. Thus, this nation is in no way justified in sending down the fire of our bombers, drones and missile launchers upon nations of other religions who oppose us.

We are to love our enemies...and rejoice!

Love our enemies, with all our heart, mind and soul. Lay down our lives for them. See after them. Live for their benefit. Seek their welfare, for they are fitted for our salvation. Even our own flesh is fitted for our salvation, hallelujah! We must love!!!

Throughout His ministry JESUS LOVED THOSE WHO HATED HIM, suffering affliction at the hand of His enemies and then rescued them by dying for all.

He freed the worst prisoner (Barabbas), saved the most hated tax collector (Zacchaeus), saved the thief on the cross and forgave those most scandalous religious leaders, they along with the soldiers who killed Him, though He was more innocent than they all. Additionally, He spoke no evil against any of them.

There is a reason that many of us are perceived as mean, unsympathetic and untrustworthy by others, and act as counter-Christians. We don't love other people who aren't friendly or familial - thus we exclude, rather than include others.

At a time, South Korea was going through a depression, a Korean girl exclaimed on a Christian radio station that while she was thankful that the nurses and helpers at the Christian center saved her from her illnesses, they weren't very warm or friendly towards her. This is why we must learn to care for others from our heart. It is why we must become a church that is interested only in this and that is that we love our enemies with the sufficient love with which The Master loved His enemies.

What is The Point of Our Earth Walk?

THE BIBLE SAYS WE THE SAINTS OF THE HIGHEST, will soon become kings and rule the kingdom under the whole heaven forever, Daniel 7:27 NIV. "Then the sovereignty, power and greatness of all the kingdoms under heaven will be handed over to the holy people of the most High. His kingdom will be an everlasting kingdom, and all rulers will worship and obey him."

"God had not placed the angels as rulers over the new world to come-the world of which we speak. Instead, as it is said somewhere in the Scriptures: What are human beings, O God, that you should think of them; mere human beings, that you should care for them? You made them for a little while lower than the angels; you crowned them with glory and honour, and made them rulers over all things." It says that God made them "rulers over all things"; this clearly includes everything. We do not, however, see human beings ruling over all things now, (Hebrews 2:5-8 GNB). We don't rule all things now, but apparently our earth walk is to prepare us for the rulership of all things in the future.

We can surmise that in order to be a good ruler we would need some form of training. On any job of some responsibility we would need a great deal of preparation which would entail education, testing, hands-on project based learning and real-life trial situations, Luke 22:31. For such a position of rulership we would need some sort of severe boot-camp and some severe obstacle resistance courses to prove our mental, emotional, and spiritual competence.

Our boss would have to be confident that we can work in line with his policies and that we have a sincere heart and attitude that reflects his own. Since we are in line to rule others He has to know that we will do it His way and not do our own thing. We must thereby exhibit the same heart and desire that He has as ruler of the universe. He has to know that we trust Him and thus we can be trusted. This may be why The Master repeatedly uses the Master-Servant and King-Steward analogies throughout the gospels. He wants to know what quality of steward we are and what He can expect from us when He leaves us alone to carry out the tasks He commands of us.

The Master did not die; give up His Undie-able Eternal Indestructible Infinitely Powerful Life that we might be Undie-able, Eternal, Indestructible, Infinitely Powerful rulers with Him over all the Kingdoms under Heaven, all the universes, all the billions of galactic systems under the infinite skies to risk us destroying it due to our inability to be obedient to His rules.

Therefore, we must not be covetous, a slave to pleasure, controlled by lusts, liars, fornicators, adulterers, sexual deviants or lovers of men more than lovers of God. We can't be quick tempered, wrathful, irrational, insensitive or oversensitive, prone to beat down people. We have to exhibit good character, fidelity, wisdom, generosity of spirit and purpose. We must adhere to honesty and live by the spirit of the law and hold others accountable to the same. We must learn the proper way, God's way to do all things in love. We must not be easily deceived nor persuaded by wrong messages. We must not be enticed to do evil and we must be true and virtuous in our walk. We must be always humble, teachable and obedient as is a little child. We must prove we can follow all of His commands.

So, the point of our earth walk is to realize God! We should be looking for Him. We must realize Him. To realize Him is to see a clear demonstration of who He is. To see why He declares Himself to be "Love" (I John 4:8).

The point of our existence is thus to realize the immeasurable measure of God's love. In order for us to realize this immeasurable love God must purify us so that we become more like Him. To be more like Him we must go through tests and challenges. Even though we want to do only what is good we often find ourselves torn between two choices. We must learn to delineate His goodness from human goodness.

We are effectively walking this earth in order to learn to obey Him and Him only. God's ultimate goal is to give us a heart to help the marginal folks in this world. God's definition of love is one who joyfully serves another at his own expense. In having a heart for the marginal, we demonstrate that we have the same rulership values that He has. God came to lay down His life for everyone and we are here to learn to lay down our lives for everyone also. He came to save. We must become slaves to all that we might save some.

In serving all, we serve God. When we actively operate our whole life in this manner He can see that we are properly readying ourselves to rule with Him in His Eternal Kingdom of love.

To become perfect, we must start by admitting some things. We must clearly realize our own depravity. The apostle Paul said it in Romans 7:18 "for I know that in me (that is in my flesh) dwelleth no good thing:" Verse 24, "O wretched man that I am, who shall deliver me from the body of this death?"

We realize that "the heart is deceitful above all things and desperately wicked: who can know it?" Jer. 17:9 "For there is not a just man upon earth, that doeth good and sinneth not", Ecclesiastes 7:2. "Behold I was shapen in [depravity] and in sin did my mother conceive me", Psalms 51:5.

Obviously, I am not espousing a new age feel good doctrine. Rather we must look realistically at our true state of being before we can begin to appreciate the amazing love God has for us.

Look at how we really are, "Every man at his best state, is altogether vanity, Selah", "But I am a worm, and no man: a reproach of men, and despised of the people" Psalms 22:6. "For there is not a just man upon earth, that doeth good, and sinneth not". Explanation: all the good we may do, if we can even be considered just, is canceled by the sins that we habitually commit on an ongoing basis in spite of our "good deeds".

"But we are all as an unclean thing, and all our righteousness is as filthy rags; and we all do fade as a leaf: and our iniquities, like the wind, have taken us away." Isaiah 64:6. "Ye when ye shall have done all those things which are commanded, you say, we are unprofitable servants we have done that which is our duty to do", Luke 17:10.

The Messiah the son of God who was Himself without sin asked the Jewish leader, "why do you call me good? There is none good except God alone" Luke 18:19 GNB. So if this is the criteria of who is good, how can we even imagine we are good? We all attempt to do good, but only God the Father is good. What about the Pharisee who was praying in the temple and said, "I thank God, that I am not greedy, dishonest, or an adulterer, like everybody else. I thank you that I am not like that tax collector over there. I fast two days a week, and I give you a tenth of all my income." Notice he was thanking God...but was using that idea in vain, in the vanity of his heart, exhibiting a 'form' of godliness. The righteous have less chance of making it than do the sinners, obviously. Yes, our Father has great plans for us, but we must always remember we are unworthy.

Anytime we know the truth and have stated the truth and back up and compromise that truth, we are worse than a Godless person.

The Bible tells us the truth of who we are, and what we are, but even at our best, our sins negate any good that we would do. We who are subject to suicide and self-annihilation, are subject to this for the perfecting of our souls, Romans 8:20-21. God is demonstrating by making us thus, that despite our condition, which is opposite of who He is ...He still loves us!

We must learn to appreciate the depth, breadth, scope and immutability of His love. He died for haters; He died ahead of time knowing we'd be born hating Him. If we can get a glimpse of the immeasurable permanency of the death that our depraved state deserves, then we can get a glimpse of the infinite, unlimited and immeasurable permanency of the redemptive love God has exacted upon our lives.

Said another way, if we could see the certain non-existence, irreversible eradication, void, black hole, everlasting expulsion death state that is come upon us, but for God's love, we would completely pass out. We then begin to obtain a 'tinkling inkling' of what real love is all about, and how we are so loved.

If we could just get a glimpse, a flash of the scope of how much we are loved, loved by all the power of the universe which is all the power, and all the universe, all the permanency and total perfection and supreme good that is, which is without limit, exponentially infinite, then we would begin to get happy!

The magna of this love would kill us if we understood it. This is a love that makes it impossible to die. We cannot know it in our flesh state for we would be destroyed by the simple magna of realizing it! And yet I surmise it would kill us to life, eternal life!

Herein lie the beginning fragments of the example by which we must begin to live. Yes, we should learn to love ourselves as permanently dead in our own sins as God loves us as permanently dead in our own sins. This realization then reflects the magna of the love that God has for us as sinners, filthy rags, that deserve to be ever deposed into the black hole of the darkness of the void of hell.

We may even get an 'tinkling inkling' that life has forever existed, and cannot not exist, because there is a holy God who cannot be destroyed nor voided, be prevented, nor lessened, reduced nor subdued, nor in any sense negated, captured nor contained, but makes everything ever living by the ever living, everlasting power that is Him, and loves us in opposition to the death sentence we deserve.

By this He who is boundless joy loves us by what He is, which is eternal boundless existence. His eternal boundless presence literally saves us from our predetermined death fate.

Dead Man Walking

We may not realize it, but at this point in our lives we are "'Dead Men Walking". The terminology "dead man walking" refers to a person who has been selected to die by means of some form of capital punishment, whether by firing squad, hanging, beheading, electric chair, lethal injection, crucifixion or stoning.

These people are prisoners who are destined to die at a time appointed by the judicial system. Their life is to be terminated by means of a lethal implementation. It is the intent of the judicial system to make them pay, with their life, permanently, for a crime that they've committed that deserves death.

There are also hundreds of thousands of others in prison right now who are there until the day they die. They will never be released but will die in jail for crimes they have or have not committed.

Many of these prisoners claim innocence of the crimes for which they've been accused. Many know they are guilty of the crime but wish for pardon. Some so rebel against what is happening to them they end up in "the hole" or a place away from the general population called solitary confinement. What we who experience the earth walk may not be aware of is that, we too are living the same destiny as these prisoners who are destined to die in these physical jails.

These prisoners who have no way out, are also us since we were born in iniquity and so our sins have merited us a death sentence. Therefore, God wants us to have pity on those who are locked away in prisons. When we become conscious of the parallels we share with those in literal prisons we begin to obtain the heart of compassion that we need so that we can be forgiven for the spiritual crimes we have committed. We then learn to sympathize and even empathize with the plight in which they find themselves because of the parallel plight in which we find ourselves.

The truth is that sin is the breaking of God's law. The breaking of God's law is a crime. For the crime we've committed, we must pay. The law we've broken is the law of love.

The Bible says God is Love. So since God is Love it is Love that created us. We were thus created by Love. Being created by Love we were created for Love. Being created for Love we were created to love. Whereas when we perform something that is contrary to Love we "death" our self.

Put another way, God is eternal life. He has no beginning and He has no end. So, God who is Love is Eternal Life. If we love, we have Eternal Life because Love is Eternal. If we do that which is opposite of Love, if we break the law of Love, we lose Eternal Life.

This is why we are asked to receive Love as our Lord and Saviour. If we receive Him, because He is Eternal Life, we receive Eternal Life. After we have "deathed" our self, if we receive Love as our Lord and Saviour, because of His sacrifice for us, He saves us from eternal death. And that eternal death came because we broke the code by which we were made; we broke the code of Love. We broke the code of Eternal Life. Upon being made by a certain code, if we violate that code we will be in peril of the consequences. We would thus cease to operate properly. It's like any machinery that is programmed to function by a certain code. If it operates in alignment with that code it continues to function well. But if it goes against that code the machinery will fail to properly function.

So, the code that is set in us is the code for the law of Love. Since we were created by Love we are made to love. If an intruder comes along and convinces us to 'death our self', it would be reasonable to infer that the intruder wants to get us to cease operating, by convincing us that the code is unimportant, silly, non-doable . He might get us to feel that the code of Love is for ignorant, regressive, unattractive, individuals and that we could do without it.

So, we choose to be smart, wise, beautiful, rich, prideful, intelligent, intellectual individuals and live against the ways of the simple and mundane code of Love. We grow to believe this law of Love is uselessly stupid and we feel that we deserve excitement and hype over pedestrian Love. So, we choose the immediacy of excitement and thrills over the mundanity of the delayed gratification Love would bring us in terms of eternal life. We choose the quick thrill over life eternal with all power and unlimited and infinite knowledge, wisdom and understanding. We choose to die now rather than to stay grounded in faith and live forever. We refuse to be grounded in the faith, to believe that Love cannot and will not fail.

That Eternal Life which created us for eternal life will succeed in us if we trust our maker and live according to the code upon which we were manufactured. When we truly treasure our eternal life, we can easily sell all that we have and give it to the poor. We can take care of our neighbors especially our enemies. Visit the sick, the prisoner, the widow and the fatherless. Feed the hungry, clothe the naked and make a home for the homeless. Fight to free the oppressed and bring justice to those who are defenseless. Be a voice, an advocate for the voiceless. Keep our temple clean because it is holy, refrain from lust, fornication, adultery and that which defiles and makes our temple unholy. We can now be truthful even to our own detriment. Now if we manifest these things and do them with all our heart, mind and soul, and forsake greed, pride and material pursuits, we will live according to the code of love and thus live forever. The goal of Love is for everyone to lay down their lives for everyone else, (Galatians 6:2).

Theologians use the word sin as a substitute for the word crime. Thus, breakers of God's law of love are sinners or in more contemporary secular terminology criminals. The penalty for breaking Love's law is death. That is how we got to be "dead men walking", in the first place.

Once we realize our dilemma, we understand that our hands are in chains, our feet in shackles, and we are shuffling from one location in this prison called earth to the next until one day we walk down the final corridor in life, and the prison guard yells, "Dead Man Walking!"

Yes, we who pretend we have such self-determination over our lives and can do anything and be anything we want to be, don't realize our participation in the death-walk of this prison called earth.

Our destiny is to cease to exist. No matter how good an impression we've made during our lifetime, when it is all said and done, we are 'dead men walking'.

Since Adam and Eve chose to listen to the voice of pride and vanity, or self-seeking and self-serving, we have all been destined to die.

Yet in opposition to the choice of death that we through Adam and Eve intentionally chose for ourselves, Rabbi took on the penalty of our crimes and died in our stead in order to save us from our own deliberate bad choice, so that our predetermined death sentence could be waived, and we could have life everlasting, anyway. This is love.

It is easy to look down on prisoners and jailbirds and incarcerated folks who've done some of the stupidest things that have caused them to be locked up, many for life, and some to the fate of state execution.

Do we yet realize that those who are in prison are simply mirroring our own destiny? Do we yet realize that they are walking reflections of ourselves, because there is a spiritual death sentence that is also upon us? Do we realize how trivial and stupid have been the sins we've committed, the errors we've made, the faulty choices in which we've deliberately invested, hoping we'd get away with them somehow, believing we are invincible or immune?

Do we yet realize in what ways we've hated Love, that we've gone against Love's operating instructions for us? Do we realize how many times we've tried things for ourselves because we wanted to do it our own way? Do we realize the penalty of death that sinning against Love has incurred? And yet we will at this very moment, due to faulty and failing reasoning again do something to err against Love.

Do we see ourselves as "The Judge" sees us, as "dead men walking"? That we're shuffling through life up one corridor and down another, from one location in a prison facility to another? Our destiny is to die in jail just like everyone else, whether we become prison trustees or land in the "hole".

Yes, man was doomed to death ever since we chose to disobey the code of Love which is the code that dictates how we are to properly function. And yes, Christ the son of Love came to pay the penalty for our crimes, in our stead so that we would not have to suffer death for eternity. However, whether we receive that pardon or reject that pardon is demonstrated in how we repent and walk a new way, walk according to the code of the law of love. Whether or not we allow the code of love to change our hearts, and we get about the business of visiting the widow, mentoring the fatherless, serving the foreigners in their needs, visiting the sick and fighting for the rights of the oppressed and imprisoned.

If we simply pay lip service to the code of love, but fail to operate in it, we demonstrate that we do not believe in Him who died in our stead (John 3:16), we then violate our parole and confess by our inactivity that we have not received the pardon Christ died to give us. In this way, we return to the death walk from which we were released. We demonstrate that we in fact agree with the decision that Adam and Eve made to eat of the tree of pride and the knowledge of good and evil, ultimately rejecting Eternal Life.

But once we know we've been pardoned and we agree to change and operate according to that law of Love, then we receive eternal life and we live free from the death sentence that had us bound. We can then operate in the Kingdom righteousness that make us a "live man walking", "running", "dancing" and "leaping". We demonstrate we believe in Him who died in our stead and confess by our activity that we have accepted the pardon Christ died to give us. Once we are freed from the penalty of breaking the code it doesn't do away with our need to adhere to that code.

God has great things in store for us, He has given us a myriad of promises, but we must see His promises, His word as true, life and light. Even when the dark and deadly tests and trials of the "lie" come against us, we practice living by that code.

Heaven and earth may fail, heaven and earth may pass away, but God's word does not and cannot fail (I Corinthians 13:8).

He swore by Himself because there is none greater that He would keep His word (Hebrews 6:13) and He made a promise to us nobodies, that we would receive eternal life in the Kingdom of Heaven, the everlasting "promised land".

Oh, how great is this love, how unfathomable? Yes, the Matthew 6 obedience will throw us into a wilderness of bewilderment but remember the experience will get us to the promise land if we don't fear, don't doubt, don't complain, don't faint, but trust Love.

When what we see is what we know, this is very shallow
When what we know is what we see, this is very deep
Do you know what you see?
Or
Do you see what you know?
I don't see God, so I don't know Him?
Or
I know God, so I see Him?
So why do I act like I don't see God?
I must first love God!
Then I will see what I know, and act like I see what I know.
To pretend God is not in the room is to be more comfortable without God around.
To see God is in the room is to be more comfortable in His presence.
We've been trained one way or the other.
One way is love, the other is denial.

Love is ever reaching and has no limits, despite all signs to the contrary, love will come true. The word must be true; thus the promise will be kept.

Thus, no matter our station in life; if we've been promised something, we are loved enough that the promise will absolutely happen.

God gave His life in order to keep a promise. God kept His promise to give His life, this is love. Therefore, we even if it cost us our own life, must keep our promise, so that we demonstrate infallible love. This exercise is possibly the greatest builder of self-love and love period, which is under all conditions, to keep our promises.

So, what God promises must happen. Every promise will be fulfilled which proves His love is infallible. Upon this rock our confidence is built, and we become lovers and not haters.

Abraham was given a promise by God, and it was his duty to believe the promise that God would not and could not lie, to endure (through sufferings, setbacks and discouragements) patiently until that promise would be delivered, Hebrews 6:13-15.

This is how our love becomes perfect. So that we become perfect even as He is perfect. We love those who hate us and under all circumstances, always do what we promise, no matter how much it cost.

"In the past, God spoke to our ancestors many times and in many ways through the prophets, but in these last days he has spoken to us through his Son. He is the one through whom God created the universe, the one whom God has chosen to possess all things at the end. He reflects the brightness of God's glory and is the exact likeness of God's own being, sustaining the universe with his powerful word. After achieving forgiveness for human sins, he sat down in heaven at the right-hand side of God, the Supreme Power. The Son was made greater than the angels, just as the name that God gave Him is greater than theirs. For God never said to any of his angels: "You are my Son; today I have become your Father."

Nor did God say about any angel, "I will be his Father, and he will be my Son." But when God was about to send his firstborn Son into the world, he said: "All God's angels must worship him." But about the angels God said, "God makes his angels winds, and his servants flames of fire." About the Son, however God said: Your kingdom, O God, will last for ever and ever! You rule over your people with justice."

"You love what is right and hate what is wrong. That is why God, your God, has chosen you and has given you the joy of an honor far greater than he gave to your companions."

He also said: "You, Lord, in the beginning created the earth, and with your own hands you made the heavens, They will disappear, but you will remain; they will wear out like clothes. You will fold them up like a coat, and they will be changed like clothes. But you are always the same, and your life never ends."

God never said to any of his angels: "Sit here on my right until I put your enemies as a footstool under your feet." What are the angels, then? "They are spirits who serve God and are sent by him to help those who are to receive salvation" (Hebrews 1:14, GNB).

Shakespeare wrote, "to be, or not to be, that is the question: Whether 'tis nobler in the mind to suffer the slings and arrows of outrageous fortune, Or to take arms against a sea of troubles, And by opposing end them?" The 'Americanized' church teaches it is nobler in the mind to suffer the slings and arrows of outrageous fortune…fancy that!

The Bible also teaches, "And having food and raiment, let us be therewith content. But they that will be rich fall into temptation and a snare, and into many foolish and hurtful lusts, which drown men in destruction and perdition.", I Timothy 6:8-9.

The answer to Shakespeare's question is that it is better to "take arms against a sea of troubles, And by opposing end them", "loose the bands of wickedness, to undo the heavy burdens, and to let the oppressed go free, and that ye break every yoke?" Isaiah 58:6.

"…supposing that gain is godliness: From such withdraw thyself." I Timothy 6:5.

Many of us will miss eternity because of our penchant toward 'gain', a woman's body, a sleek car, some mind-altering substance, a house, status or our refusal to relinquish chasing money. 'Gain', is not godliness. (Colossians 3:5) The rich fellow who would not sell all his riches and give the funds to the poor is dead today. He is dead and his riches have dissipated. That brief vapor-long moment called his life is gone…forever. He failed to see the value of living life eternally having all power to do anything immortally. He was suckered into knowing only what he could see rather than seeing what he could know. He was short sighted. Therefore, Christ said, give it all away, and follow eternity.

There's nothing here worth losing eternity over. Even if it means giving up a life of ambition. If music trips us up to the point we're so attached we're taken down bad roads, we need to give up music. Whatever it is, it could be certain television shows or movies, well then we got to let them go. We might have to cut off our eye, hand, ear or mouth if necessary.

People are beautiful and the gifts we have are awesome to behold. But those gifts and talents don't belong to us. They're on loan until that point in our lives that we die. Then they return. The earthly aspirations we have are also temporary until we decease. It is our job to improve the planet so that all people might enjoy this fleeting life we have here. It is then that we're doing the work God has given us. Improving the planet is kingdom-like work. It is the work of rulers of those who have a heart for the Kingdom. Improving life on the planet is an example of the heart and mind set of those who want to rule with Christ.

If we orient our lives to helping on this earth, then we are in training for helping in the Kingdom for eternity. This is why Immanuel said our role is to be servants. We are to see how we can help the neediest. We are to train ourselves in how to bring about change for the good of those who live on the fringes of life. This is how Love operates, this is the work of the Kingdom. It is the work over which we will preside in eternity. For we will be kings and priest and rule forever. Revelations 1:6 KJV, "And hath made us kings and priests unto God and his Father;". "You have made them to be a kingdom and priests to serve our God, and they will reign on the earth." Revelations 5:10, NIV. "And His name shall be in their foreheads" (22:4).

The Kingdom of God and His righteousness is the poor, the needy, the desolate, homeless, the prisoner and the oppressed. Getting help to these people is Kingdom business. It has to do with the Godly concerns for righteousness and justice. It demonstrates that our hearts have the same interests that our Lord who created all these things has (Hebrews 1:10; Col. 1:16). We are these servants and stewards and managers of the Kingdom universe that He created. (Revelations 22:3-6; 6-21. KJV), NET Bible, "And so the one who conquers (himself) and continues in my deeds until the end, I will give authority over the nations-", Revelations 2:26. Notice the word "works" or "deeds", we must obey His commands by doing the deeds He's told us to do. What would these deeds be? Love God and our neighbor, heart, mind and soul. How? Serve the least of them. The Father may have in mind having us rule unlimited universes. The universes are unmeasurable. Let us take heed lest we fail.

Meekness and lowliness, that is what is required. Eternity should be the theme of our lives. Eternity or no eternity, that is the question. Greed, drunkenness, whoredom, lying, thievery addictions won't inherit eternity. The reason why is because our attachment or the attachment of these things to us demonstrate the hold, "things" have on us. Coming off "things" is like coming off alcohol or drugs, we'll experience a terrible, horrible withdrawal. It's the hardest action we could possibly face, like persons who are in a rehabilitation program, truly we will suffer withdrawals and setbacks and more withdrawals and setbacks.

Most everything going on in our world is about the here and now having nothing to do with eternity. The goings on in this earthly world appeal to our fleshly sensations as a test to prove whether eternity has enough value to us for us to forsake it and follow Christ. The temptations are here to test whether we will serve God or materialism. "Things" are here to distract us from that which eternity is concerned, which is a heart of love for those who live on the fringes of life.

Most of us are spiritual whimps. Do we see Abraham endure twenty-five years of doubt, waiting and waiting for the promise of a son through Sarah, at 90 years of age?

What about Joseph, 13 years in a dungeon, or Moses, 40 years in the wilderness, Job suffering to the bone 8-12 years, Ezekiel, lying on his side 390 plus 40 days, eating food baked with human dung, are we even aware? Hosea married a harlot, John the Baptist beheaded, Peter hung on the stake, upside down, Paul stoned to the death...possibly beheaded, and we sit around because of a loss of income and question the most High?!

Most promises made to many of these men did not come through. They weren't coming through. Abraham could've been killed by Pharaoh, who wanted to take his wife, Jacob was tricked by Laban, almost killed by Esau. The promises were under extreme duress. Isaac almost sacrificed by Abraham. King David told he'd be the next king, nearly killed by Saul twice, hunted continually, gave up his best friend and brother Jonathan. We're spiritual whimps, lock stock and barrel, how dare we...Peter and Paul and Barnabus, were locked up in jails, and sang hymns. Steven was stoned to death. John was exiled till death. Thousands were slain, never having received the promise, and we curse the most High and challenge his integrity, with our bellies full of food, walking free?

We fall ill and question the most High – concerning things we caused mostly by our own lusts. We've never sweated an ounce of blood for the gospel, whimps...don't deserve the name Christians, Acts 5:40...and when they had called the Apostles, and beaten them... Yes, the Apostles (12), were beaten...with whips...

Let'sbePerfectlyClear, Can I be Frank?

IS OUR LIFE GOING TO BE WITHOUT SUFFERING, without strife, without worry and without want if we live the way God is telling us? Unequivocally no!

What we don't understand is that the children of Israel experience is more like the experience we will have to endure in this life today. When The Master says, seek ye first the kingdom of God and his righteousness and all these things shall be added unto you", in Matthew 6, we are being asked to leave Egypt, to get away from our enslavement to the "good life" we see all around us, and to go into the wilderness of lack, doubt, conflict, grief, bewilderment, loss, despondency and allow God to lead us by day and by night (as he led the children of Israel).

In this the children of Israel experience, we will not necessarily receive fine houses, fine cars, eat caviar, drink fine wine, and acquire fine clothes, but we may have to scrap and scrape for our physical stuff.

What it will definitely do however is give us time to help people who are needy. It will also give us time to learn to love self, despite our circumstances.

When the Lord God says, "He", will provide all of our needs, how can he prove it if we don't get to enjoy the wandering in the wilderness experience, as did the children of Israel?

The children of Israel had just come out of slavery and by means of the baptism they symbolically experienced by walking through the supernaturally parted Red Sea, were thrust into a 'wilderness' experience.

They deserted the finest kingdom man has ever known in the world, which was Egypt, and found themselves alone, in the desert. This was not a very upwardly mobile experience. We're talking about no food, no water, no shelter, much less an automobile or even a donkey to ride, neither heating in the cold nor air conditioning in the heat.

Oh, and they had only the clothes that were on their backs. They did not even have a job. In the desert, they could not build a house, or grow food.

They were vagabonds that could only wander from place to place. Even after getting out of a harsh and cruel slavery, this wilderness experience felt as if they were getting nowhere fast, felt worse than the slavery! Many of us are yet slaves to our Egypt, we idolize the society in which we live and feel that we deserve a "piece of the pie". We reason it's okay to seek, and enjoy, the niceties, perks and creature comforts Egypt offers. However, God wants us to have our heart fixed on the future promised land. People tell us that we're fools for hoping for the hereafter and that what we should be concerned about is getting all we can in this life now. They snicker at our befoolery, for believing in something we cannot see. We live in a western world that exalts human reason and embraces materialism, rationalism and reductionism.

It must have felt quite demeaning and frightening for Israel to be wandering around in that desert where there were vipers, scorpions and large frightening flying insects.

Their only resort was to cry out to the Lord God for everything, which turned into bitter complaining and disgust. On top of that there were hostile nations all around them and the children of Israel were of all things unarmed. They had no fighting weapons, nothing to fight with. No swords, spears, shields, knives, nothing. As a matter of fact, the children of Israel did not even have an army or fighting force.

Upon running up on these vicious nations out in the wilderness, the children of Israel had to learn to watch as God fought their battles for them and defeat their enemies in various ways, one by one. A fascinating story.

Oh, and upon arriving at the promised, Promise Land, the land flowing with milk and honey, guess what? There were giants occupying the land. Giants, so large and so strong, and the land so well fortified, that it appeared impossible to overtake. This kind of experience would certainly have disheartened even the brave-of-heart. After all of this suffering that Israel had gone through and then to reach the "promised land" kingdom they'd been promised and to see that it was fully fortified with mighty people twice their size and three times or more their strength had to be disheartening. How impossible, how frightening, frustrating and futile.

It was difficult for them to believe that their God was larger than all of the mountains that they faced.

The lesson that they needed to learn was the lesson of love. That love means that you do not break your promise. To learn that our God does not break His promise and that He is the guarantee, the seal of His love for us. First of all, His love is that He would even stoop low enough to promise we who are "dead men walking", anything. His love is that His promise to us will not fail. Matthew 24:35: "Heaven and earth shall pass away: but my words shall not pass away". His love is so great that He will demonstrate how impossible it is for His promise to be kept and then go ahead and keep it anyway, remarkable!

The word is life. Life is the word. The promise is truth, the broken promise is the lie at work. The lie tries to kill life, it tries to prove that it the "lie" is the truth. The lie tries to prove that there is something other than the truth, that there is something other than life. Hebrews 6:18 says that it is impossible for God to lie. The word is not a lie but rather the word is the truth. The truth cannot thus be a lie, that is impossible. This is an immutable fact that God cannot lie, so that we know that He loves us and He cannot, not just will not, but cannot fail; can't miss it by a little bit.

The immutable truth is He will absolutely deliver His promise. His promise is Word, it is Life, it is Light, it is Truth, and it is Love.

God promised Joseph that he would rule the world and that his brothers would be his subjects and kneel before him. Immediately upon having received this promise Joseph was hated by these same brothers and his life nearly ended. He was cast into a pit and brought to Egypt into slavery. He was then elevated because of his good spirit to a place of trust and leadership in Potiphar's palace, but because of a challenging event was thrown into prison, locked-down and jailed in chains. The Bible speaks of a good spirit that Joseph had about him. It is that spirit that prevailed even in those unjustifiable circumstances, and it is that spirit after a time that got him elevated to the promise that God made to him, because it was the spirit of love. Love is the spirit of Eternal Life. Love excels above the physical and values itself supreme. Joseph loved above all his circumstances and was confident that God would keep His promise, he was confident that God could not lie, and that God would work out His promises despite how it looked at the moment and for many, many moments.

Our first goal is to love all of our circumstances, good or bad. Loving our bad circumstances is also to love our enemy, as self. Love turns our bad circumstances into good and constructive challenges. So in the spirit there are no really bad or destructive circumstances. People who are hooked up with a bad mate can be more in love than those hooked up with a good mate. So, there is no bad or negative circumstance in the spirit. Harvard University can be achieved in a community college in the spirit. The spirit of love makes everything as great as you "love it" to be. Our own doubts are the only limitation to love. The saying you can be anything you want to be, is true. For instance, we may not be a great singer, but if we learn to love self as a not so great singer, in the spirit of love we are the greatest singer there has ever been.

Yes, we can become in love whatever it is we want to be. Not out of hate for our deficiency but out of love for our deficiency. My wife calls me handsome and strong in the spirit of love. She calls me that despite my deficiencies in those very areas, because love makes it so, because love is the sufficiency for all deficiencies.

Because I am from the City of New York, the City of San Bernardino strikes me as the pits of an environment, especially the city itself. In hate of the City of San Bernardino I become every bit as much the pits in the spirit that I see the City of San Bernardino to be. But in telling myself to love San Bernardino anyway, San Bernardino becomes as fine a city in the spirit as I love it to be.

When I love myself being here in San Bernardino and applying the sufficiency of love to the perceived deficiency, the experience will be in the spirit the greatest experience of all-time! Because love is all-sufficient, it seeks for voids or deficiencies to fill.

What did Old Testament Israel have to do? They wandered in a desert wilderness for God's sake! San Bernardino, wilderness, wilderness, San Bernardino! Where there's a void, like air, love is the sufficiency to fill the void. Again, this is why loving the imperfect, is the area which increases our love. Therefore, we must learn to love our enemy whether that be in terms of people or circumstances.

God has great things in store for us, and He has given us a myriad of promises, but we must see His promises, and His word as truth, life, and light. Even when the dark and deadly tests and trials of the lie come against us, we learn to use the infinite sufficiency of love to overflow the deficiencies of lies, deceit, pain and discomfort, just as the ocean's waters overflow the great chasms of the sea.

Something Is Wrong

When churches fail to advocate against the destruction of children in all phases, but especially in pedophilia, there is something wrong.

When a church will not fight for the rights of all immigrants legal and illegal, there is something wrong.

When a church will support military aggression against other peoples for reasons other than emanate self-defense, there is something wrong.

When a church will not fight against the unequal treatment of minorities in all phases of existence particularly as regards equal access to jobs, education and housing, something is wrong.

When a church is not engaged in politics to protect the weak, poor, vulnerable and the underserved, then there is something wrong.

When a church will not preach truth to power, there is something wrong (Isaiah 58:2-7).

When a church will sell-out its support of the male population in its congregation because women give the most financial aid, something is wrong.

Yes, some churches have a form of pimp-daddy for a preacher, who essentially fleeces the women congregates, who majorly financially support the church. In such congregations, men are barely second-class citizens, although they pretend to have clout. Castrated is more the reality of how men function politically and in substance in such churches. The males are in effect caretakers of the pimp-daddy's emotionally and financially supportive stable. Such congregations are mainly social clubs with male props for visual balance. This is why so many churches have ineffectual influence in their community because the activism if any, is feminine or nest protective.

Biblical applications are thus feminized and not pertinent to the whole reality of real world challenges. The 'granmotherization' of many churches has rendered them impotent.

It was not the American Christian Church which fueled the civil rights movement for social justice in the 50's and 60's but grassroots indignation, tempered with the philosophy of Gandhi.

The American Christian church wore a skirt in the movement, and so what credit it gives itself in that role is mostly self-serving. There is a need to understand love. That true love is both passive and violent as is life. There is a place and time for each thing.

A politically impotent church, or a church that supports the oppressive party is also a part of the blame for the poverty and inequities that exist in the society today.

A church cannot be the "right wing" or the "left wing". Just as it takes two wings for a bird to fly properly, any successful venture needs both wings.

God is not the God of one wing or the other, God is the God of the whole body. He is socially liberal and morally conservative. I don't believe God is for subversive elements that may influence either wing to hurt vulnerable peoples.

"God is Love", I John 3, and thus I believe He wants the good for all His peoples, which is everyone, for from His view we're all His children.

Preacher's Wives

And where does it say that preachers have the right to have extramarital affairs? Where is it permissible for preachers to disrespect their own wives, take advantage of them and use them as props to hide illicit affairs with other women?

Again, the church must protect, not hurt and destroy, the weak and the vulnerable. The church should rather understand that the woman, the "weaker vessel", and the children are to be given honor, shown deference, and held in esteem. They are not there to be cheated nor stabbed in the back.

Preacher's wives are such a vulnerable group because they must put up such a front to the public, whereas privately some live in horrid hypocrisy. And in what way is this behavior in the least sense supposed to be tolerated?

It is this very conduct that also causes the church to be disreputable in the greater community. It is this conduct that makes the children of such unions become the worst of the worst, whether gang leaders, party animals or addicts.

A church that doesn't care about those it is supposed to protect is a false church and operates in the shadows of death. Malachi 2:13-17, "And this have ye done again, covering the altar of the LORD with tears, with weeping, and with crying out, insomuch that he regardeth not the offering any more, or receiveth it with good will at your hand." The offering becomes unacceptable when the hearts of the preachers are corrupt.

Preachers are crying over the altar and bringing folks to Christ and weeping, yet dealing treacherously with their own wives. The Lord hates putting away of a mate who shares a portion of the godly seed and the holy spirit with the husband. "Yet ye say, Wherefore?", The preachers ask in amazement, "what did we do wrong?" Answer: "Because the LORD hath been witness between thee and the wife of thy youth, against whom thou hast dealt treacherously: yet is she thy companion, and the wife of thy covenant. And did not he make one? Yet had he the residue of the spirit."

And the preachers ask: "And wherefore one? That he might seek a godly seed." Answer: "Therefore take heed to your spirit, and let none deal treacherously against the wife of his youth. "The man who hates and divorces his wife, says the lord, the God of Israel, does violence to the one he should protect, says the lord almighty. So be on your guard, and do not be unfaithful." (NIV).

God considers this wrong dealing towards preacher's wives, violence, and a poisoning of the spirit. "Ye have wearied the LORD with your words. Yet ye say, Wherein have we wearied him? When ye say, Every one that doeth evil is good in the sight of the LORD, and he delighteth in them; or where is the God of judgment?" Mal. 2:17 (KJV). Preachers make excuses and condone evil. This speaks of preachers doing badly.

Pacifists vs Activists

A pacifist church can no longer be passive, it must become pro-active. It must fight not for its' own rights, but for the rights of the sick, the imprisoned, the marginal, the weak. It must pray, protest and mobilize to make its' voice heard.

The church must permit suffering upon itself by refusing to bow down to Nebuchadnezzar's idol and be willing to step into the fiery furnace.

This is where it is extremely important the church prayerfully and properly investigates the social justice cause of interest.

A case in point, it is quite possible that Martin Luther King and the civil rights movement (or rebellion) fought for the wrong goal. It is possible that their efforts to achieve integration for people of color was a vital mistake. It is possible that segregation made the blacks a stronger force because then they had to handle their own businesses for themselves. They were able to be together and thus produce their own lawyers, doctors, bankers, insurance companies, import/export companies, manufacturers, transportation operations, schools, colleges and the like.

Durham North Carolina and Tulsa Oklahoma are two of many examples including the Central Avenue district in Los Angeles, where blacks as a segregated group produced entrepreneurs and business leaders. Jim Crow caused many blacks to lack equal access to many of the opportunities accorded white America which resulted in blacks having to defer, kowtow, and live in inferior circumstances, and often in fear of their lives. The alternative was that blacks had the opportunity to have more jobs within their own segregated communities because there were needs that needed to be filled and no other racial groups was there to fill those needs.

Essentially the main problem was not the segregation of blacks from whites, but it was the demeaning "Jim Crow" laws, the spirit which perpetrated the attitude of inequality. Blacks were refused access to some of the same public facilities to which whites had access. Buses, trains, bathrooms, water fountains, restaurants were segregated. Public facilities including schools were separate and unequal in quality (Read Jim Wallis, America's Original Sin). A form of punishment for violating these laws would often lead to black folk being hung from trees, an act called lynching, along with the burning of their homes and businesses to the ground. There were literal riots of persecution called "race riots", headed up by white folks to seek and destroy black folks and their property.

In an effort to solve this problem MLK and the civil rights movement fought for equality which involved ending Jim Crow and ending segregation. Ending Jim Crow was one thing but pushing for integration may not have necessarily been the best thing in itself. Ending the fact that blacks had to ride at the back of the bus, drink at separate water fountains, were denied access to restaurants and forced to use inferior bathrooms and the like was right to fight for. However, insisting they amalgamate into the greater white society eventually hurt them because it dissipated their strength as they lost positions of employment to the larger white community.

When blacks were seen by whites as doing well or better than the whites, the whites would find ways to crush or even kill the blacks. This caused regression in the black community, the same regression we see today. In addition, when the blacks were allowed to integrate, it economically defused and eventually dissipated the force of their own community. The fight of the civil rights movement may have been better if focused on equality which MLK espoused, while maintaining segregation which is what Malcolm X espoused. Segregation would've kept the blacks strong economically and allowed their dollars to remain in their own community for longer periods of time.

Equality (not integration) would have permitted the blacks to stay alive without losing their businesses, their homes and their lives. Integration caused blacks to separate and get swallowed up into the greater white society, losing the advantage of unity, solidarity and nationhood. Ironically, we pray for the protection of Christians from persecution overseas but fail to fight against the persecution of black Christians here at home in the streets of America.

It is important that when the church does fight for social justice it researches the most advantageous righteous outcomes for whom they are fighting. It would do well to note that it was the average white church in the south, in the so-called "Bible Belt" that led in the oppression of and condoned the violence against the Civil Rights movement either actively or by its' silence. It was the members of these very churches that populated the KKK, the police departments and the justice systems that oppressed their neighbors who were brother Christians.

These same Christians also elected the "Dixiecrat" officials who fought against equal rights in Washington and supported the maintenance of the confederacy and the flag which represents it. Christians are to seek an eternal abode. The settling of the war between the North and the South is not our goal, it's not pertinent to our Christianity. It's not important who won the Civil War, that's an earthly habitational concern. We're to be about the profession of loving our brother, especially the least of our brethren. The church is not yet mature to fully recognize that this is not our world. That physical earthly territory doesn't matter, that its' only the Kingdom of heaven territory that matters.

The church is to be wise as a serpent and gentle as doves, militant to stand for the rights of the weak, helpless and disenfranchised. The church must fight for righteousness, not with weapons of warfare, but with the weapons of the spirit. And suffering as a result, suffering for doing good is how we imitate our Lord and master, The Messiah. Self-interest rules the day in American churches today. God's interest are subjugated to selfish concerns and long-time traditions of men.

A church should defend others while not defending itself, as was the nature of King David. That is why it will not fight for the rights of fatherless, nor will it fight against the abortion of children, which sources back to its acceptance of fornication as a norm.

The church supports capitalism, which is why it will not fight for health care for all peoples. The church wants to downplay those acts that will cause it to be despised in the eyes of the government, IRS and the general populace because it doesn't want to suffer. It doesn't want to alienate the wealthy members either. It doesn't want to exact upon itself punitive retribution even though that be for defending the rights of less blessed peoples. They'll fire an upstart audacious preacher who supports this matter.

It's more interested in adding members to its rolls, rather than fighting for the rights of disenfranchised peoples and risk the loss of congregants and thus revenue. Many influential members would disagree with socialist sounding "commie-like" policies and therefore the church would lose revenue. "Got to keep the lights on, don't we?", a pastor exclaimed to me once. "Got to pay the bills first or we'd have to shut the doors", he went on. My question is, is not God capable when we are obedient to Him of keeping the lights on and making sure our bills are paid? That church has rendered itself ineffectual anyway, the lights might as well go off.

Many churches that fail to practice the faith that God requests of them preach to the congregants as if they have it all together. The Bible says that our God wants obedience and wants the people to bear good fruit. If we reason we don't want to lose members who might otherwise be saved, we should also realize we might be blocking the salvation of many, many more members who are waiting to be called by God, if only we'd trust Him and get out of His way. "Got to keep the lights on, don't we?" I'm sure there are many churches that have gone out of business because they've maintained such a position.

The problem is also that there are many churches who are not doing Kingdom business. They are effectively a 'country club'. Rather than stand-up, these churches choose to remain silent on issues of controversy. They do not take sides in order to curry favor with the wealthier elite minded in its congregations. The very members who benefit from the oppression of the poor, James 2:6.

Such a position of omission makes the church therefore an accessory to the crimes and oppressions against poor and weak peoples, an enemy of the needy and a tool for the abuses perpetrated against them.

Thus, the church becomes a party to crimes against oppressed peoples' women, children, fatherless and elderly. However if such a church does seek to feed and aid these neglected folks, due to its own failure to advocate for their social justice, it is ultimately a church that may be considered in God's eyes, self-serving.

When that church is by omission consenting to the injustices that create the despondent populations it neglects, it is helping to create the problem that keeps it gainfully employed in charitable works. Consenting to the atrocities which could curb the numbers of hungry and destitute for which it receives funds to aide, is a self-serving action that keeps that church in business.

Such a church often acts as a wolf in the sheep's clothing when it comes to being charitable. That church calls down awesome private and corporate funding which means the church is feeding the hungry, not because people need food, but to stay in business.

Some such charitable churches take a conservative right-wing posture in a spirit of condemnation regarding social justice movements and yet neglect to preach against injustice. Moral permissiveness leads to babies out of wedlock, STDs, abortions or single parenting, and as a consequence, poverty, hunger, homelessness and disenfranchised populations of people. We must question then the heart as to why a given organization is in the charitable business. Is it simply to be employed? Is it simply a career path? Yes, we must be careful to give all to feed the poor but do it because we truly have a heart of charity (I Corinthians 13).

Thus, lacking the component of fighting for justice, which would curb the numbers of the despondent, and applying only a band aide to the problem results in feeding people fish without fighting for their right to fish. An activist church needs to sit on the boards of city planning meetings. We must make ourselves known to those who are the movers and shakers in our community.

Churches could set up breakfast food feeding programs for kids in areas where families need that level of assistance. Churches could set up home upkeep programs in areas where widows and elderly cannot afford the cost of regular contractors.

We must understand that decisions are made by the rich and the so-called elite that directly produce homeless in the streets. We must understand, that we have to understand, that corporate and governmental officials make specific decisions that alter the supply and demand, production and consumption chain or the order of the universe on the ground level, and that they are well able to calculate that they will by implementing certain policy decisions dispossess great numbers of people. Homelessness is not an accident. Homelessness is legislated and construed by design. Self-interests "rules the day", and the fallout is suffered by those whose trust they have betrayed.

Municipalities want to dispose of the homeless, make them disappear out of their areas. "Bad for business"; "unsafe" (after all they don't vote). The whole idea is to rid themselves of homeless, send them somewhere else, and thus mask the problem instead of changing the circumstances that led to the homelessness in the first place. And now laws are being written to prevent them from sleeping in their own vehicles. My God! "Send them where the other homeless are...", "but get them away from here!" "Don't feed or clothe them or they'll never go away. Don't permit them in our parks, it's not safe for our children." The church will hand the homeless religious tracts and pray for them, but who is intentionally taking care of their needs? Who's housing them? The municipalities then set ordinances that prevent housing them even temporarily.

Why are there insufficient mental and physical health centers to care for their needs? "The money is drying up", they all say. But don't we have a state lottery? Why isn't a minimum of 10% of the revenue from the lottery allocated to homeless rehabilitation? Why aren't the corporations and businesses taxed to fund the cure to the homeless dilemma? Where is the heart of love, the heart of flesh, the concern for the dispossessed and the despondent? Why is everybody afraid of the banker elite? Guns? Assassinations? Certain death? Seventy-one or more bank employees died in recent years and none from natural causes. This does not include the assassinations of public officials who have not cooperated with the banks. This must change. We the church must confront the bankers and advocate for change or we will all be destroyed. Yes we will suffer persecution, but we must at all costs see that justice is done.

Those who have the public trust don't protect the interest of the voiceless public. They fail to uphold the public trust in lieu of the selfish greed of the few brutal rich. We must be that voice. Homelessness was created by the powers that be, just as starvation and poverty were created in China and India, when the colonial invaders from Europe dispossessed them of their natural resources, and interrupted their agricultural and economic systems, which previously had adequately fed their populations. Now their supply and demand chain got corrupted by the invaders, leaving multiple millions hungry and starving.

We did this to parts of Africa as well. Meanwhile someone has convinced the churches to "sit-down". The churches must RISE UP! The general attitude of the American church goer is to scapegoat the deeds we have done so we can feel morally superior. Realize the church is wealthier than all the corporations put together. Our capital could immobilize them.

We could stop the exploitation of peoples and countries by investigating the policies of each corporation and enforcing change where needed.

We could stop global warming, if we were willing to give up much of the creature comforts these very corporations provide, or better yet, if we were willing to challenge them to make their products in a holistic "green" conscious way, removing top profits as the biggest motive and making people's welfare top priority. We could stop air and water pollution in their tracks, stop homelessness, stop starvation and poverty world over, stop an innumerable array of diseases including cancer and diabetes. We could stop the sex slave trade, stop joblessness and prevent wars and the merciless killing of innocent women and children.

These problems and more would no longer be issues if we took the considerable billions raised in church each month and applied them to fighting the ills created by corporate and governmental greed! Of course, the greatest opposition to this idea will come from fellow churches. In fact, the biggest persecutions will be other church organizations who will be "in-bed" with the corporations and government leaders (many who are in-bed with them now) and have been bought and sold to oppose any social movement for justice.

Indeed, the persecution against the activist church will majorly come from within the church itself. Many factions of the churches treasure the very riches Christ told us not to treasure. Many will take an "offering" from rich special interest groups just as readily as they will fleece funds from needy widows in their own congregations. Additionally, some of our strongest opposition will be those members of our own household. "For I have come to turn a man against his father, a daughter against her mother, a daughter-in-law against her mother-in-law, a man's enemies will be the members of his own household" (Matthew 1:35-36 NIV). Bringing down this evil system will be painful, but it is our responsibility. It would be more painful to sit by quietly and let it continue. Painful for those it hurts and painful to our eternal salvation. The pain of hell would be much worse. This pain or that pain? I vote, let's face this pain.

With God as our guide and intercessor we can please Him and promote the Kingdom here on earth in our lifetime. Our job is to care for those who are God's heart, this is our public trust, we the members of His great Kingdom. We must advocate for the voiceless, weak, ignorant, deaf, blind, disabled, poor, uneducated, oppressed, imprisoned, homeless and helpless. Yes, the enemy will infiltrate our organizations with spies, counter-agents, naysayers and subversives whose goal it is to turn us against each other. They will offer us money, bribes, blackmail, pay offs, buy outs, tap our phones, poison our organization with disinformation, and lies, then cause our best, brightest and most trusted members to betray us. That is why the scripture says, only the pure of heart will see God.

At many rallies, the police will meet us with tear gas, dogs, and Billy clubs. Some of us will be bloodied, some placed in jail and some lose our lives. It will take great courage to stand up for Christ. He would rather have our obedience in this than to have tithes and offerings and we do nothing to free the oppressed from their oppression. This is the essence of what is called laying down our life for our brothers (John 15:12-14).

Great consideration should be taken as to how much of our funds can be used to buy back our politicians. We must put up monetary roadblocks to stop special interest groups from having their way. Consider how we can also economically boycott even the banks and businesses that don't line-up with God's heart for the needy.

God has given us the power to do these things (Isaiah 42:6-7). When the congregations are taught to have a heart for God, to have a heart that seeks after the things of God, that value what God values, that congregation will get off considerable amounts of expendable capital and go to war for the causes of social justice.

When congregations plural, denominations and nations of churches reach out to each other and combine together to agree on one common denominator, which is to create mighty streams of justice in the lands, then not only will the congregations pour out the funds necessary to win these battles for justice, but the unbelievers and church doubters who sit on the sidelines will come to the table and join the fight with their considerable resources.

The resources will pour out from the public in mass, like the mighty waterfalls of the Niagara or the powerful and deafening Victoria water falls in Zimbabwe, Africa.

"God created the heavens and stretched them out; he fashioned the earth and all that lives there; he gave life and breath to all its people. And now the Lord God says to his servant,":

"I, the Lord, have called you and given you power to see that justice is done on earth. Through you I will make a covenant with all peoples. Through you I will bring light to the nations. You will open the eyes of the blind and set free those who sit in dark prisons." (Isaiah 42:6-7).

Exportation of The Americanization
of God

THE CRUELEST JOKE BEING PLAYED ON THE WORLD TODAY is when the church exports itself or better said when it proselytizes "Americanized" religion to the world. When The Master told Peter to "make fishers of men", he did not intend for Peter to disciple men into deeper corruption than they'd already known and yet that is what is going to on for the most part today, 2 Peter 2:19-22. A capitalistic and monopolistic church with prejudices, biases, as well as racism and greed is being exported to the world stamped, "Made in America", and being pawned off as representing Christ our Lord.

The evidence is extent everywhere. The clearest examples are in Africa and Korea where gigantic mega churches are created to enrich one man and his family. Thousands flock to the church in reverence of the preacher who often flies a jet, rides a limousine, and has multiple houses. The man is honored as a man of God and his people are no better economically well off after coming into the fold, than they were previous to becoming a church member.

Why is it the people should not be delivered from squalor while the preacher excels in riches? Why does the preacher heap upon himself the gifts of the people, because he is a man of God, and the people are not simultaneously enriched? Is the preacher the only one capable of receiving such enormous blessings from God? Are the people just not getting it? Try as they may, are they so broken that they cannot be blessed also?

Yet as sheep the people pay high tribute to the man of God and sacrifice their own well-being. Whereas the Lord says, the man of God should be blessing the hireling in his wages, the widow, and the fatherless, and the stranger (Mal 3:5). Yes, the congregation should be funding the rest of the congregation. Tithes and offerings should go to the members who are "the church", and not solely to the ministers. The preacher should be no richer or poorer than any congregant. All should be shared with all. "And I will come near to you to judgment; and I will be a swift witness against the sorcerers, and against the adulterers, and against false swearers, and against those that oppress." Who was the Lord talking to here if he wasn't talking to these preachers? Luke 12:17 "And he thought within himself, saying, What shall I do, because I have no room where to bestow my fruits? 18 And he said, this will I do: I will pull down my barns, and build greater; and there will I bestow all my fruits and my goods. 19 And I will say to my soul. Soul, thou has much goods laid up for many years; take thine ease, eat, drink, and be merry."

The ministry ought to be sharing the tithes with the hired hands, the widow, the fatherless and the immigrant, illegal or otherwise instead of taking tithes from the hired hands, the widow, the fatherless and the immigrant, illegal or otherwise, because the funds are their "right", verse 5. If you want to know what love is, then do that!

It is their "right", according to the ordinances of old, for the wage earner, the widow, the fatherless and the immigrant illegal or otherwise to receive monetary assistance from the ministry on an ongoing continuous basis. Ministries that neglect to pay their musicians preach a false doctrine also when they say the musicians ought to work for free. This too is not biblical and flies in the face of what the bible clearly teaches (see the books of Ezra and Nehemiah).

I use the term ministry here because the church is actually the people. Ministry is the board of trustees and assistant ministers, deacons and the like who serve the people, who make "church" policy and therefore knowingly and mostly unknowingly condone the corruption noted above. And God says He is tired of all the crying, weeping, tears, prayers, singing and wringing of hands, when our hearts are far from him. And then we export this stuff around the world, "But ye are departed out of the way; ye have caused many to stumble at the law; sayeth the Lord of hosts."

Many ministries "peddle the word of God for a profit" (2 Corinthians 2:17 NIV). In short, they use the awesome message of The Master as a wedge to extract funds from our pocket books to financially enhance themselves. Many of these same ministries use the phrase "sow a seed, reap a harvest" to excite people to give to their ministries. However, if we read carefully the context of this scripture, we see a completely different scenario unfolding from these words.

The apostle Paul acting in the capacity of a cheerleader, advocate and motivator was urging the Corinthian church to keep the promise they had made to give of their blessings to the poor church folks down in Jerusalem (I Corinthians 9). So, since the wealthier Corinthians were a more 'urban' bunch with many distractions, he had to persuade them to 'man-up' and keep their promise, so that the glowing report he had made about their generous heart would not end up becoming egg on his face. So Paul said, that just as the other church from Macedonia had enthusiastically donated help to the church in Jerusalem based on the proposition that the Corinthians would do so, that the Corinthians now had to come through, anti-up and keep their commitment.

To sell the Corinthians on the principle of giving to the poor, Paul used the analogy of "sowing and reaping". But note, the sowing and reaping had to do with helping the less blessed. This principal did not concern itself with enhancing a ministry or minister for a "profit". Many of today's ministries have misconstrued this analogy to enrich themselves. So yes, Paul said, "If you sow sparingly, you also reap sparingly; if you sow bountifully, You also will reap bountifully" (2 Corinthians 9:6 NIV). Notice he says v. 7, "Each of you should give what you have decided in your heart to give, not reluctantly or under compulsion, for God is able to bless you abundantly..." But we must read the context, v. 9 He says, "As it is written, 'They have freely scattered their gifts to the poor; their righteousness endures forever."

So again, the sowing and the reaping a harvest does not concern itself with the support of a ministry and we must acknowledge they need support also, however the use of this analogy in II Corinthians 9:6, is purposed to help those who are closest to God's heart, the poor. When we exude a heart of generosity in helping the poor, God will bless us abundantly.

The cruelest part of the proselytizing of Americanized Christianity is not only does our disinformation deny help to the poor, needy, widows, fatherless and foreigners, and enrich the preacher and key officials up the food chain, but this same form of religion anesthetizes the new converts into passivity against the colonial forces that come to oppress them.

This American brand of Christianity sells democracy, which is a manipulable governmental construct, which permits American capitalism to thrive in foreign countries with almost no resistance. This situation creates a people who are captivated by the idea that a fight for their own social justice is not what a true Christian should do. They're frozen with the idea that helping those who have been disenfranchised by the democratic-capitalist model is not the main goal of Christianity. With this flawed premise mixed into the Kool-aide, the American capitalist oppressor is free to enact his economic exploitation of the nation almost unimpeded, because the people have been anesthetized by this disinformation, served to them through the propaganda of Americanized Christianity. The strategy is well known, "To conquer a nation first disarm its citizen", Adolph Hitler.

However, an even crueler construct of this idea is that the American Christian church sees this whole scenario as a good thing in furthering the gospel upon the colonized nation. So, the American Christian church won't lift a finger to fight against the oppression of people of other nations, instigated by the leaders of its' own American- corporate-military-industrial-complex, to exploit, oppress and suppress people around the globe, using the tool of religious disinformation to poison the Kool-aide and anesthetize them. Instead of being a help to the well-being of the people of these proselytized nations, we've become major contributors to their destruction. Instead of being a reliever of their poverty as Christ would do, we further impale them in their poverty while further enriching ourselves.

This loyalty to "God and country" theme the church purports is a "misinformation" tool to throw the American Christians off of God's heart, a "misdirection" drug floated into our belief system to blind us to the evil intentions of the bankers and selfish rich who will want to further gorge themselves with treasures at the expense of religiously sedated co-matose poor people who desperately cling to anything that sounds hopeful enough to deliver them from their demise. The idea of "One Nation Under God", and "In God We Trust" are misnomers added by capitalists corporations in the 1950s who feared they were being blamed for "The Depression" and thought it clever to counter that negativity with these Christian sounding phrases. So they sought to bring capitalism and Christianity together to create a capitalistic Christian sounding construct called libertarianism.

Missions and missionaries since King Leopold II sent his first missionaries to the African people have continually been used as pawns to conquer and control the resources of colonized peoples.

"As early as 1493, the Vatican gave Europe permission to violently invade, conquer, then divide among themselves the wealth of so-called "barbarous nations" under the disguise of Christianizing them (Papal Bull Decision) and then return to finish the job via the Berlin conference in 1884." (Jahkia Taureg).

This very country the United States as well as the rest of the Americas north and south are a prime example of this very thing. Hundreds of years ago the Catholic church sent missionaries to this very land to sedate the people while Spain and Portugal; then France, plundered the land. Did Vasco De Gama, Columbus and others share the wealth with the natives who were proselytized into the church? No, the wealth was extracted from this land and sent back to Europe and the Vatican. The poor plebeians of this country are as a whole still poor plebeians to this day. They were introduced to Jesus Christ as being part and parcel to their eternal salvation but were denied economic inclusion in the considerable wealth the church was extracting from their own inherited lands.

The tendency of Europeans to look down on the poor is hypocritical because the wealthy Europeans got rich in the first place by exploiting the poor peoples we look down upon, around the world. So, these riches are nothing to hold our heads up about. Our heads should rather be hung down in shame for how our wealth was acquired. Then we look askance in mockery at the backwards poverty of those who have not so exploited their fellow human beings to become wealthy as we have and so we jeer and point the finger at them mockingly in derision.

These same poor plebeian farmers were prevented from being also enriched when the colonial forces upset their entire economic systems which had been in place for thousands of years plunging many of the natives into deep poverty because so much of their crops and produce were exported to the European lands for mere pennies. This left the small farmers devoid of the resources upon which they for thousands of years had relied on for their substance. It threw off the economic balance of their society and as a result threw most of them into a poverty, hunger and starvation they'd not previously experienced. These conditions of course created a greater dependence on the church for mere survival, a condition the church itself in part aided in creating. So not only did the church help extract the wealth from these lands and export them to Europe, the church simultaneously impoverished a vast majority of the people into deeper economic ruin and dependency. We must mark the fact that Europe has no gold sources germane to the continent to speak of. It extracted most of its gold from foreign lands.

We supposedly professed concern for the spiritual needs of the people, but failing to address their physical well-being, we proved that we did not preach the gospel to the people because we loved the people. We demonstrated that we preached the gospel to the people because we wanted to save ourselves. We are preaching the gospel to buy our own ticket into heaven. This approach smacks of a way of bribing God. This absence of love for the people's well-being and the assuaging of our own guilt for past sins of the fathers is the antithesis of what the gospel of Messiah Christ actually is. The Messiah loved the people, the human beings He saw in front of Him. The Messiah fed the 5000, plus and at another time the 4000, plus, with real food and not just spiritual meat. The Messiah did not send them away to find their own food. He took five loaves and three fishes and addressed their immediate physical needs. These are just a couple of examples of the many miracles He performed to address the physical and social needs of those to whom He preached.

We come to a land where the people are hungry, dirt poor, poorer than any poverty we've ever seen in America and talk about the saving grace of Christ The Messiah, and mind you we come from the richest country on earth. The new convert must wonder, why isn't some of the considerable resources of the land from which this missionary comes, making its way over here? The proselytized new convert, if ever placed in a position of access to some resources himself, will then have been taught to deny his brothers and other peoples of their physical needs, due to how he himself was denied when proselytized. That is why we see many wealthier peoples in these impoverished lands, who've obtained access to wealth, treat their own people like dirt. This they've been taught to do by the colonial powers and the example of the church. They have been taught to despise the immediate needs of the poor when they are in the prime position themselves, to help their own poor people. This is not the heart of The Messiah being spread, but the crooked ploy of the evil one, denying people's urgent plight and telling them to call on "Jesus" to save them in the hereafter.

Telling people everything is going to be alright when they get to heaven, but failing to do our utmost to relieve their present burdens when we have the bread available to address that human being's dilemma is heretical. Our Creator relieved the physical burdens of people, whether of hunger, illness or forgiveness of sin.

God in His word asks, how can you say you love me whom you can't see when you do not love your brother who you can see? There will be weeping and gnashing of teeth. Indeed, we have great folks spreading the gospel of Our Creator throughout the world. These individuals are highly commended soldiers for Christ. Many have sacrificed their entire lives, sold-out all for Him and are walking in obedience for the calling He has placed on their hearts in sharing the gospel. But the church; but the church; O, but the church; the ministries fail to understand that they must equip these soldiers of the gospel with the resources and produce necessary to enrich the needy of these lands.

We see this same church model operating in the slums and ghettos of the American cities today. There are many churches planted in these areas, some rich, some beautiful, while the surrounding areas are completely devastated. The churches receive the tithes and the offerings of poor people without improving their physical environment. By the fruits it is obvious, the church is a tool to extract funds from the people without enriching them physically. This very same model has been in operation for centuries. The propaganda is that if we feed the people "spiritual food", it will bless them physically. A big bold-face lie!

There is a depletion of the wealth in the impoverished areas of our land which makes these areas fair game for drug and alcohol abuse, which further cripples and depletes them of wealth. The same thing operates in impoverished lands near and far.

The church needs to stop extracting funds for itself and begin pouring out funds to the needy so that the impoverished can be supported, not only spiritually but also physically. Christ said that if we've done it to the least of these, we've done it unto Him also. This is the fruit that we must produce, that would be the rock-solid evidence that we love God, whom we cannot see, for if our brother is begging bread and we do not address that need when we have so much bread, how is the love of God in us?

Instead, as a rule, we teach these new converts to give, give, give whatever 'widow's mite' they may have, to the ministry. Instead of giving to the poor, we are a culture of extracting from the poor. Sadly, so many blindly follow the blind creeds of their conquerors, not knowing they themselves will also be missing out on eternal life. They will say, Lord, Lord did we not do all these things in your 'name', and He will say I don't even know you, get away from me you workers of "iniquity". Iniquity has to do with inequity, inequality, unequalness, the failure to physically level the playing field.

Security in the accumulation of earthly things should not be our goal, rather our values should be about heaven and not earthly empire. But, our hearts are about earth and not heaven if we fall lockstep for the propaganda which we've been conditioned to believe. We have to get up off of our own stuff and give it away. If we're not inconvenienced continuously with these efforts, then we're not doing the work that manifests Christ's saving grace in our lives.

Even the tax collector Zacchaeus, whom was hated by the people gave half, a full half, of all he made to the poor, and Christ counted that as worthy of salvation. That ought to tell us a lot about what counts for eternal life. If we have jobs, and we're not working to give it all or most of it all away to the poor, we haven't yet arrived as Christians. Any other ideas are not "Jesus", they are unrighteousness, and our hands are bloody, no matter how much offering and tithes we place on the altar at church, no matter how many church services we attend, and how many sinners we bring to Christ. And if we're counted among the silent majority, we are also guilty. We will say when He comes, "Lord, Lord" haven't we done all this in your name, and He will say, "I never knew you", you "evildoers", Matthew 7:21-23.

Why Does God Keep So Many Unconverted?

The reason God keeps so many people on this earth unconverted is so that we can develop the same perfect love the Father has for us, Matthew 5:43-48. Christ exhorts, "Be ye perfect as your Father in heaven is perfect." When we love both good and evil, our friends and our enemies, we achieve perfect love. We achieve complete love because we love both sides of the spectrum, good and evil. Another way to say it is that perfect love denies no one love. That's what makes it perfect, complete, pure and whole.

So, the way scripture uses "perfect" simply means complete - whole, total...so we begin to understand that good and evil are companions, two sides of a complete whole...perfect. Thus we should love both good and evil - perfect. God loves both. He acts good in companion with evil, or perfect. He obviously allows evil or He'd have disposed of the devil long ago. Our God allows evil for a purpose.

Why or how is this? Well not until we love a "bad" God, do we prove that we love God...for what love is it to God if we love Him, only when He is a "good" God?...that's not love in His eyes...that's conditional...real love or perfect love, is to love Him when He is also "bad", our adversary, and hating us…

When His loving seems hating!!! If you can love an evil God, you have achieved perfect love.

When He is evil is when He is our adversary! Job experienced God as an adversary. God allowed Satan to 'jack him up!' God got the 'credit' for the whole scenario, because not once in the book of Job, did Job, or any of his consultants blame the devil. It was God who allowed it. God apparently does not do the evil, but as the one in charge will allow the evil to be done. God can apparently work as an adversary also against our enemies, Exodus 23:22. When He wants to seem hateful He sends humans or other forces who are hateful to do the job!!! Which is why He keeps so many unconverted!!!! We who love only the good but are partial to the evil or the unconverted, have imperfect love. We're in trouble because we don't also love the evil. True love is to love the evil enemy and the good friend alike. This is complete or perfect love. It is truly unconditional, unfailing love, not based on circumstances, immutable.

He keeps so many unconverted for an additional reason: Romans 11:30-33 "For as ye in times past have not believed God, yet have now obtained mercy through their unbelief: Even so have these also now not believed, that through your mercy they also may obtain mercy. For God hath concluded them all in unbelief, that he might have mercy upon all. O the depth of the riches both of the wisdom and knowledge of God! how unsearchable are his judgments, and his ways past finding out! "...for he is kind unto the unthankful and to the evil. Be ye therefore merciful, as your Father also is merciful". Jonah wasn't very merciful because, he wanted to see Nineveh go down. He avoided going because he didn't want them to have the chance to repent and be let off the hook by God. He wanted them to be punished for their sins. If they weren't punished it would be like they got away with a lot of stuff without paying for it.

Jonah's love was imperfect. He loved the people of God but hated the sinners. He loved the good folks but hated the evil ones. He was so frustrated regarding the people of Nineveh repenting he wanted God to kill him. Jonah wore the badge of righteousness on the outside but did not have the circumcised heart of righteousness on the inside. We must not get caught in Jonah's trap, therefore we must learn to love the sinner. God loves everyone, sinner and saint. Luke 6:35-36.

And so, God keeps so many unconverted, He keeps so many sinners in the world as is necessary so that His 'called out ones' might have plenty opportunity to develop mercy.

The book of the Bible is not written to the "world" or the unconverted, it is written to the called-out ones from out of the masses.

The masses are not responsible for not obeying God, but we the called-out ones are. They will suffer little to no judgment but the judgment will be upon the "household of God". The church must stop blaming the evil that goes on with us on the problems of unconverted peoples. Sometimes the called-out ones use the uncalled as an excuse to say, 'we're not so bad, look at what they're doing'. This is very immature on the part of the church. The judgment and punishment will be upon us, especially the so-called ministry.

If we take the book of Matthew 19:28-29 literally, we've been selected to rule at the right hand of God over the people in the world, We don't know if unconverted people will be required to change or not. Love exists to forgive sins. So-called sins exist to be 'loved-over'. So will a perfect world be a world where everyone is righteous, or will it be a world of many, many unconverted sinners who need to be 'loved-over'? And thankfully our sins will be included in that group of sins that need to be loved-over, however all indications are that our punishment, will be more severe if we don't repent since we're supposed to know better. Listen to the warning of God, Malachi 4:1 "For, behold, the day cometh, that shall burn as an oven; and all the proud, yea, and all that do wickedly, shall be stubble: and the day that cometh shall burn them up, saith the LORD of hosts, that it shall leave them neither root nor branch."

Some of us will disagree with the changes God is challenging us to make. We want to preserve a Christianity we think is the cornucopia of loving and good works, a bastion of joy and serendipitous acts of goodness toward mankind. I don't believe we should delude ourselves into thinking we have arrived there yet. I have witnessed the fact that the church has enough self-hate that one Baptist church will denigrate another Baptist church. I attended such a church and the put-down was akin to saying the other Baptist church was blind and hell-bent. And they were both Baptists! I've seen churches exclude everyone else but themselves from the Kingdom of God. I've seen churches claim that white Americans are descendants of Israel and profess they're the only pure race, so they have a special place in heaven. I've seen a church say only 144,000 will make it to heaven. Some churches believe people will be tortured before making it to heaven or hell.

Many denominations hate certain other denominations; hate Catholics, hate Jehovah Witnesses, hate Adventists, hate other Episcopalians, hate LDSs, hate Universalists. Then beyond that hate Muslims.

Some churches hate the Televangelist and publicly castigate them. Right wing Evangelical churches "strongly disagree" with Left-wing liberal abortion loving, gay loving churches.

I've witnessed a church tear-up another churches' literature over doctrinal differences. Sundays are still the most racially segregated days of the week in America.

If you want to see hate in action, attend a Christian church board meeting and watch us get into a "church fight". Some of us know what I'm talking about. It ain't pretty. So if the way things are going is correct, and the world is benefiting, then keep it.

But the earth is no longer flat, the sun does not revolve around the earth and at the Salem witch trials the witches that those Christians decided to burn to their deaths were other Christian women of faith (martyrs). The Christian church leads the world in divorce. God loves marriage more than anything else. Marriage depicts the marriage of His son Jesus Christ to we the church. God would not want an unfaithful bride to marry His Son. Neither would we. So marriage is serious to God, because He wants a pure and faithful, serving and loving bride to marry His Son Jesus the Christ. Faithfulness to our vow is preeminent in God's mind. We have to have the character to be faithful till death. Divorce to Him is a violence akin to murder.

IN GOD'S EYES, once married always married til' death, even if you obtain divorce paperwork. We'll even protest abortion, but quietly accept divorce as something that can't be helped. Our twisted doctrines are producing single parent homes at a rate that is beyond the worst ghettos in America. We the church and particularly the evangelical arm of the church lead the world in divorce because we've been programmed into believing a selfish me first, materialistic covetous and greedy form of Christianity. There is little servitude, little janitorial humility, little tolerance for inconvenience, no patience with unhappiness; it is all CEO upwardly mobile images, and laughter around cocktail tables "mentality".

Wives talk of not having their emotional needs met yet hate the idea of meeting the needs of others. Some can't accept instruction from their husbands. Many husbands live in a fantasy world of wishing we could get with some supermodel or Hustler porn star. We don't fully practice laying down our lives for each other. Humility is out the window because it so pedestrian, undesirous, backward, immobilizing. Giving up earthly wishes and dreams is counter to being progressive and outstanding.

We don't want to wait tables, clean floors, scrub feet. People whose mate become injured or incapacitated have big emotional issues. The Americanized superwoman or superman fantasy of "you can have it all", warps us into puffed up stinkin' thinkin'. We become testy, impatient and upset all the time. We begin to feel life is passing us by. Our life becomes a worthless humdrum of activity, and unexciting repetitiveness. We begin to pull out our hair, and engage in tantrums, pouting and murmuring. Wives leave their husbands, husbands leave their wives. The neglect of the poor, of the needy, of the stranger, of loving our enemy leads to this type of arrogance. On top of that when we add scriptural knowledge to that mix, then ka-boom!!!

Often those who are most into the word are most vulnerable for a breakup. That may be because the spin that taints the word that comes from the pulpit may misdirect us as to the true meaning of the word when we're reading it and makes us vie for unrealistic goals, and bang, the marriage is out the window. It really is not about the here and now but about the hereafter.

If the mentality the church has today is that of true love, then I guess I'm confused.

Our demise in this physical realm of matter is our release into eternity. Our purpose in the flesh is to grow in love so that our treasure in the next life is the measure of love we've produced in this life. By loving the one who sends the evil, we are freed from that which enslaves us to the limitations of this illusory world. Love unconditional is perfected when we love the evil as well as the good...to resist the evil we are resisting He who sent the evil who is God...also known as Love, so the idea is to cooperate with the sender and be willing to lose our lives as does a seed planted in the ground so that we might gain true Life. Thus: Resist not evil (Matthew 5:39).

What Is Wisdom?

For who am I that I should not suffer? Who do I think I am that I should avoid suffering? Only the arrogant seek not to suffer. We have rather come to this world to expect to suffer, in order to be molded and shaped into that pure spiritual man that our Lord seeks for us to become.

The Savior our example, our master, came to suffer affliction. If His spiritual character had to be shaped and perfected by affliction, so our spiritual man must be shaped and perfected as we follow His example.

"We glory in tribulations also: knowing that tribulation worketh patience, experience, hope." Romans 5:3.

Wisdom is not to seek gold and silver and rubies, which are here today and gone tomorrow, but seek to rejoice in trials, and be buffeted in tribulations. It is through trials and tribulations that we learn to endure and are made gold. It is not the external gold we should seek, but the internal gold of the spirit.

"Happy is the man that findeth wisdom, and the man that getteth understanding for the merchandise of it is better than the merchandise of silver, and the gain thereof than fine gold." Proverbs 3:13-14.

"My brethren count it all joy when ye fall into 'diverse' temptations; Knowing this, that the trying of your faith worketh patience. But let patience be worked in you completely, that ye may be perfect and entire in perseverance, lacking nothing." This is wisdom, so if ye lack it, then ask for more of it, being not wishy washy. James 1:2-6

Wisdom is that we must also endure temptation. That temptation, which is the lust that is pulling us against God. But we must not give into that temptation, but must resist it, endure it, and then we shall receive the "crown of life". v. 12-13.

I denounce all things. I disown all things. I want nothing. Nothing to possess me. Only the most High God.

It is what is being born in us for heaven, that should be our only concern. Heaven, not earthly things must truly be our goal. Scams can be found everywhere. Everyone in this country is trying to take our money. Con artists are incessantly ripping off people, especially elderly folks, and God hates that. We must not be naive, once we are known as a 'giver' or philanthropist, sharks will come after us, and they do not bode us well. They are simply out for themselves, not trying to help needy folks, or worthy causes.

We are not to give money over to thieves, for they again would cause us to fail to fulfill the gospel, which is to sell all and give it to the poor. Do not give it to thieves who should be working for a living, but instead decide people owe them something, so they come up with schemes to trick well-intentioned folks out of their money. There are thieves in almost every area including banking, finances, governments, courts, businesses, charities and churches, many who have subtle tricks to steal our funds (Micah 7:2-6).

There are charities that are thieves, that fail to appropriate the money to the problem they claim to be in business to address, or they appropriate such a small percentage of it to that problem that it is essentially enriching itself. There are churches that mishandle our funds also. We as Christians are exhorted to be "wise as a serpent" when it comes to fulfilling our role to help the needy.

Even though we are well-intentioned, it is very important for us to vet these organizations, study them, obtain reputable references to ensure that our funds are being handled to bring the maximum help to the problem we intend for that organization or person to address. Our loyalty is to the hurting, underserved and dying and not to the organization or solicitor. If we are elderly it may be best to have a trusted person have power of attorney in this area of our finances. Personally visiting sick, and skid row, as well as physically going to an orphanage, or a care facility, or finding people one-on-one, are direct ways to ensure our aid is getting directly to those we want to help.

Capitalism Is Not Biblical

The Bible teaches 'socialistic' economics. Apparently, The Savior wants all His creatures to enjoy equal access to the goods and services of life the earth has to provide. Capitalism teaches that at the expense of others it is okay for wealth to be accumulated by the best, brightest, luckiest and smartest. That's not what Christ taught. His main concern was for the poor and the downtrodden, the lowly, disenfranchised and the handicapped.

The Creator wants the goods provided by the planet to be shared by all. The problem is men don't agree with The Creator.

The American Church does not agree with The Creator. The American church teaches capitalism, which is the accumulation of wealth by the fittest and the best at the expense of wealth for the weak, dumb, lazy and unlucky.

The Creator provided bread for all and did not send them off on their merry way to survive for themselves. The Creator told the young rich ruler to relinquish his wealth so the poor could have their fair share. He spoke against the man who decided to build more new barns.

While the American church extols the virtues of capitalism, the Bible clearly despises capitalism. It was Lazarus and not the rich man that Jesus loved. It was Lazarus who would make it to heaven and not the rich man. It was Judas the treasurer of the group who betrayed Jesus and then hanged himself, not the other disciples. While Jesus was interested in the tithe going to the fatherless, the widow and the foreigner the priest wanted the full quota or all of it. They deprived the less blessed. This is the mindset of capitalism, which is anti-biblical. There'll be no rich men in the Kingdom of Heaven, for it is easier for a camel to go through the eye of a needle than one of them to make it in.

God despises the payment of minimum wage to people, who are worth far more than wages, for a business to exist. Mal 3:5; James 5:4.

Denying people the essential goods and services necessary for their wellbeing is profane, is profanity, pornographic. It is using God's name in vain. The starving masses of populations in various nations through various eras of our lives are the direct result of capitalist exploitation. Suppressing goods and services and manipulating prices creates a tidal wave of deprivation and vulgarity throughout the world.

The entire lending industry is a violation of basic human rights. The entire lending industry is criminal in its existence. Debt creation is the creation of sin, of evil, of corruption, of hate, of slavery, of vulgarity, it is the dehumanization of life. Capitalism depraves the earth and depraves the soul. Life becomes a system of commodities, instead of the spiritual experience it was intended to be.

America takes capitalism to an extreme. It is a system that creates its own enemies, and then demonizes them for being the enemy it created. The motif is, that if we cannot control a foreign government's economic enterprise system, and exploit it, and make top dollar within it, then we will topple it in the name of democracy, which we really mean 'capitalism', so we can bring destruction to that nation and build a new economic system, that we'll use to further enrich ourselves. We call this taking care of "American Self-Interest", which usually means self-interest at the unfair and undesirable expense of others. It is not to keep our country safe, and free, it's to enrich the top 1-5% of our already enriched population.

This system that worships capital above all else will exploit everything coming and going for its own self-interest and will readily dehumanize others to enrich itself. This is pornography in its fullest sense. This is an anti-Christian value that the Christian church supports, even extols as righteousness. If the church is simply quiet in this regard, it is by its' silence supporting a perverse system. It is a system of exclusion rather than inclusion, which makes us think we are important so long as we are helping these industries achieve their goals, even and especially if it is at our own expense and to our own demise. We have industries and oligarchies that upon reaching a level of wealth that is spellbinding, will stop at nothing to retain it.

For instance, the American medical "industry", rather than curing cancer for which there are a myriad of natural cures, it to maintain capital enrichment, will divert, and if necessary destroy anyone or organization that presents an actual real cure. Other nations have cures for cancer. The United States of America's medical industry will veil the cure in order to maintain the spellbinding wealth cancer research garners. Meanwhile hundreds of thousands of men, women and children die of a curable disease in order to maintain the wealth status of the shareholders in this elitist "industry".

This too is an example of "blood money". There are many ways the rich murder people to enrich themselves, and the medical industry along with their insurance company accomplices have made a science of it. We've heard of blood diamonds, blood gold, blood for oil, blood for food and there is a blood health industry. An industries' chief goal is to stay alive and to stay alive it must make money, and that by any means necessary. Making money at all costs most often means making it at the expense of human lives; how ironic. In short, it's addition by subtraction. And while all this is going on we go to church to assuage our conscious, and so we place money into the offering plate to pacify our callous heart and try to bribe God in lieu of our inaction (Deut. 10:17).

The church must advocate against such genocidal atrocities that occur on our own doorstep. We need to stop pointing the finger at foreign nations for their indiscretions and look at what's going on right under our noses right here in America.

I will not even touch the heinous crimes the judicial and prison "industry" are committing daily. Prison sentences are traded as bonds and other instruments on Wall Street, making the statement "crime doesn't pay" a fallacy. Crime does pay for many a shareholder. The incentive is to incarcerate as many human chattel as possible, because crime can pay-off in big dividends.

But back to the medical industry. Even more death defying is the thought of tackling the cause of cancer in the first place. If an industry causes cancer or contributes to the cause of cancer that industry should be shut down or corrected. But the cause is impossible to stop because everybody is in bed with these industries including we the consumer, and that is because in America money is "god". Money is the "god" we trust. When money is "god", it translates into death to people.

In many cultures of old, human sacrifices from children to adults were offered to appease the gods. Different day, same problem. So to support or even extol our system is for us to have blood on our hands. Even to silently permit such a system to thrive makes us worthy of eternal capital punishment, each and everyone of us who do nothing about it. Every church and every church person who sits silently by and permits this blood for money system to exist has blood on their hands. Isaiah 1:15 GNB, "When you lift your hands in prayer, I will not look at you. No matter how much you pray, I will not listen, for your hands are covered with blood." v.17, "-See that justice is done-".

Lending with collateral is anti-Biblical, anti-Jesus, anti-righteous and totally and blatantly sinful and evil. The use of usury is clearly evil, and forbidden in the Bible, and the idea that some few make their fortunes on the misfortunes of others is Satanic. Our King's only display of overt physical anger was with the money changers in the temple. This is the key to understanding the source of why people suffer in this world today.

The entire civilized system that is in place in this world today is thus a savage evil and fraudulent system. Essentially the fraud has to do with the economic system as it is spearheaded by the western world. The economic system is bereft of goodness, throwing the world into the darkness it is experiencing. We the average person often fail to have time to fight the powers that be because we are so strapped with subpar wages while working longer hours. We often travel greater distances while absorbing inflated prices for goods and services. This condition drives us to take out loans to pay for all this inflated stuff, having insufficient funds to pay for the hyper-inflated loans. We are left with not enough time nor energy. So the oppression continues unchecked. We're thus rendered 'slaves'. Yet if we don't oppose this system we support this system, which is to support the greatest evil that man may have ever seen.

Germane to the sin of drugs, alcohol, sexual immorality, abandonment, lying, cheating, murder and a host of other sins is the banking system which is in place in the world today. Lending with insufficient controls and no moral guidelines is a violation of basic human rights, an inhumanity to man.

"Greed gives rise to selfish or wicked actions" (Proverb). "For the love of money is a root of all kinds of evil. I Timothy 6:10 NIV

The apostle Paul writes, "But you, man of God, flee from all this, and pursue righteousness, godliness, faith, love, endurance and gentleness. Fight the good fight of the faith. Take hold of the eternal life to which you were called when you made your good confession in the presence of many witnesses. Command those who are rich in this present world not to be arrogant nor to put their hope in wealth, which is so uncertain, but to put their hope in God, who richly provides us with everything for our enjoyment. Command them to do good, to be rich in good deeds, and to be generous and willing to share. In this way they will lay up treasure for themselves as a firm foundation for the coming age, so that they may take hold of the life that is truly life", (I Timothy 6:11-12, 17-19).

Many other nations do not operate from a debt perspective as do we here in these North Americas, many people operate by paying for goods and services as they are able. Americans live in a delusion that they're monetary system of investments and debt accumulation makes them a first world country, when nothing could be further from the truth. America is vanquished, conquered and bankrupted. The ministry encourages a covetous eye in its people by calling the obtainment of material things, "blessings".

The collateral damage caused to the billions of disenfranchised peoples that share this planet is incalculable. Yet the American Church supports this egregious culture of filth and calls it good, sophisticated (which it is [fake]), and tries to attribute it as being Godlike or some sort of gifts from God. We believe having all this stuff is a blessing from God and are the fruits of being a successful Christian. Such lies as these enslave us and numb our senses whereas we lose touch with facts and reality and live in a state of superstition and sorcery. This hedonistic state gives license to debilitate and anesthetize our hearts and minds. We become the living dead and become worthless rather than worthwhile and fully empowered. Buying into this debt system is the antithesis of righteousness.

Let's breakdown the system under which we reside in America. If we are paying a monthly or weekly loan payment on a vehicle we are a slave to the bank. The bank owns that vehicle until such time as we pay them in full. If we own a house and took out a loan for that house, a bank loaned us that paper and that bank owns that house until such time we pay them back in full. The business down the street more than likely got the goods it needs for inventory by obtaining a loan from the bank. So, the business, store, restaurant, church building is owned by the bank until such time it pays off all its debts in full. The amazingly tall skyscrapers we see in giant cities are owned by the banks also. Until such time the borrowing entity pays them the paper in full. Our military is financed by the banks so that all the purchases of equipment dedicated to fighting wars belongs to the bank until such time the military pays its debts in full. So, the phrase "In God we trust" is better spelled, "In 'god' we trust".

The bank is the "god" of this country and everything in America is owned and run by the bankers, seen and unseen. They're not using gold or silver which is the only real money there is. They are using "paper". In fact, the banks don't have a legal right to lend us paper and retain a legitimate claim to what we bought with the paper, but because the government and the courts support this felonious system of paper exchanged for paper, the banks can win most challenges to their claims. If a bank does not lend us gold or silver, then we owe them nothing. But the system in place is setup to support the deception. Besides they own enough fire power to ultimately settle all disputes in their favor (Micah 2:1-9). When a nation's leader attempts to introduce real gold into the economic system that leader if he doesn't at some point relinquish his attempted introduction of that gold will find himself in a grave.

The same vain economic and lending system that is propagating the poverty all over the world today is promoting the gay proliferation. The same system that denies the human beings their economic rights, vulgarizes the soul and denies the human being the right to be heterosexual. Many gays fight for the rights of the poor and oppressed naturally because the gay is also the poor and the oppressed. The oppression against people, their economies, their beings and their sensibilities is the same oppression that perverts people and sexually changes them. It destroys the nuclear family because the woman is out of the house working, pressured to help bring income as well as feed the household. As a result the children are under supervised, morals and structure evaporate, and protections are removed.

The abusive power of the oppressive rich sexually castrates the human being, it re-sexualizes them and renders them a neuter or sexual non-entity. It is a form of human GMO or human genetic modification through the pressure of generic hate.

The church should be fighting to force the oppressors out of office and out of business. The church should fight for the welfare and benefit of all peoples.

"Money has become a sort of language. It has emerged as the communication system of an entirely new way of seeing the world: The entirety of God's creation becomes capital to be exploited and property to be owned by individuals and corporate entities. As a natural outgrowth of this worldview, today every square inch of the earth is theoretically owned by someone. Every living thing, every natural feature-every rock, bird, mountain and forest-can be quantified in terms of economic value. Even people are measured in dollars and cents.

What effect does this all-pervasive economic worldview have on our lives? How are we affected by living in a society where virtually all of our activities are assigned monetary values? What are the long-term effects of a system that aims to operate entirely on the free market principles of calculated self-interest, where even human love is reduced to a transactional exchange?" (Money is our Language and our Love, by Micah Bales)

The reductionist destruction and vanquishing of the spirit and soul of human beings rendering them hopeless commodities, and mechanizing them into throw away products alters, changes, perverts perception and realities, heightening the weird aspects of our human development by stunting it, causing remasculinization and refeminization, materializing our inner core foundational human aspects all because gold is our god. The neuter-human, a gen-X, relegated powerless and distracted, is the end-goal of those who seek unchecked absolute power. We have a droopy American church that won't stand up for the rights of others or its own rights. We are either too busy, too lazy or too faked out by false propaganda or and preaching to get up and stand up for our own "condemned" rights.

Everyone can have plenty to live on, the earth can support it. The creation allows everyone to live at a good economic level. It is a lie that in order for some to be rich others have to be poor.

Everyone can be well to do, but the abusive economic oppression must be stopped. There is enough to go around if we all have a heart to share. It has been calculated that the entire population of the planet could all fit into the state of Texas and be adequately sustained. Generosity breeds generosity. Exploitation of others as a means of existence always has and always will bring destruction on humanity unless we the Christian church snap out of our malaise and unite to stop it.

The rich folks at the top of the food chain, the corporate heads, shareholders, paid government officials, military and financial folks have poisoned Christ's message with what amounts to feeding the people heroine. Some of us are so duped by the false doctrine that has come down from on high, otherwise known in the military as 'disinformation', which is a form of brainwashing, that we're drunk with it. God calls people who dupe people sorcerers, liars, perjurers, adulterers. They have most of American church folks believing that social justice betrays the creeds of Christianity, and that capitalism makes you a better Christian. The term used to reinforce that idea is "God and country". That is not a biblical term but is accepted as such by most American Christians. That term is a part of the 'cyanide' being slipped into the Kool-aide. It is a patriotic sounding term which inculcates the religious sounding overtone "God" in it so cleverly framed it serves as a tool to recruit the church to back the United States military in its exploits even when they are evil.

Capitalism does not connote spiritual righteousness either, because it is secular, which means godless or profane. It is a commercial construct, a theory really and it is preached in order to further empower the oppressors even if it's at the expense of the poor. Its learned in school at a very young age as being "American" and affirmed by our educational system as a pillar of American democracy, an exciting idea promoted by our forefathers, specifically credited to Adam Smith, which gives it a sort of sanctity in our hearts. The church then picks up the ball and runs with it without even investigating its origin, its slant, and whether it aligns with what Christ would do. The fact is, Christ is a social justice advocate. That fact is the key to the entire word of God.

The true Christian church is in the streets protesting against the oppressions of the rich and powerful. Those advocating for human rights against the abuse of the poor are the Christian church today because they are DOING what Christ said they should be DOING, and those who are found sitting on the pews in the auditoriums of church buildings each Sunday/Saturday/Friday are the silent majority who have supported by their silence the bloodletting murderous and vile actions of the military industrial complex called America.

One Lie Leads To Another

A church that would lie about the heredity or racial lineage of its God on earth is a church that will lie about what it truly represents...that it represents the works of the devil. It hates helping foster children, and hungry souls, and homeless folks, its own elderly parents and people of other faiths. It supports the exploitation of other countries to benefit itself; it even supports the death of women and children to gain economic advantage and empire.

To paint Christ as Neapolitan, or Anglo-Saxon invalidates the charac teristics of non-white peoples and inverts their god-likenesses as traits of inferiority. The paintings of Michelangelo have voided "Jesus" of even His Jewishness. So, who is this idolized image hung in our churches and homes today? If he is not the Jewish Savior, then they promote a false idol.

Until a non-Jewish Jesus is removed from the psyche of the American people, the American people and all other peoples will be enslaved under the false mental image that their "god" is a European. Indeed, this image may be the one most important factor we need to help eradicate. I see my African brethren come to this country and hang that same non-Jewish image in their churches and in their homes. This Jesus image is their "god", it is their "idol". It is the crux of their lives, that in which they've invested their faith, the essence of their hope, that which consumes their reality. Yet the image is a fraud, feeding the concept of white supremeness. It and the spirit behind it supports the non-Jewish European man's most effective tool for control over the minds and hearts of those he wishes to colonize. This image is in up to 90% of all churches in America and Africa.

The false European non-Jewish Jesus presents a false Church. A Church that is impotent in protecting the rights of the poor, the widow, the fatherless, the foreigner and the oppressed. The Greco-Roman empire Jesus represents a militant Church interested in exploitation of wealthy lands for its own self-aggrandizement. One lie always leads to another.

It is not the original Church based on love, but is a Church based on the concept of empire. It is not a Church of suffering for the good of others but a Church that causes others to suffer for its own good.

An American Church which looks down on the negro race because it is negro, is a Church that denies its very Saviour and what its very Saviour taught it to do, which is not to condemn but save people. The hate of the negro has caused us to deny our true Lord and Savior because that Savior is a negro, of the tribe of Judah, and the people that hate negroes therefore hate Him (Matt. 10:33-35).

Thus, the church worships a Jesus, they've made up in their own imaginations. It is a foregone conclusion, those who hate Christ will not make it into His Kingdom.

So if we despise His people, his kinfolk, we despise Him; and we do despise the negro people in America. Thus, we don't worship the true Christ, but an invention after our own hearts, an idol, a false god…appearing as an angel of light.

A Church that looks down on the yellow and the brown and other disenfranchised races is a Church that hates Christ, and loves itself, when its own scriptures tell it to love its enemies and do well to those who spitefully use them. A church that supports white supremacy, its' principles deeds and actions is a church that cannot be a church of the living God. A church that fails to fight against white supremacy, by its inaction, supports white supremacy.

Such a Church uses its power to control, enslave and abuse its control over vast populations of peoples so that the peoples are economically no better off than before they came to that church. Those people are used to build-up that Church to their own detriment and personal demise.

The refusal of the negro to change the image of Christ into one of their own is the proof pudding that they are permanently enslaved in their minds. They'll never come out of their dismal state of captivity, until they admit that Messiah was a Hebrew, and the Hebrews had dark skin and negroid features. In many nations, it is customary to hang the picture-image of the current dictator of that nation on their walls. It is important, because it impresses his power upon their psyche; it enforces his control over them and weakens their resolve to defeat that image. This same power, this same influence is accomplished in the postings of a Greco-Roman Jesus in our churches and homes. This image must be defeated. It's not even good for European descendants to continue doing. It's also messin' up their heads.

It encourages all peoples to remain enslaved to a false god and all the false ideas and perceptions he brings. In fact, God hates images worshiped in His name, He calls them idols, "Do not make idols or set up an image or a sacred stone for yourselves, and do not place a carved stone in your land to bow down before it. I am the Lord your God" (Leviticus 26:1; Exodus 2:3-5; Psalms 115:3-8). Paintings are being posted in churches and homes and statutes of so-called "Jesus"; giant monuments are being erected in various countries today, but God says don't do that!

Whites who otherwise mean well are duped into believing that what other white people do is righteous according to God's will because after-all Jesus is white like the whites who are running things. On top of that he is a white Jew, like the so-called Jews who are running things in Israel. However, it is of utmost importance that we recognize the Ashkenazi Jews of Europe are a new Jew on the scene, and they are not the bloodline of the Jews or the Hebrews of biblical lineage.

Thus, the so-called white Jews who order the events in this world to-day are not the Jews that Jesus was (Revelation 3:9). In fact, these are not even the Pharisee or Sadducee Jews of the Bible. These present-day Jews did not exist as Jews back then. So, once we overcome this lie, we question all the hoopla that is going on in the nation of Israel as to the veracity of the claim of its inhabitants that that land is their Biblical God ordained inheritance. This of course is a lie also, and the region is in flames because liars are lying and others who should know better are supporting the lie. Verily one lie leads to another.

However, when well-meaning American whites awaken to realize that they've been duped on several levels, to realize that our Savior isn't European, but a Hebrew who are black men, we can begin purging our hearts of "racism", which is "haticism". Further, the Jews of today don't speak Hebrew, but speak Yiddish, which we mistake for Hebrew, but is a German dialect. Thirdly, the depiction of Jesus in the pictures as white do not even favor him being of what is of Ashkenazi Jewish ethnic origin, which also compounds the fabrication. We agree, Our Savior is not Italian or Eastern European or Anglo-Saxon. Fourthly, since Our Savior is properly pictured as a black Jew throughout eastern Europe, along with a black mother Mary, those who are giving orders in the western Churches today have no real authority to do so, therefore their purposes and aims must be examined.

What were the goals and purposes of the western Roman emperor Constantine and the Council at Nicaea in 335? Were their goals and purposes ordained of God? Were they the authorized descendants of the twelve apostles The Savior left here on earth? And if so, how so, because Paul preached the gospel in Rome, and some accepted Christ as did Constantine? Well does the fact that instead of being martyred, the church now became the martyrs, and martyred hundreds of thousands over a period of 1,200 years, who refused to become Roman Catholic and abide by their doctrines; any indication that something had gone awry in the thinking of so-called Christians of that day? That Jesus' followers are now executing, torturing and hanging on stakes, people who violated church doctrine, is not a problem? Has an imposter, an interloper slipped in and deceived the Christian world today? We say yes!

Is there a problem in that the persecution and enforcement of the Christian religion was so bad that thousands from Europe fled to America so that they could practice Protestantism without their lives being threatened? That the ones being murdered became the murderers is not a problem? Is the fact that the persecuted Protestants that then fled to America and martyred, tortured, mutilated, murdered and persecuted millions of native Americans because they were not white, nor Christian, not a problem? Don't ignore the Native American. This was his land before we got here. If we celebrate Thanksgiving, we should celebrate it with the perspective that the blood of millions of Native Americans was spilled on these lands, and we must be grateful for God's forgiveness, for the atrocities we visited on those Native Americans.

We must repent, stand up and fight for their rights, for they who we consider foreigners are actually the original inhabitants of these lands. We must fight for their justice, and for the justice of millions of displaced and despondent blacks in this land, many who are original inhabitants also. The Bible is not democratic, it is theocratic. That means, God oversees the government; not the people, the king, congress, the president nor the bankers. When God oversees the government, He loves each of His human children, made in His image, equally. He sees all of us as having equal rights. He does not grade us by who is the richest, best looking, smartest, fastest, or strongest, but by how we love one another.

He's most concerned with the sickliest of us because the sickliest needs the most care and protection. This is not the animal kingdom of the survival of the fittest. We're not to be eaten if we're not fit! Those are animalistic realities. This is the Kingdom of God which professes, "they will know you are my disciples if you love one another" (John 13:35). So now we can properly access that today we are not Christ's disciples. We can now honestly assess that God's Kingdom is not like man's kingdom, His Kingdom is about justice for the needy, justice for all. And now after all this assessment, we can change and do something about it.

Why Fight For The Foreigner?
A foreigner desperate to get across our borders is usually one of two people. He got wealthy in his native country and seeks to increase his wealth,

even protect his wealth over here, because certain policies favor his position, Or... Our country has so impoverished his country that he cannot survive in his country, and must desperately seeks to find work over here. He is driven to come here to have a life. He prefers his native land, family, culture, music, food, traditions and all, but is forced to choose between poverty and survival.

When he comes to the United States its often because our country has plundered his country by exploiting their natural resources or and wealth production systems, rendering a majority of his people impoverished. As a result, the jobs are over here. We'd do the same thing if in his shoes. We need to give the foreigners love.

What happened? What changed? The gospel of Messiah where He states I came not to destroy but to save has absolutely gotten twisted, flipped on its head, "For the Son of man is not come to destroy men's lives, but to save them", Luke 9:56. The disciples who stated that anyone who did not profess Messiah is the enemy, and Messiah's response that we are to "save not destroy", those type of disciples are in power today. The Master told them to wipe the dust off their feet, not to "dust" them.

The idea that we are to love our enemy has been overwhelmed by a terrible group of bigots today. The gospel which gives Christians the license to kill others and then justify the killing because the "others" are non-Christians, is an insidious evil in vogue today.

The Redeemer preached a gospel of love, not of loss. The true gospel was twisted by European empire builders who maimed, enslaved, robbed and destroyed peoples, "In the Name of Jesus", a white Jesus who doesn't even look like a modern "so-called" Jew, and is definitely not a Hebrew of biblical lineage, but an impostor.

This same group of empire builders claims to want to disciple the lost, when their fruits bear witness that their real aim is to anesthetize those whom they colonize, enslave and capture, so that they might enrich themselves. This religious opium is sold to the non-believers and then those who are high on the drug sell it to others of their own nationality, until everyone becomes drunk on it (Revelations 17:6).

This is the brand of Christianity which has engulfed the world and has the tag, "Made in America" attached to it. Is there a correlation when we see white Christians, feeling justified, when they hang a black man on a tree? "Gotta put the fear of god in those negroes"? Christ was hung on a tree.

American churches today support the bombing of Muslim nations because they're not Christians, just like they supported bombing Communist nations because they're atheist. The root of this mentality is lust, greed, control, supremacy. Doesn't it sound like something has gone radically wrong with this level of bloodletting in the name of "Jesus"? The Redeemer did not come to destroy, but clearly to save.

The Christianity of today comes to destroy. We have a Church culture today that does not fight for the weak, the fatherless, the widow, the disenfranchised, the hungry, the homeless, the foreigner, but rather neglects them, and uses the scripture, "the poor you will always have with you", as an excuse to extort them for our own gain. This is the Americanization of God.

Teaching Christians to passively sit by while the nation's militant factions destroy the oppressed at home, as well as abroad, is unacceptable. This Americanized Christianity preaches lethargy in the face of violence and evil, teaches apathy in the face of injustice, teaches there's nothing you need to do once you are saved. That all the scriptures that state that God will judge us by our deeds, by the fruits we bear, by the commandments we keep, what we do for our brother, by how we treat our enemy, by the actions we take on behalf of the oppressed are not important. The scriptures that state that we must do these works until the end and not quit, and then we will receive the crown of righteousness promised us, mean nothing...to visit the widow and care for the fatherless are not really true, and make no difference as it pertains to receiving or missing out on Eternal Life. The churches teach that if you keep a certain day holy day or attend Easter services, or be baptized by fire, or pay tithes regularly, or you are a Baptist, Catholic, Mormon, Jehovah Witness, one of thirty-four thousand denominations, or simply receive Jesus into your hearts, if you're with that one right church, you're "sitting pretty", you're in the 'honey pot'.

You'll make it simply because you are with the right church. All you have to do is ride along with that church, and you can "honey pot' your way into heaven. As regard to the Kingdom and Everlasting Life, you are surely set! You may do some tweaking of some of their procedures, but pretty much if you're with the religion that makes it in, then you're a sure bet to make it in. I call this the belief that you are sitting in the 'honey pot", or as in the vernacular, "sitting pretty".

God clearly does not look at it that way.

The rulers of this land love having a passive Church that permits them to do almost any heinous thing and get away with it unchecked. It's the same cyanide that is mixed into the Kool-aide of the American brand of Christianity exported to foreign lands.

The lie is spread like this: The deceiver whispers in our ear with his hand partially cupped over his mouth so we can't see his lips moving: (programming us)

When you hear that: 'think this'!

When they say that: 'think this'!

When you read that: 'think this'!

When you don't understand that:

'think this'!

They've already preprogrammed us what to think.

When you think that, "think this"!

We've been misinformed by the powers that be, to act and react in ways that keep us passive toward them and divided, in fear, hate, toward one another. This is also the Americanization of God.

In Jeremiah 5:2-31, the key to this entire diatribe is verse 28, "judge with justice the cause of the fatherless and make them prosper and defend the rights of the needy. This is not a secondary option. This is Christianity if nothing else. This is the primal, primary thing. We must make a widow in a hospital bed or fatherless child in need, our life's work, period. No other priority, there is no exception.

There is a widow who is in pain lying in the hospital as of the writing of this very book. Her name is Charlotte. She is eighty-three years of age and has pneumonia. She prays for everyone and loves-on everyone. She is a bedrock of our congregation, attends all Bible studies. She has two 'unsaved' daughters. We must not assume her daughters or some friend will see to her. We must make sure she's okay. Miss Charlotte needs to be visited and the church members must be about knowing what the hospital staff is doing 24/7, until she's out of that hospital.

Then once she's out of that hospital, we must assure ourselves that when she is at home, that she has everything she needs to fully recuperate from her distress. We who can cook need to prepare the meals, the folks that clean need to clean her domicile, and everyone needs to be at the "ready" to meet her needs. If there is a dispute with the hospital bill or a problem with payments, the church must fix the discrepancies in the charges and if she lacks coverage for the bill's full payment, then the church must pay the bill. Any problem with utility bills and rent should be taken care of if necessary. Miss Charlotte should have no ancillary worries about her hospitalization because we, her brothers and sisters in Christ are "Johnny on the spot" in the fullness of care for her situation.

And to take this even further. The church or and churches across the board, across denominations should be networked to the point that if a wife, mother or sister's vehicle breaks down, that one phone call would go out, and all Christians are alerted so that if any are in the area of the break down they can assist.

Imagine if Ms. Naomi is driving and her car runs out of gas. She's stranded in an area where it is dark and she couldn't afford AAA this year. Her husband is disabled or unable to assist her. What should happen? A Christian Amber-Alert-like action-line should call all connected congregants, no matter the denomination, and alert whomever is in the vicinity that Ms. Naomi needs help. Within a short time two, three, four vehicles should show-up and give her assistance.

Mrs. Carol Barksdale attends a community meeting and the mayor states that the DA is thinking of prosecuting homeless people. Mrs. Barksdale is enraged at this prospect and calls the Christian Amber-Alert-like-action-line. A petition is formulated and emailed and texted to all Christians in that community. Immediately five thousand or so protest signatures are obtained and placed at the DA's doorstep.

If a widow is evicted from her house, the Amber-Alert-like-action-line notifies all members of all the churches that there is a need to move her belongings and find a place for her immediately. If rental assistance is needed then we take up tithes and assist widows, fatherless or strangers until funding can be acquired from other sources. The same thing that applies to church members in distress applies to the unchurched widows, fatherless and strangers in distress. Our funds must be applied to help them until they can get on their feet as well. In the case where a family is evicted, the various members of the church need to take them in, even if they have to divide a large family on a temporary basis until permanent housing can be acquired.

Another glaring problem in this country is the lack of sufficient rehabilitation services for the many prisoners we have locked away in our prison system.

The U.S.A. has more prisons and prisoners than any nation or group of nations in the world. The churches need to initiate and run rehabilitation programs to help prisoners to never have to return to prison again.

Youth church might be encouraged in regard to their career choices to orient themselves to becoming a rehabilitation counselor, psychologist, legal assistant or the like for the primary purpose of assisting in creating inmate rehabilitation programs to serve the prisoners of our land.

Many of these rehabilitated men and women will become rehabilitation counselors themselves, each one teaching one. The churches need to set-up "houses of honor" for released prisoner's re-entry into society.

We must encourage the agencies that are available to assist in each prisoner's reentry. We as a body of believers must fight for the rights of those who are on the fringes of society, for the weak, the marginal and the oppressed.

Again, we must encourage our youth and devoted members to take on professional careers that prepare them in these multiple areas of need.

Denominational difference and biases must be locked away in a closet somewhere and true believers with God's love need to reach across denominational divides, grab hands and become the "living crosses" for our Creator Christ. If churches would team up, we could crisscross this whole nation and the waters of righteousness would pour down like a flood.

Christ said take up your "cross" and follow me. We must educate folks in preventative lifestyles, that will keep them out of the doctor's office. We must help educate the sick into altering dietary habits that may further harm them.

We must promote education in morality and family values. A counter immorality course must be implemented to show that there is another way. We must make people aware of the vices that are tripping up folks at all levels, that work to their detriment mentally, physically, emotionally and spiritually.

We must be pro-active in our efforts to show the world we are the body of Christ and that He is our Head.

Our jobs are not to be placed in the way as a roadblock or interference as to why we cannot go see that people in need are immediately and fully cared for 24/7. God is the source of our lives, not our jobs nor our work. He gives us jobs and, He Can Take Them Away! We surely have sick time or vacation pay. If nothing else, we must put God over money and exercise our faith.

Condemning people for the various situations they've gotten themselves into is not to be used as an excuse not to help them, that's why He gave us instructions not to condemn.

We'll have to risk losing our jobs. It would be better than risking our eternity. Our treasures are not about what's on this earth. Our treasures are about heaven. It's about eternity, yes or no. This is not an option. Christ says we are to keep His words, to obey His commands and then He will consider us His friends. He says we are to lay our lives down for one another. Down means put down whatever we had planned and pick-up our "cross" and follow Him no matter what it cost. This is the tithe, the offering, the fasting that God is looking for and no other.

Do we have a fatherless child that we mentor or physically care for? Do we speak to them every day and make sure their needs are taken care of? Are we on their case about how they are living their lives helping others? Are we demonstrating to them the gospel of Christ regarding helping others who are in their same situation? Are we inviting them to church and making sure they're treated special? Do we esteem them better than our self? Do we feed them, clothe them, tutor them, mentor them, take time and effort to take them on trips and outings and build events for them to interact with our own family?

Is our church partnering with the local orphanage and assisting in their needs? Are the fatherless the priority work of our church? Are our biological children being taught that cliques among themselves are the new non-existent crime, that the inclusion of the fatherless is their new life's work? Have the fatherless become number one priority in every church member's life, so that if they're struggling in any phase of their life, it is known and addressed by all? Notice the scripture says fatherless, not motherless. They may have a mother but they are still orphans if there is no available father.

Does every qualified man in the congregation have a boy they mentor? Every qualified woman have a girl she mentors? There is no other gospel than this, that the widow and the fatherless be cared for at the platinum level of care. That they receive the best of everything. Not the preacher, not the ministry, not the elders, not the wealthy, but the needy, the poor. This is the good news of the Kingdom of God, and no other. It is the demonstration of love, that will bind us as one people, and "they" will see our "good works", and glorify our Father in heaven.

The widow, fatherless, stranger, should be at every congregants' house for dinner week to week, every week, the poor also should eat every congregant house, " they (Christians) are waxen fat, they shine (they're flashy)" yea; they overpass (surpass) the deeds of the wicked: (how?) they judge not the cause, (they pretend the problem is not there) (they do not make right the cause on behalf of the fatherless, yet they prosper) (they're building their empires); and the right of the needy do they not judge (in building empires they overlook the needs of the needy) (the oppressed situation is not fixed; their problems continue), "Indeed, there are wicked scoundrels among my people. They lie in wait like bird catchers hiding in ambush. They set deadly traps to catch people (fishers of men, but with the wrong intent) their houses are filled with the gains of their fraud and deceit as a cage full of birds. That is how they have gotten so rich and powerful", Jeremiah 5:27 NET Bible.

Leadership classes, conferences, seminars, revivals and the like should be centered about helping the needy, centered on training and equipping the saints to serve those closest to God's heart, centered on strategizing the best way to fight for justice for the oppressed. This is where salvation starts and ends. This is for what we are to forsake all.

"And whoever has left houses or brothers or sisters or father or mother or wife or children or fields for my sake will receive a hundred times as much and will inherit eternal life", Matthew 19:29 NET Bible. The jobs at our workplaces are secondary, and we're to do them well mind you, however in America we're taught the subtle lie that our jobs are primary and most important.

What we must grow to understand is that our jobs exist to support our primary purpose in life, and that is to advocate on behalf of those who cannot advocate for themselves. Our profession as believers is to promote the gospel of Christ to the world by our action of loving those closest to God's heart and prioritizing their situations above our own.

We have the Kingdom in us, but is it manifest to the world for its benefit? We are to practice the good news of the Kingdom of God which is to preach the good news to the poor: (feed them and remove their poverty) to heal (see justice is done on behalf of the brokenhearted), to preach deliverance to the captives (rehabilitate them, Matt. 5:4), fight for their release, and recovering of sight to the blind (open the eyes of all people to the truth), to set free the oppressed (fight for righteousness to all who are disadvantaged and abused). Whereas the American culture makes our jobs our number one priority, God makes the fight for justice our number one top priority. Thereby work, and working hard on our jobs is secondary, unless the line of work we do is altruistic, charitable work.

Put first things first. Our treasures for eternity are "priority one". We start by loving God with all our heart, soul and mind. We prove this by loving our neighbor who we can see (I John 4:2), with all our heart, mind and soul (Matthew 22:37). The summation of this thought is to love our neighbor who is the least like us, with all our heart, soul and mind and we will have loved God as we ought.

"Speak up for people who cannot speak for themselves. Protect the rights of all who are helpless. Speak for them and be a righteous judge. Protect the rights of the poor and needy" (Proverbs 31:8-9). These are the commandments Christ gave us to keep (John 14:15).

How To Love Yet Fight For Justice At The Same Time?

How do we love the sinner and hate the sin at the same time?

King David might be a good example of someone who had deep passionate love for God and for people, especially Israel. Yet when people including Saul and David's own son Absalom attacked him personally, he was a 'wusp' (a chump). He did not defend his person, he did not see himself as being important, but conversely when the enemy attacked the things of God, David was a terror, the best warrior that ever was, and he was passionate about destroying the evil. King David set the example. If you came against him personally he wouldn't defend himself, but if you came against almighty God or one of God's concerns, you had a fight on your hands.

We're to love our enemy and greet them with kindness. When they are hungry give them food and drink, when thirsty and when naked clothe them. Also esteem them better than self (Philippians 2:3). However, when it comes to the oppression of marginal people, we must love the marginal people more. If the enemy is found oppressing the poor, fatherless, widow, foreigner, weak, sick or challenged, children or elderly, then as King David would, see that justice gets done. We are to free the oppressed, the prisoner, the poor, the under-served populations. It's about equality, in the church and in the world at large.

Warning: The book of Ecclesiasticus 12:3 probably gives us the best perspective as to how we are to apply the principle of giving in this real world, full of so many con men, rip-off artists, drug addicts, thieves and murderers. "There can no good come to him that is always occupied in evil, nor to him that giveth no alms. [However] Give to the godly man, and help not a sinner." Repeat, "help NOT a sinner". Do well unto him that is lowly, but give not to the ungodly." Repeat, "give NOT to the ungodly". "Do well unto him that is lowly, but give NOT to the ungodly: hold back thy bread, and give it [NOT] unto him, lest he overmaster thee thereby: Why? "For [else] thou shalt receive twice as much evil for all the good thou shalt have done unto him." The conclusion of the matter is found in verse 7: "Give unto the good, and help [NOT] the sinner."

Next, some of us have jobs, careers, stock holdings, occupations that pay us well. Many reading this book make well into the six figures or more, either as individuals or as a married couple. The trend is to 'max-out' the level at which we can spend materially. By max-out I mean that with such a wash of funds coming in each month, our sights focus on bigger and better and more costly material things. We go after the bigger house in the nicer neighborhood driving the maximum vehicle our finances can sustain.

The only reason we don't purchase an even more expensive house or car is because we just can't. But given enough of a pay increase, we'll precede to obtain it or multiples of them. We tend to shop at better more expensive exclusive luxurious stores and purchase better clothes, shoes, jewelry and so forth. Our programming is to max-out or 'maximitize'. This is what the commercial advertisements are teaching us. And we find ourselves obeying them hook, line and sinker. Everything in our flesh screams that we "deserve" these conveniences, because we have worked hard to put ourselves in a position to obtain, obtain, obtain, them!

But who of us who pulls down let's say $120k a year says, we can live comfortably on $60k, if we are frugal and manage our money properly, so that we can give the rest to support a cause or two for social justice, a cause to feed the hungry, a cause for improving the lives of millions of orphan children in lands near and far away?

How many of us realize we can purchase a decent pre-owned auto for $10k cash and obtain a decent house or town house for a mortgage of up to $2,500 a month or rent payment of up to $1,800 a month (even in So. California, Florida and some parts of NYC) and still have enough leftover to eat well, save and spend time at the mall? Or are we caught up into "mansion" building and coveting the sleekest of sleek autos? Let's face it, we're either serving one "god" or serving the other. A couple with two or three kids and a couple of pets does not need a house over 2,500 sq. ft. We just don't unless we're housing fatherless, widows, elderly and infirmed throughout that house.

If enough of us lived like this, floods of income could be going towards the overthrow of this evil system. With the 'de-maxitized' available income of Christians, we could actually outspend the corporations in order to get 'people-first' policies implemented into our society. The social service agencies announce cut-backs in aid for the poor, disadvantaged and under-served people perpetually. Because of these endless cutbacks in funding, the under-served have become doubly and triply under-served and we sit around feeling silly, useless and powerless to do anything about it.

This is the very reason God warns us not be caught up in our own lusts (desires for comfort and sensation); because when we are free from that, we can figure this thing out.

We the church must help the poor, disadvantaged and under-served because that is our role on this earth. The behemoth corporations use loopholes to escape payment of taxes. The payment of these taxes would only be them doing their fair share, not their excessive share, but their "fair share". These tax payments would be a boon to our infrastructure and aid in the support of tons of marginal folks. We have the clout to stop this also. Why are we buying what these hucksters are selling us in regard to the ideology of a smaller government, more tax loopholes and free or unregulated enterprise? People with money and without watchdogs will not act right! It's obvious!

Think, when we are buying things that we really don't need, we're in fact feeding these behemoth corporations the fuel that gives them life. We make them stronger and harder to defeat when we purchase their products in this system of covetousness and greed. We essentially vote for these out-of-control behemoths with our own dollars. It is we the people that feed them the fuel that make them big and strong enough, to be unstoppable in abusing "we the people". This occurs when we are caught-up in "maxing-out".

We as a Christian church body, instead of feeding these oppressors of the people, should be denying them these funds, which gives them the power to oppress "we the people". And since we've already enlarged them to the degree we have, we owe it to those who are being exploited and hurt by these entities to redirect great amounts of our income streams and aid the exploited. Or are we so caught up with our conveniences, drunk on our pleasures, that we drink the blood of those who are killed due to our indulges?

The corporate giants send jobs overseas and exploit the workers of other lands because we allow it. They deny our own people employment while they enslave poor workers overseas because we're too addicted to do anything about it. We must wake up, snap out of it! We're stoned out on the pride of our high, like addicts in a crack-house, oblivious to our surroundings and the collateral damage we're creating. We remain comatose. There is no excuse. We the church body of Christ have the monetary advantage if we join our funds together and form an economic block. And so it is time to use our advantage. "If my people called by name would humble themselves and pray, then I will heal their land", 2 Chronicles 7:14.

We who claim we are Christians, disciples of The Creator Most High must prove it by how we actively love Him. The proof of our love of God is shown by the measure of our compassion for the least of our neighbors. It is demonstrated by our actions. We cannot be a child of God and be a conformist. We cannot be a child of God and simply covertly keep the commandments which is the avoidance of doing wrong. We can no longer live by thou shalt "not" do this or that.

We must keep the new commandments by overtly doing good. We must feed the hungry so that we don't murder him. We must actually sell all we have and give it to the poor, so we don't steal from him. We assist our neighbor's mother, wife, daughter, sibling when in distress, so we don't commit adultery with them. We must intentionally lend to our enemies and let things be stolen, so that we don't covet. We must neglect fellowship with family and friends in order to serve the wheelchair victim, so as not to bear false witness. We must exempt ourselves from our excesses, 'maxing-out', in order to fight for the justice and rights of minorities, immigrants and voiceless, so we do not commit idolatry. When we fail to visit the sick, we murder, when we fail to free the prisoner we murder, when we fail to feed the hungry we murder. When we claim to be a child of God, a chosen people and we fail to do any of these commandments, we murder. When we break one, we break them all. The new commandment is overt, pro-activist, whole heart, mind and soul.

We cannot be a child of God and be a "closet" commandment keep-er. We cannot be a child of God, saved, sanctified, filled with the Holy Ghost and be a bystander. We must overtly love our neighbor as our-self. Neither can we be a child of God and be a bigot. We cannot be a child of God and be a racist. We cannot be a child of God and be a supremacist. It cannot be so. We cannot be a child of the living God and do nothing about the racism, bigotry and exploitation imposed upon others, by our own people.

If we love God, it is manifested by how we treat our least worthy neighbor. And who is our neighbor? Our neighbor is everyone who is most not like us. We can't sit idly by, but rather we must stand in the shoes of those being oppressed and stand in their shoes and receive their oppression in order to help defeat the oppression against them. When Christ was being crucified the disciples ran away. We cannot now deny Him again today and run away, for the least of our neighbors is "Christ". Matthew 25:4 NIV, "The King will reply, 'Truly I tell you, whatever you did for one of the least of these brothers and sisters of mine, you did for me.'" "The world will not be destroyed by those who do evil, but by those who watch them without doing anything", Albert Einstein. Total love is for everyone to lay down their lives for everyone else.

Will we the Christian church miss the call? Will we be so strung out on the heroine of this life that when Christ comes to get us we won't recognize His voice, John 10:27? Will we the Christians who are invited to the wedding banquet be so busy and self-absorbed that we refuse to go? Or, are we the folks in the streets who have prepared ourselves to answer the call when it comes (Matthew 22:1-14)? What choice we make from this point on is critical.

We should not condemn those who are suffering. We should not even condemn our enemies. However, we can discern who is doing the evil to those who are suffering and take the appropriate action. We can discern because discernment means "perception in the absence of judgment or condemnation." Indignation is righteous "anger aroused by something unjust, unworthy or mean."

Be angry and sin not, Ephesians 4:26. God condemns the wicked, Psalms 7:11. God gets angry and wrathful and will punish. Does He love us? Yes! Will He punish? Yes! 2 Thessalonians 2:8-10. Exodus 22:21-24, This is what we also must be angry about, especially when it comes to the affliction of the stranger, widow and fatherless. We don't get angry at those who hurt and persecute us, we must love them for they are our enemy. However, we do get indignant at those who hurt others. Another way to say it is, 'we get angry, but we do not hate.' Like a prizefighter, we need to obtain proper training so that we can master the skill to become an effective pugilist, against those who oppose whom God loves.

Since we're in this world, and should not be of it, we should be busy making the world better, rather than enjoying its sinful fruits, even for a moment. God can determine if we're Kingdom material by the demonstration of our Kingdom-like works here on this earth. Who do we think the Father would choose, someone who has no experience in negotiating on behalf of those who are suffering, or someone who is actively gaining experience advocating with the powers that be, on behalf of the suffering of others?

Do you think He will choose someone who is generous with his time and resources or someone who barely has time for others? If we are using what talents we have to do kingdom work here on earth, God can multiply our talents to do greater Kingdom works in heaven. In fact, He says that if we multiply our gifts here on earth, He will make us rulers over cities, Luke 19:16-17,19. The Bible also says He intends for us to rule over nations, Revelations 2:26-27; Psalms 2:8-9. He can trust us in this rulership if we've built up a track record with Him in this life. He can trust us not by what we say, but by what we actually do. We cannot afford to bury our talents.

We today have the opportunity to reverse the wrong choice Adam and Eve made on our behalf and eat of the fruit of the tree of life that grows in the garden of God (Revelations 2:7).

Our opportunity for on-the-job training is in the here and now. Are we exercising and honing our diplomatic skills in this lifetime and advocating against "the Establishment" on behalf of the marginal of our society, or are we letting life slip out of our hands? How will He approve of us if we've had no on-the-job training here on earth? How will He know that His best interest is our best interest and that our best interest is His best interest? How will He know that we have the loving heart to get along with our fellow king and priest rulers over other nations, if we cannot skillfully negotiate with our fellow brethren here in this life?

We will be wielding way too much power in eternity for there to be dissension and fighting one with another. If we're not proven to be obedient servants of the Master now, then how can He trust us later to behave over the nations to which He wants to assign us rulership? Christ said to Peter, He doesn't want us to be deceived by false righteousness, he doesn't want us to fall for earthly deceptions. He wants us to follow the instruction of the only Father. Remember the devil used scriptures his way to trip Messiah. Messiah used scriptures the correct way, to defeat the devil (Matthew 4:14).

A lesson we can gain from that is, that we are not to obey an evil source, even if it is telling us what sounds like the truth, and that is because we are to obey only the most High (Matthew 16:23). It is by their fruits we will know them, Matthew 7:16.

Just as a good tree cannot give us bad fruit, a bad tree cannot give us good fruit.

"Among those who claim him to be Lord, few will be saved..." (Paul Washer) "the way is narrow that leads to life and there are few that find it." "Not everyone who says Lord, Lord..."

Today many are saying Jesus is Lord, and are deceiving many, with those words.

To discern their fruits, we must honestly know for certain, what good fruits look like in the first place.

We have to understand that the Master wants to guarantee a fail-safe no disaster eternity. Therefore, our proving ground has to be here and now on earth in this life. Messiah exclaimed to Simon Peter, "Simon, Simon! Listen! Satan has received permission to test all of you, to separate the good from the bad, as a farmer separates the wheat from the chaff", Luke 22:32 GNB.

We must become dispassionate, free of all covetousness, lust, unswayed by deceptions, "things", pleasures, greed, and wrong desires, meaning, we must have God's heart for the oppressed, the suffering, the needy, at all cost; because our eternal life is at stake. We can do none of this, if we don't do it through the power of the holy spirit of the most High God of Israel, our Lord and Saviour. We must not hesitate, we must not fall asleep, we must not turn back.

To exist, or not exist? We do, get to decide.

The question is, how do we inherit the Kingdom The Messiah has prepared for us since before the creation of the world? Asked another way, how do we obtain the favor of the Master to rule over cities, nations and kingdoms forever? And the answer is...

DAILY DEVOTIONALS
TRAIN FOR RULERSHIP
PRAY, READ, PRAY, MEDITATE

Recommend Ten A Day

* Obey the word, it'll make you happy. Luke 11:28.
* Passive Christians are sinners. James 4:17
* If faith includes no actions, it is dead. James 2:17
* All of our Christianity, worship and religious participation means nothing if we don't practice this level of love. Isaiah 1:15-17
* God doesn't care about the size of our offering in church or our noisy praise and worship and shouting, He is interested in our delivering justice to those who are in need. Amos 5:21-24
* Employees don't pay tithes. Widows don't pay tithes, they receive tithes. Malachi 3:5
* Tithes must be paid to foreigners, widows and fatherless.
* How many times does God have to say it? Don't take advantage of widows, foreigners and fatherless. Exodus 22:21
* What if the policy of all individual Christians was to take care of the least? Matthew 25:40
* The Savior is not just talking to Himself here! Matthew 25:34-39
* Taking care of needy is critical! Matthew 25:40
* Got to forsake the relatives and follow The Savior. Mark 10:28-30 The tithe which is required every three years, not every year, is to be paid to the widows, fatherless, immigrants and Levite (if you can find one). Deuteronomy 26:12-13

* God is not interested in church or church offerings, He is interested in His church doing justice. Isaiah 1:13-17
* We'll receive eternal punishment, why? Matthew 25:41-46
* If you do it to one of the least of these,.. we need to be concerned about caring for The Savior and not the other way around. Luke 9:58
* Once committing to this Christian walk; we can't look back and second guess our decision, because the slightest hesitation can kill us. Luke 9:62
* The slightest hesitation can kill us. Luke 9:60
* Don't make the excuse, if I have more money, I can do the work, when if we do the work, we'll have the money. Matthew 6:31-34
* We can't let our beloved family talk us out of selling everything we have, giving the money to the poor, and following The Savior. Luke 14:26; Acts 4:36-37
* We must reject our own family if it interferes with the work He told us to do, Matthew 12:48.
* The justice the church is to fight for is justice for the oppressed, poor, prisoner. Amos 5:21-24; Read Luke 4:18.
* "My tongue also shall talk of thy righteousness all the day long." Psalms 71:24
* Instead of obtaining we must be losing, we don't win unless we lose. Matthew 16:24-25
* Hate your life in this world. John 12:25
* We can't let anyone or any circumstance block us helping the poor, the widow, the fatherless, the stranger, the sick and the needy. Luke 14:26
* Plan carefully our decision to follow The Savior and count the cost. Luke 14:28-29
* Plan ahead, so we can endure to the end. Luke 14:31
* Be good to the ungrateful. Luke 6:32-36

* It's not love if it incurs no personal deficit to self. Proverbs 19:17
* To neglect the oppressed is the same as doing evil. Isaiah 1:15-17
* What are the proven traits that we might emulate that made Job know without a shadow of a doubt that he was righteous?
* Never, Never trust riches or take pride in wealth. Job 31:24
* Love our enemy. Job 31:29-30
* House the homeless. Job 31:31-32
* Do not look upon any woman to lust after her. Job 31:1-12
* a) help the poor, b) help the widows, c) help the fatherless, d) clothe the naked. Job 31:16-18
* Treat our employees justly. Job 31:13
* Greed gives rise to selfish and wicked actions. I Timothy 6:10
* God keeps His promises. Deuteronomy 7:9
* Don't be afraid, be still. Exodus 14:13-14
* God keeps all His promises. Joshua 24:45
* Sinners are those whose loyalties are divided between God and the world. Wash and purify self. James 4:8
* Purify self by prioritizing the serving of those most underserved. James 1:27
* By my deeds, I show my faith. James 2:18
* It takes faith not money to do these deeds. Matt. 6:33
* God don't lie. Numbers 23:19
* a) foreigners b) fatherless c) widows = overwhelming blessings. Deuteronomy 27:19
* Bear fruit, produce results. John 15:16
* Naked and you clothed me, thirsty and you gave me drink, sick and you visited me. John 15:8-16
* We are ordered to bear the fruits of righteousness, taking care of God's kingdom which include widow, fatherless, foreigner, poor and prisoner. John 15:5
* We are being purged right now. John 15:2
* I did not know what the commandments were til' now. Not the "10", but yes, the "10' by assisting the needy, and helping the poor,

and even our enemies, with all our heart, mind and soul, we fulfill the "10", commandments of love. John 14:15

* a) The Savior cared for the people's needs, then b) pointed them to the Father. John 14:12
* Every day we do good works is our Sabbath day of Rest. Luke 6:9
* This is the "Secret', Matthew 6:33, this is the narrow path. Matthew 7:14
* The righteous are Abraham's seed. Galatians 3:7-9
* These are the commands we are to teach the whole world when we bring them to Christ. Matthew 28:20
* It's not about church offerings. The church says it is, God says it's not. Micah 6:7-8
* Obey God's commands. Deuteronomy 1:13
* Fear and obey with all heart, soul and might. Don't obey half-heartedly, but one hundred per cent. Does God want 10% or 100%? Deuteronomy 10:12
* God accepts no bribes; we cannot bribe Him with offerings. We must do the work. Deuteronomy 10:17
* Even a perfect Christian is not saved if he does not sell all and give to the poor. The poor are the heart of our Christian walk. They're the key that opens the door. Luke 18:22
* We must do what God says do. Luke 6:46
* We're blessed when they separate themselves from us; it means we're following God. They'll say we are the ones doing the evil (causing churches to go broke, ministries to break-up etc.). Luke 6:22
* Calling on the name of The Savior is not enough, we must also do his will. Fatherless, widow, foreigner, hungry. Matthew 7:2
* This is what the rich have done to be rich, and we who do not sell all benefit, and are just as guilty of having blood on our hands. James 5:5-6
* Employees are always mistreated, they are worth a share of the profits and not just a meagerly wage. Without them the business would collapse. James 5:4

* The rich look proud, but woe unto them. James 5:1, 10
* Sin is to neglect doing the good. James 4:17
* We must not dishonor poor people by preferring rich people. James 2:6-7
* We break God's commandments when we show favoritism to the rich. James 2:8-9
* We must also teach obedience to The Savior's command to do good to the needy when we preach the gospel to the world. Matthew 28:19-2
* Don't be friends with the enemy, the world, it's riches. James 4:4
* Faith alone is nothing without works of righteousness. James 2:24
* We will be kicked out of churches and murdered by them for this book's contents. John 16:2
* Others are more important than self. John 15:12-13
* We are to have an attitude of servitude and humility toward one another; foot washing level humility. John 13:14
* The Savior came in an animal feed box called a manger. Luke 2:7; Luke 2:12
* The Savior describes His own nature Himself, Matthew 11:29
* The Savior grew up poor in the Nazareth slums, John 1:46
* Jesus our master is our greatest servant. Matthew 23:11; Luke 22:26
* We will have trouble. John 16:33
* Love is infinite. Being kind only to our friends, our friendly neighbors is not enough. We must also be kind to the wretched, thieves, murderers, bad-drivers and low-life trash. Matthew 5:47
* Next level of perfection: Love not just neighbor, but also the neighbors who hate us. Those of another religion, sect, culture, nationality, race, class, ethnicity, gender or anyone you'd naturally hate back. Matthew 5:43-44
* Deeds should shine. Matthew 5:16
* Deeds should be secret. Matthew 6:3
* Our walk with The Savior requires we be different from everyone else. Matt. 5:11

* God doesn't care about how much offering we give, He is concerned with our doing justice and showing mercy to the poor; the needy, the challenged; the invalid, the sick, the foreigner. Our God cannot be bought. We can't say I am giving my big offerings to the church to increase the message of the gospel to the world and think that that buys us not having to personally feed, clothe, serve the poor and needy. We can't buy God by giving funds to a ministry. Micah 6:7-8
* What did The Savior tell us to do? Love our enemies, do good to those who do us badly, lend to our enemy, hoping for nothing back. Matthew 6:46
* Why do we not care for the widow, the orphan, the foreigner, poor and needy? Luke 6:46
* Give to others and receive full measure, pressed down shaken together and running over. We can't sidestep this by only giving the church offerings. Luke 6:38
* Give up our lives, our time, comfort, resources, for others. Mentor others to do the same. John 15:13
* We are appointed to bear much fruit. John 15:1-6
* God gets glory from the fruit we bear. Naked and you clothed me, thirsty and you gave me drink, sick, in prison and you visited me. John 15:8
* The fruit we must bear are the fruits of righteousness, taking care of God's kingdom which include, blind, the deaf, the indigent, physically and mentally challenged, the widow, the fatherless, the foreigner and the prisoner. Multiple sclerosis, palsy, cancer, epilepsy, Cronin's disease. John 15:5
* We are being purged right now. John 15:2
* His words: Clothe the naked, feed the hungry, visit the prisoner, sell all, give to the poor; God over money, lend hoping for nothing in return, even to our hated enemies, turn the other cheek, be a good Samaritan to strange nationalities; all ethnicities. John 14:23
* Share with others. Sacrifice something of yours, things, time, life, money, energy, brain power, heart and soul. Deut. 6:4-9

* This is the crux of the Christianity for which the book of Hebrews was written. Hebrews 13:1-5
* Honor marriage. Hebrews 13:4
* Be content with money we have. God cares for us. Hebrews 13:5
* Motivate each other in good works. Hebrews 10:24
* God will reward. Hebrews 6:10-12
* The Father and Son will come and abide with us if we obey their commands. John 14:23
* We love God if we do his commands. John 14:21
* Obey. John 12:15
* The Savior took care of people's needs and encouraged them to believe in the Father. John 14:12
* We must believe God will compensate us if we enter into His Rest by caring for the needs of others. Hebrews 3:19
* We are to do good deeds on the Sabbath day every day. Luke 6:9
* To enter God's Rest, we must give up selfish work. Matthew 7:14
* This is the narrow path few tend to take. God will compensate us if we work for Him and not for money. Matthew 6:33
* You can't really do both things at the same time. Matthew 6:24
* To enter into His rest is to do Kingdom works of righteousness instead of selfish works for money and security. Hebrews 4:1,10
* Do right things. Romans 12:17
* Practice hospitality. Romans 12:13
* We are the Master's servants who must distribute to the other servants. Luke 12:47
* There'll be no peace, even in our homes for doing this. Luke 12:51 The failure of the ministry to teach us these things is why we the people will perish for a lack of this knowledge. Here's why so few American Christians will make heaven. Hosea 4:4-6
* And when the master calls we'll be so busy with our own interests we'll decline to come to the wedding banquet table. Luke 14:17
* Who are my brothers and sisters and mother who are doing the will? Mark 3:34-35.

* It is a lack of this knowledge which will cause God's people to perish. Hosea 4:4-6
* We must believe; belief is everything. Luke 8:50
* We are seeds, destined to die; die to live. I Corinthians 15:36
* Choose the poor. James 2:5
* The Kingdom goes to the poor. Luke 6:20
* We're not saved by good works but are created to do good works, which is the evidence of our salvation. Ephesians 2:8-10
* God vowed He'd keep his promise. Hebrews 6:17-18
* Stop accusing the victims, by pointing fingers. Isaiah 58:9-11
* Take up our cross; lose our life. Luke 9:23-25
* We can't hesitate; Act instantly. Luke 9:61
* Faith demonstrated; Not talked. Genesis 22:12
* Giving to the poor is the criteria for salvation. Luke 19:8
* We must forgive those who owe us, we must serve God with His money, and not serve money. Luke 16:11-13
* He is not angry forever. Psalms 13:8-9
* Don't faint. Galatians 6:9
* We must do the first works and not get tired. Revelations 2:4-5
* This is what the righteous do to win. Psalms 112:9
* Lend generously, to the poor of course, and to those who despise us, and whom we despise. Psalms 112:5
* This is how to get blessed, we are to fight for justice. Isaiah 58:9-11
* Our actions are evidence of whether we have eternal life. Matthew 25:34
* Apparently, our deeds are evidence of whether we are saved to eternal life. James 2:14-16
* Feed your enemy; Love includes our enemy; or we don't love God, heart, mind and soul; Perfect Love is unrequited. Romans 12:20-21
* Perfect love is unrequited. It's 100% not hating. Matthew 5:46
* Be perfect as our heavenly Father is perfect. Matthew 5:48
* Give to the needy in secret. Matthew 6:3

* Be hungry for instruction; weep for the tragedies we see; don't be filled; don't be rich, be empty, not full of self. Luke 6:21
* The poor are open for help, the rich don't need God's help; so be poor, don't miss out on eternal life. Luke 6:20
* What did He say do? People who call on His name but fail to follow His instructions will not be known by Him when He returns. Luke 6:46
* Notice that sowing a harvest and reaping a harvest has to do with giving to the poor. 2 Corinthians 9:9
* Biblical criteria for righteousness is to give to the poor. We emphasize this less and emphasize sharing the gospel verbally more, because in sharing the gospel verbally all we have to do is talk, but we don't have to give up nothing. Luke 11:39-41
* The tithe should go to the fatherless, widow and foreigner, but we must not neglect social justice on behalf of the weak. Luke 11:41-42
* Do not fear. God will uphold us. Isaiah 41:10
* A claim of faith is nothing without physical deeds of love for the needy. Apparently, our deeds are evidence of whether or not we are saved; whether we enter heaven. James 2:14-16; Revelation 2:12
* To neglect a brother is the devil's work. I John 3:8
* If we don't share with our brother, we murder him. I John 3:15-16
* To lay down our lives it must cost us something. We must lose in order to win. I John 6:16
* Love is to lay down our lives; this is how through a brother or sister we love God. I John 4:20
* Actions of giving are proof of whether we love our brother. I John 3:17-18
* The only tithe with a promise of blessings; The only tithe with that promise. Deuteronomy 14:28-29

* This is why we do this, we fight for the fatherless, widow, homeless and the prisoner; we imitate the Father. Psalms 68:5
* Is anything too hard? Is anything impossible for God? Genesis 18:14
* God's promises are not limited by time. Thankfully God's promises are not dependent on our belief or lack thereof. Genesis 17:17
* Mere mortals? Psalms 118:5-6
* What can mere mortals do when God is on our side? Hebrews 13:6
* We're called to do good even if we suffer for it. I Peter 2:20-21
* Hear His voice, be doers. John 1:27
* We can't get started and hesitate or regret or second guess. Luke 9:62
* It is Christ living in us that must be doing the works and not ourselves. I Corinthians 13:3
* We must persevere in the work we must do; don't faint. James 1:4
* Why our churches are so segregated today. Luke 6:32
* Give to the poor, freely. Luke 6:3; Eccl. 11:1
* Love our haters; then our love is perfect as is the Father's. That after-all is what haters are fore. Haters increase our capacity to love. Luke 6:27-28
* Is it wrong to do good on the Sabbath day? Luke 6:9
* Loving enemies by doing good for them, helps make it easier for us to do good for the benefit of all. Luke 6:35
* We must share our bread with the poor and hungry. Luke 6:25
* Luke 6:30
* Can we imagine everybody talking to everybody no matter who they are? Matthew 5:47-48
* We must let down all our defenses. We're called to enjoy both sides of the equation. Matthew 5:39
* We are "rich" when we are inconvenienced in order to help the needy, widow and fatherless. Luke 6:24
* All our giving is in vain if we hate any part of the equation; if we hate any peoples or persons all whom are God's creation. I Corinthians 13:3

* If we would let them be oppressed and do nothing about it. Isaiah 1:17
* The yeast is that which puffs up and dazzles our pride, our sense of self-esteem, and appeals to our sense of importance. Mark 8:15
* We must lose in order to win. The burden we need to carry must cost us something. Mark 8:34
* Sell all we have, help the fatherless and widow. Mark 8:35
* This is active love of our enemy, of the poor and needy. Luke 1:25-28
* If we give vigorously to one group yet hate in our hearts another group we are unworthy. I Corinthians 13:3
* The Samaritan was active. Luke 1:33-34
* We can't judge by appearances; don't condemn. Luke 1:3
* We must practice this; perfect love in action; love the foreigner as ourselves. Leviticus 19:33-34
* If our enemy is hungry, feed him. Romans 12:2
* We can't serve two masters; purify self. James 4:8
* As much as lies within us, have peace with all God's creation and do everything possible. Romans 12:18
* Don't let the world change us from this; corrupt us from this. James 1:27
* We show faith by doing the deeds of faith. James 2:18
* Praise God! Numbers 23:19
* When we hear; don't be stubborn; thinking we're safe because we heard it; but failed to act. Deuteronomy 29:19
* Deuteronomy 27:16
* Conversely, if we give justice to foreigners, fatherless and widows, God promises overwhelming blessings. Deuteronomy 27:19
* Don't be afraid of God's intentions for us. Luke 12:32
* He's not just talking to the rich ruler here! (Luke 11:52) Luke 12:33-34
* Declare The Savior publicly as we do in this book. Luke 12:8

* Sell all and give to the needy. Luke 11:52; Acts 4:33-37
* Justice, mercy and the love of God is #1. Luke 11:42
* We must hear and obey; and DON'T mute it. Luke 11:28
* We're not acceptable on the inside if we don't give gifts to the poor; the poor is God's heart; Blessed. Luke 11:38-41
* This is the true work of the church that God requires. Isaiah 58:6-7 NLT
* God is not impressed with our righteousness; our celebrations of the truth; rather He wants us to do the truth; the church services fool us into thinking we're doing the truth. Don't be hearers only, but doers. Isaiah 58:3 NLT
* Churchgoers today are doing the same thing and missing the same point...! These are ancient prophecies for today's realities. Isaiah 58:1-2 NLT
* The justice the church is to fight for is justice for the poor, justice for the prisoners, justice for the weak, the ignorant, the challenged, justice for the oppressed. Luke 4:18, Isaiah 61:1, to free the captive, give good news to the poor, this is what the "Spirit of the Lord' shows us! Amos 5:21-24
* The good feeling the Holy Spirit gives us is just the first phase of our conversion. Next, we must allow it to propel us into spiritual activity.
* "A-ha! We've got him now!" Psalms 70:2-4 NLT
* You will restore me to even greater honor. Psalms 71:20-21 NLT
* Anything? Genesis 18:14
* To enter God's Rest, we must give up selfish labors. Matthew 7:14
* This is the narrow path few tend to take. God will compensate us if we work for Him and not money. Matthew 6:33
* We are to do good deeds on the Sabbath day; Sabbath deeds every day. Luke 6:9
* We must believe God will compensate us if we enter into His Rest. Hebrews 3:19

* This is talking about giving love and lending to our enemies; not to the church. Luke 6:38
* Even when The Savior spoke to the rich man about giving, He did not ask that the money be given to further His ministry; He told him to give the money away to the poor. Luke 18:22
* If you are rich in spirit, you have no room for The Savior, Luke 6:24 NIV.
* For God accepts no bribes; we cannot bribe Him with money or offerings. We must do the work He requires. Deuteronomy 10:17-19
* Do the service with all our heart and soul. Deuteronomy 10:12
* Obey! Deuteronomy 1:13
* We cannot hesitate when called to follow Him. Luke 9:61
* Money is a medium used by God to determine the measure of our faith in Him. Luke 18:22
* Loving sinners is a deep concept. Loving those who have no love for you is a deep concept. Luke 6:32
* Do good to them who hate you. Lend them things, give things away, and run from compensation or repayment. Luke 6:35
* Share our bread with the poor and hungry. Luke 6:25
* Be quick to give... Luke 6:30
* We are poor as when we fail to make ourselves uncomfortable in order to help the needy widow and fatherless. Luke 6:24
* The yeast is the pride of life; BMW, Gucci, diamonds, mansions, education. Mark 8:15
* We must lose in order to win. The burdens we need to carry must cost us something. Mark 8:34
* Sell all that we have, help the fatherless and the widow. Mark 8:35
* This is active love of enemy, poor and needy. Luke 10:25-28
* Our neighbors are our enemies; love as self. Luke 10:33-34
* We must extol foreigners. Leviticus 19:33-34
* Don't be upset, always concerned about what we will eat and drink. Luke 12:29-31

* We are not to show partiality or favoritism to oppressors. Psalms 82:2-4
* Practice justice, mercy and faith. Luke 12:35
* We'll hear the knock only if we're serving. Luke 12:36
* Be a slave to the needs of the needy. Luke 12:43
* If we fail to escape, shame on us. Luke 12:47
* This we must be doing as servants. Luke 12:42
* Let us work to enter into His rest. Luke 12:43
* Or are we this fig tree which was looking good but was found without fruit? Matthew 21:19

(50) FIFTY INDICATORS THAT A CHURCH IS "AMERICANIZED"

1) The congregation is thriving with numbers but a visitor is left standing alone for more than two minutes when services end, and leaves without being noticed even after being greeted maybe once or twice.
2) The congregation almost doesn't exist, and there are almost no kids.
3) An actual physically needy person doesn't feel comfortable asking for actual physical help.
4) You couldn't get a loan of money from a deacon a pastor or any of the church leaders if you were sitting there dying on the front steps.
5) Your pastor hasn't darkened the doors of a homeless shelter, prison, orphanage, hospital or nursing home, food giveaway or battered women's shelter in the past two weeks.
6) If your pastors haven't done the same on their own, aside from church assigned visits in the past month.
7) When a drug addict, prostitute or pimp can't walk into your church service and feel comfortably received.
8) When every dwelling unit within a mile of your church doesn't know you are there.
9) When you speak so much religiosity a new person doesn't understand what you are saying.

10) When you have no working relationship with even one local school in the community.
11) When you have no relationship with several other churches in your community.
12) If your church has no access to a local food bank, can't distribute or obtain food from any sources i.e. supermarket, local restaurants, etc.
13) If your church has no official programs that paints, repairs, widow's houses or moves them when needed.
14) When your church hasn't reached a prostitute, pimp, drug dealer, substance abuser, homosexual in the last month.
15) If your preacher's bank account, house and car is on average greater than the average accounts of your composite church members.
16) When the population of females outnumbers the population of males by a full one-third.
17) If people in your church think they're pretty good. Jeremiah 17:9
18) When the teens get old enough, they don't stay, or return to the church.
19) If the church is lifting tithes from the people and not distributing 100% of it for the sustenance of the fatherless, widows and aliens.
20) If the church is not operating a homeless shelter or supporting convalescent home or orphanage.
21) If the church is not a partner with a charity.
22) If the church is not a partner with a social justice organization.
23) If the people are not inviting, lame, maimed and blind to supper on regular basis, preferably weekly (not just to conduct a Bible study)
24) When you hold a church picnic or banquet you include, at least five homeless or strangers.
25) You do not have the same proportion of handicapped attending as is available in your community.

26) Your church is not multi-racial in proportion to the demographic breakdown of your community.
27) If your church does not have a monthly clothing drive distribution for distribution of clothes to poorer people especially children.
28) If your church facility is not opened to the community other days of the week other than on worship day.
29) If less than 10% of the congregation are visiting prisoners.
30) If the ministerial staff is not active in local community activist groups.
31) If your beneficence fund is less than 5% of your budget.
32) If your giving to poor and needy people outside your membership is less than 10%
33) If you're giving to poor and needy people inside your membership is less than 10%.
34) If a child molester is being tolerated within its leadership.
35) If an adulterer is being tolerated within its leadership.
36) If a fornicator is being tolerated within its leadership.
37) If your people are not helping with a battered women's shelter.
38) If you espouse one political party over another.
39) If you agree with the secular government and its policies of hurting other people.
40) If you are not participating in the fighting for the rights of immigrants, illegal or otherwise.
41) If less than 10% of your people are caring for foster kids and orphans.
42) If less than 10% of your monies goes to missionary workers.
43) If from 80-90% of your offerings and tithes go to administration cost.
44) When you laid hands on someone to heal them, the problem goes away but returns the next day.
45) When someone comes up for healing who has a real need and won't get allowed on stage.

46) The dress styles of your female population aren't more chaste than that of the surrounding society.
47) When the majority of husbands aren't the spiritual leaders in their own homes.
48) When the majority of kids don't like the Sabbath/Sunday School teacher
49) There are many scheduled church activities, meetings, conferences etc., there isn't time or money to care for the poor, needy or to fight for justice.
50) When most of a member's giving ends up supporting the preacher and his level of living and maintenance of the physical church facility and activities and less than 15% supports an actual ongoing charitable cause.
51) When people have a physical need and make a request, everything goes weird. People feel they're bothering the church when they have to make a request.
52) A church teaches that the way to be blessed is by tithing to the church.
53) When it emphasizes being blessed with wealth over being blessed with the power of God, the power to heal the sick, to restore sound minds, to calm the storm.
54) If the church emphasizes laying up treasures on earth rather than the laying up of treasures in heaven.
55) If the church fails to teach that the way to be blessed is by selling all and giving to the poor.
56) If the church fails to teach that the way to be blessed is by seeking first the Kingdom of God and his righteousness.
57) If a church teaches you to obtain wealth in order to give to the poor.
58) If a church doesn't recognize that the important thing is not wealth or success, but power and faithfulness.
59) When the church supports a suffer-avoidance gospel.
60) When too many of these points describe your church.

Let's eliminate 10 indicators as not applicable to your church situation. How many of these indicators does your church exhibit?

    2 of 50
    5 of 50
    10 of 50
    15 of 50
    20 of 50
    25 of 50

Finally: Do we individually participate?

Steps Toward The Mobilization of our Christian Walk

Intentionally:

1) Seek social justice organizations to support financially (google them).
2) Seek watchdog organizations that rate the top charities (google them).
3) Seek social justice organizations to support physically (google them).
4) Seek social justice churches to support financially (google them).
5) Seek social justice churches to support physically (google them).
6) Seek to take in a fatherless child.
7) Seek to feed and mentor a needy fatherless child.
8) Seek to help a widow in some way, each week (neighborhood or / and church).
9) Seek to visit a sick person each week.
10) Seek to feed the hungry or give directly to the poor each week.
11) Seek to feed the hungry and the poor through feeding organizations foreign and domestic.

ABOUT THE AUTHOR

RONALD BARKSDALE is the most exciting author of this time. And what a perilous time this is. While most Christian books are going down the broad path, Barksdale takes us down the narrow path, the one least traveled. Does not the Bible say, "Broad is the way that leadeth to destruction"?

Originally from Brooklyn, New York, he studied theology and comparative religion at Ambassador College, Pasadena, California, and earned a BA degree in theology. A devoted husband and dad of two beautiful offspring, Barksdale excels in the exploration of the practical application of the principles of spiritual living.

So, since "narrow is the way that leadeth unto life, and few there be few that find it", Barksdale seeks to put us onto the narrow path that leads to Life.

Given a God inspired edict to publish this message, he probes into the tougher areas of our Christian walk. With the flare of the artistic talent he displays as a musician, he also paints his ideas well on the canvasses of this fine book. His own personal communique with the creator has prompted him to pen this work, certain to be coined a classic in the near future, *The Americanization of God: Come Out of Her My People.*

His contact address is starbaze1@yahoo.com.

www.ingramcontent.com/pod-product-compliance
Lightning Source LLC
Chambersburg PA
CBHW070952040426
42443CB00007B/481